ASPEN PUBLISHERS

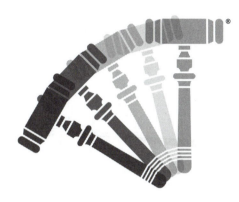

Casenote™ Legal Briefs

INSURANCE LAW

Keyed to Courses Using

Abraham's
Insurance Law and Regulation

Fifth Edition

Wolters Kluwer
Law & Business

AUSTIN   BOSTON   CHICAGO   NEW YORK   THE NETHERLANDS

This publication is designed to provide accurate and authoritative information in regard to the subject matter covered. It is sold with the understanding that the publisher is not engaged in rendering legal, accounting, or other professional services. If legal advice or other expert assistance is required, the services of a competent professional person should be sought.

— From a Declaration of Principles adopted jointly by a Committee of the American Bar Association and a Committee of Publishers and Associates

To contact Customer Care, e-mail customer.service@aspenpublishers.com, call 1-800-234-1660, fax 1-800-901-9075, or mail correspondence to:

Aspen Publishers
Attn: Order Department
P.O. Box 990
Frederick, MD 21705

Printed in the United States of America.

1 2 3 4 5 6 7 8 9 0

ISBN 978-0-7355-9773-0

About Wolters Kluwer Law & Business

Wolters Kluwer Law & Business is a leading provider of research information and workflow solutions in key specialty areas. The strengths of the individual brands of Aspen Publishers, CCH, Kluwer Law International and Loislaw are aligned within Wolters Kluwer Law & Business to provide comprehensive, in-depth solutions and expert-authored content for the legal, professional and education markets.

CCH was founded in 1913 and has served more than four generations of business professionals and their clients. The CCH products in the Wolters Kluwer Law & Business group are highly regarded electronic and print resources for legal, securities, antitrust and trade regulation, government contracting, banking, pension, payroll, employment and labor, and health-care reimbursement and compliance professionals.

Aspen Publishers is a leading information provider for attorneys, business professionals and law students. Written by preeminent authorities, Aspen products offer analytical and practical information in a range of specialty practice areas from securities law and intellectual property to mergers and acquisitions and pension/benefits. Aspen's trusted legal education resources provide professors and students with high-quality, up-to-date and effective resources for successful instruction and study in all areas of the law.

Kluwer Law International supplies the global business community with comprehensive English-language international legal information. Legal practitioners, corporate counsel and business executives around the world rely on the Kluwer Law International journals, loose-leafs, books and electronic products for authoritative information in many areas of international legal practice.

Loislaw is a premier provider of digitized legal content to small law firm practitioners of various specializations. Loislaw provides attorneys with the ability to quickly and efficiently find the necessary legal information they need, when and where they need it, by facilitating access to primary law as well as state-specific law, records, forms and treatises.

Wolters Kluwer Law & Business, a unit of Wolters Kluwer, is headquartered in New York and Riverwoods, Illinois. Wolters Kluwer is a leading multinational publisher and information services company.

Format for the Casenote Legal Brief

Nature of Case: This section identifies the form of action (e.g., breach of contract, negligence, battery), the type of proceeding (e.g., demurrer, appeal from trial court's jury instructions), or the relief sought (e.g., damages, injunction, criminal sanctions).

Fact Summary: This is included to refresh your memory and can be used as a quick reminder of the facts.

Rule of Law: Summarizes the general principle of law that the case illustrates. It may be used for instant recall of the court's holding and for classroom discussion or home review.

Facts: This section contains all relevant facts of the case, including the contentions of the parties and the lower court holdings. It is written in a logical order to give the student a clear understanding of the case. The plaintiff and defendant are identified by their proper names throughout and are always labeled with a (P) or (D).

Palsgraf v. Long Island R.R. Co.

Injured bystander (P) v. Railroad company (D)

N.Y. Ct. App., 248 N.Y. 339, 162 N.E. 99 (1928).

NATURE OF CASE: Appeal from judgment affirming verdict for plaintiff seeking damages for personal injury.

FACT SUMMARY: Helen Palsgraf (P) was injured on R.R.'s (D) train platform when R.R.'s (D) guard helped a passenger aboard a moving train, causing his package to fall on the tracks. The package contained fireworks which exploded, creating a shock that tipped a scale onto Palsgraf (P).

🏛 RULE OF LAW
The risk reasonably to be perceived defines the duty to be obeyed.

FACTS: Helen Palsgraf (P) purchased a ticket to Rockaway Beach from R.R. (D) and was waiting on the train platform. As she waited, two men ran to catch a train that was pulling out from the platform. The first man jumped aboard, but the second man, who appeared as if he might fall, was helped aboard by the guard on the train who had kept the door open so they could jump aboard. A guard on the platform also helped by pushing him onto the train. The man was carrying a package wrapped in newspaper. In the process, the man dropped his package, which fell on the tracks. The package contained fireworks and exploded. The shock of the explosion was apparently of great enough strength to tip over some scales at the other end of the platform, which fell on Palsgraf (P) and injured her. A jury awarded her damages, and R.R. (D) appealed.

ISSUE: Does the risk reasonably to be perceived define the duty to be obeyed?

HOLDING AND DECISION: (Cardozo, C.J.) Yes. The risk reasonably to be perceived defines the duty to be obeyed. If there is no foreseeable hazard to the injured party as the result of a seemingly innocent act, the act does not become a tort because it happened to be a wrong as to another. If the wrong was not willful, the plaintiff must show that the act as to her had such great and apparent possibilities of danger as to entitle her to protection. Negligence in the abstract is not enough upon which to base liability. Negligence is a relative concept, evolving out of the common law doctrine of trespass on the case. To establish liability, the defendant must owe a legal duty of reasonable care to the injured party. A cause of action in tort will lie where harm, though unintended, could have been averted or avoided by observance of such a duty. The scope of the duty is limited by the range of danger that a reasonable person could foresee. In this case, there was nothing to suggest from the appearance of the parcel or otherwise that the parcel contained fireworks. The guard could not reasonably have had any warning of a threat to Palsgraf (P), and R.R. (D) therefore cannot be held liable. Judgment is reversed in favor of R.R. (D).

DISSENT: (Andrews, J.) The concept that there is no negligence unless R.R. (D) owes a legal duty to take care as to Palsgraf (P) herself is too narrow. Everyone owes to the world at large the duty of refraining from those acts that may unreasonably threaten the safety of others. If the guard's action was negligent as to those nearby, it was also negligent as to those outside what might be termed the "danger zone." For Palsgraf (P) to recover, R.R.'s (D) negligence must have been the proximate cause of her injury, a question of fact for the jury.

▶ ANALYSIS

The majority defined the limit of the defendant's liability in terms of the danger that a reasonable person in defendant's situation would have perceived. The dissent argued that the limitation should not be placed on liability, but rather on damages. Judge Andrews suggested that only injuries that would not have happened but for R.R.'s (D) negligence should be compensable. Both the majority and dissent recognized the policy-driven need to limit liability for negligent acts, seeking, in the words of Judge Andrews, to define a framework "that will be practical and in keeping with the general understanding of mankind." The Restatement (Second) of Torts has accepted Judge Cardozo's view.

Quicknotes

FORESEEABILITY A reasonable expectation that change is the probable result of certain acts or omissions.

NEGLIGENCE Conduct falling below the standard of care that a reasonable person would demonstrate under similar conditions.

PROXIMATE CAUSE The natural sequence of events without which an injury would not have been sustained.

Party ID: Quick identification of the relationship between the parties.

Concurrence/Dissent: All concurrences and dissents are briefed whenever they are included by the casebook editor.

Analysis: This last paragraph gives you a broad understanding of where the case "fits in" with other cases in the section of the book and with the entire course. It is a hornbook-style discussion indicating whether the case is a majority or minority opinion and comparing the principal case with other cases in the casebook. It may also provide analysis from restatements, uniform codes, and law review articles. The analysis will prove to be invaluable to classroom discussion.

Issue: The issue is a concise question that brings out the essence of the opinion as it relates to the section of the casebook in which the case appears. Both substantive and procedural issues are included if relevant to the decision.

Holding and Decision: This section offers a clear and in-depth discussion of the rule of the case and the court's rationale. It is written in easy-to-understand language and answers the issue presented by applying the law to the facts of the case. When relevant, it includes a thorough discussion of the exceptions to the case as listed by the court, any major cites to the other cases on point, and the names of the judges who wrote the decisions.

Quicknotes: Conveniently defines legal terms found in the case and summarizes the nature of any statutes, codes, or rules referred to in the text.

Aspen Publishers is proud to offer *Casenote Legal Briefs*—continuing thirty years of publishing America's best-selling legal briefs.

Casenote Legal Briefs are designed to help you save time when briefing assigned cases. Organized under convenient headings, they show you how to abstract the basic facts and holdings from the text of the actual opinions handed down by the courts. Used as part of a rigorous study regimen, they can help you spend more time analyzing and critiquing points of law than on copying bits and pieces of judicial opinions into your notebook or outline.

Casenote Legal Briefs should never be used as a substitute for assigned casebook readings. They work best when read as a follow-up to reviewing the underlying opinions themselves. Students who try to avoid reading and digesting the judicial opinions in their casebooks or online sources will end up shortchanging themselves in the long run. The ability to absorb, critique, and restate the dynamic and complex elements of case law decisions is crucial to your success in law school and beyond. It cannot be developed vicariously.

Casenote Legal Briefs represents but one of the many offerings in Aspen's Study Aid Timeline, which includes:

- *Casenote Legal Briefs*
- *Emanuel Law Outlines*
- *Examples & Explanations* Series
- *Introduction to Law* Series
- Emanuel *Law in a Flash* Flash Cards
- Emanuel *CrunchTime* Series

Each of these series is designed to provide you with easy-to-understand explanations of complex points of law. Each volume offers guidance on the principles of legal analysis and, consulted regularly, will hone your ability to spot relevant issues. We have titles that will help you prepare for class, prepare for your exams, and enhance your general comprehension of the law along the way.

To find out more about Aspen Study Aid publications, visit us online at *www.AspenLaw.com* or email us at *legaledu@wolterskluwer.com*. We'll be happy to assist you.

Get this Casenote Legal Brief as an AspenLaw Studydesk eBook today!

By returning this form to Aspen Publishers, you will receive a complimentary eBook download of this Casenote Legal Brief and AspenLaw Studydesk productivity software.* Learn more about AspenLaw Studydesk today at *www.AspenLaw.com/Studydesk.*

Name	Phone ( )
Address	**Apt. No.**
City	**State** **ZIP Code**
Law School	**Graduation Date** Month _____ Year _____

Cut out the UPC found on the lower left corner of the back cover of this book. Staple the UPC inside this box. Only the original UPC from the book cover will be accepted. (No photocopies or store stickers are allowed.)

> **Attach UPC inside this box.**

Email (Print legibly or you may not get access!)
Title of this book (course subject)
ISBN of this book (10- or 13-digit number on the UPC)
Used with which casebook (provide author's name)

Mail the completed form to: Aspen Publishers, Inc.
Legal Education Division
130 Turner Street, Bldg 3, 4th Floor
Waltham, MA 02453-8901

* Upon receipt of this completed form, you will be emailed a code for the digital download of this book in AspenLaw Studydesk eBook format and a free copy of the software application, which is required to read the eBook.

For a full list of eBook study aids available for AspenLaw Studydesk software and other resources that will help you with your law school studies, visit *www.AspenLaw.com.*

Make a photocopy of this form and your UPC for your records.

For detailed information on the use of the information you provide on this form, please see the PRIVACY POLICY at *www.AspenLaw.com.*

A. Decide on a Format and Stick to It

Structure is essential to a good brief. It enables you to arrange systematically the related parts that are scattered throughout most cases, thus making manageable and understandable what might otherwise seem to be an endless and unfathomable sea of information. There are, of course, an unlimited number of formats that can be utilized. However, it is best to find one that suits your needs and stick to it. Consistency breeds both efficiency and the security that when called upon you will know where to look in your brief for the information you are asked to give.

Any format, as long as it presents the essential elements of a case in an organized fashion, can be used. Experience, however, has led *Casenotes* to develop and utilize the following format because of its logical flow and universal applicability.

NATURE OF CASE: This is a brief statement of the legal character and procedural status of the case (e.g., "Appeal of a burglary conviction").

There are many different alternatives open to a litigant dissatisfied with a court ruling. The key to determining which one has been used is to discover *who is asking this court for what.*

This first entry in the brief should be kept as *short as possible.* Use the court's terminology if you understand it. But since jurisdictions vary as to the titles of pleadings, the best entry is the one that addresses who wants what in this proceeding, not the one that sounds most like the court's language.

RULE OF LAW: A statement of the general principle of law that the case illustrates (e.g., "An acceptance that varies any term of the offer is considered a rejection and counteroffer").

Determining the rule of law of a case is a procedure similar to determining the issue of the case. Avoid being fooled by red herrings; there may be a few rules of law mentioned in the case excerpt, but usually only one is *the* rule with which the casebook editor is concerned. The techniques used to locate the issue, described below, may also be utilized to find the rule of law. Generally, your best guide is simply the chapter heading. It is a clue to the point the casebook editor seeks to make and should be kept in mind when reading every case in the respective section.

FACTS: A synopsis of only the essential facts of the case, i.e., those bearing upon or leading up to the issue.

The facts entry should be a short statement of the events and transactions that led one party to initiate legal proceedings against another in the first place. While some cases conveniently state the salient facts at the beginning of the decision, in other instances they will have to be culled from hiding places throughout the text, even from concurring and dissenting opinions. Some of the "facts" will often be in dispute and should be so noted. Conflicting evidence may be briefly pointed up. "Hard" facts must be included. Both must be *relevant* in order to be listed in the facts entry. It is impossible to tell what is relevant until the entire case is read, as the ultimate determination of the rights and liabilities of the parties may turn on something buried deep in the opinion.

Generally, the facts entry should not be longer than three to five *short* sentences.

It is often helpful to identify the role played by a party in a given context. For example, in a construction contract case the identification of a party as the "contractor" or "builder" alleviates the need to tell that that party was the one who was supposed to have built the house.

It is always helpful, and a good general practice, to identify the "plaintiff" and the "defendant." This may seem elementary and uncomplicated, but, especially in view of the creative editing practiced by some casebook editors, it is sometimes a difficult or even impossible task. Bear in mind that the *party presently* seeking something from this court may not be the plaintiff, and that sometimes only the cross-claim of a defendant is treated in the excerpt. Confusing or misaligning the parties can ruin your analysis and understanding of the case.

ISSUE: A statement of the general legal question answered by or illustrated in the case. For clarity, the issue is best put in the form of a question capable of a "yes" or "no" answer. In reality, the issue is simply the Rule of Law put in the form of a question (e.g., "May an offer be accepted by performance?").

The major problem presented in discerning what is *the* issue in the case is that an opinion usually purports to raise and answer several questions. However, except for rare cases, only one such question is really the issue in the case. Collateral issues not necessary to the resolution of the matter in controversy are handled by the court by language known as *"obiter dictum"* or merely *"dictum."* While dicta may be included later in the brief, they have no place under the issue heading.

To find the issue, ask *who wants what* and then go on to ask *why did that party succeed or fail in getting it.* Once this is determined, the "why" should be turned into a question.

The complexity of the issues in the cases will vary, but in all cases a single-sentence question should sum up the issue. *In a few cases,* there will be two, or even more rarely, three issues of equal importance to the resolution of the case. Each should be expressed in a single-sentence question.

Since many issues are resolved by a court in coming to a final disposition of a case, the casebook editor will reproduce the portion of the opinion containing the issue or issues most relevant to the area of law under scrutiny. A noted law professor gave this advice: "Close the book; look at the title on the cover." Chances are, if it is Property, you need not concern yourself with whether, for example, the federal government's treatment of the plaintiff's land really raises a federal question sufficient to support jurisdiction on this ground in federal court.

The same rule applies to chapter headings designating sub-areas within the subjects. They tip you off as to what the text is designed to teach. The cases are arranged in a casebook to show a progression or development of the law, so that the preceding cases may also help.

It is also most important to remember to *read the notes and questions* at the end of a case to determine what the editors wanted you to have gleaned from it.

HOLDING AND DECISION: This section should succinctly explain the rationale of the court in arriving at its decision. In capsulizing the "reasoning" of the court, it should always include an application of the general rule or rules of law to the specific facts of the case. Hidden justifications come to light in this entry: the reasons for the state of the law, the public policies, the biases and prejudices, those considerations that influence the justices' thinking and, ultimately, the outcome of the case. At the end, there should be a short indication of the disposition or procedural resolution of the case (e.g., "Decision of the trial court for Mr. Smith (P) reversed").

The foregoing format is designed to help you "digest" the reams of case material with which you will be faced in your law school career. Once mastered by practice, it will place at your fingertips the information the authors of your casebooks have sought to impart to you in case-by-case illustration and analysis.

B. Be as Economical as Possible in Briefing Cases

Once armed with a format that encourages succinctness, it is as important to be economical with regard to the time spent on the actual reading of the case as it is to be economical in the writing of the brief itself. This does not mean "skimming" a case. Rather, it means reading the case with an "eye" trained to recognize into which "section" of your brief a particular passage or line fits and having a system for quickly and precisely marking the case so that the passages fitting any one particular part of the brief can be easily identified and brought together in a concise and accurate manner when the brief is actually written.

It is of no use to simply repeat everything in the opinion of the court; record only enough information to trigger your recollection of what the court said. Nevertheless, an accurate statement of the "law of the case," i.e., the legal principle applied to the facts, is absolutely essential to class preparation and to learning the law under the case method.

To that end, it is important to develop a "shorthand" that you can use to make marginal notations. These notations will tell you at a glance in which section of the brief you will be placing that particular passage or portion of the opinion.

Some students prefer to underline all the salient portions of the opinion (with a pencil or colored underliner marker), making marginal notations as they go along. Others prefer the color-coded method of underlining, utilizing different colors of markers to underline the salient portions of the case, each separate color being used to represent a different section of the brief. For example, blue underlining could be used for passages relating to the rule of law, yellow for those relating to the issue, and green for those relating to the holding and decision, etc. While it has its advocates, the color-coded method can be confusing and time-consuming (all that time spent on changing colored markers). Furthermore, it can interfere with the continuity and concentration many students deem essential to the reading of a case for maximum comprehension. In the end, however, it is a matter of personal preference and style. Just remember, whatever method you use, underlining must be used sparingly or its value is lost.

If you take the marginal notation route, an efficient and easy method is to go along underlining the key portions of the case and placing in the margin alongside them the following "markers" to indicate where a particular passage or line "belongs" in the brief you will write:

N   (NATURE OF CASE)
RL   (RULE OF LAW)
I   (ISSUE)
HL   (HOLDING AND DECISION, relates to
      the RULE OF LAW behind the decision)
HR   (HOLDING AND DECISION, gives the
      RATIONALE or reasoning behind the
      decision)
HA   (HOLDING AND DECISION, APPLIES
      the general principle(s) of law to the facts
      of the case to arrive at the decision)

Remember that a particular passage may well contain information necessary to more than one part of your brief, in which case you simply note that in the margin. If you are using the color-coded underlining method instead of marginal notation, simply make asterisks or checks in the margin next to the passage in question in the colors that indicate the additional sections of the brief where it might be utilized.

The economy of utilizing "shorthand" in marking cases for briefing can be maintained in the actual brief writing process itself by utilizing "law student shorthand" within the brief. There are many commonly used words and phrases for which abbreviations can be substituted in your briefs (and in your class notes also). You can develop abbreviations that are personal to you and which will save you a lot of time. A reference list of briefing abbreviations can be found on page xii of this book.

C. Use Both the Briefing Process and the Brief as a Learning Tool

Now that you have a format and the tools for briefing cases efficiently, the most important thing is to make the time spent in briefing profitable to you and to make the most advantageous use of the briefs you create. Of course, the briefs are invaluable for classroom reference when you are called upon to explain or analyze a particular

case. However, they are also useful in reviewing for exams. A quick glance at the fact summary should bring the case to mind, and a rereading of the rule of law should enable you to go over the underlying legal concept in your mind, how it was applied in that particular case, and how it might apply in other factual settings.

As to the value to be derived from engaging in the briefing process itself, there is an immediate benefit that arises from being forced to sift through the essential facts and reasoning from the court's opinion and to succinctly express them in your own words in your brief. The process ensures that you understand the case and the point that it illustrates, and that means you will be ready to absorb further analysis and information brought forth in class. It also ensures you will have something to say when called upon in class. The briefing process helps develop a mental agility for getting to the *gist* of a case and for identifying, expounding on, and applying the legal concepts and issues found there. The briefing process is the mental process on which you must rely in taking law school examinations; it is also the mental process upon which a lawyer relies in serving his clients and in making his living.

Abbreviations for Briefs

Table of Cases

Introduction

Quick Reference Rules of Law

Vlastos v. Sumitomo Marine & Fire Insurance Company

Policyholder (P) v. Insurance company (D)

707 F.2d 775 (3d Cir. 1983).

NATURE OF CASE: Appeal of judgment denying recovery on an insurance policy.

FACT SUMMARY: Vlastos (P) obtained a fire insurance policy containing a warranty that the janitor lived on the third floor of the insured building, although it did not warrant that his occupancy was exclusive.

🏛 RULE OF LAW
A warranty in a policy of property insurance that a certain area is occupied by a certain person will not void the policy if the occupancy is not exclusive.

FACTS: Vlastos (P) owned a four-story building, insured by Sumitomo Marine & Fire Insurance Co. (Sumitomo) (D). The policy contained a warranty that the third floor was occupied by Vlastos's (P) janitor. This was the case, but a portion of the floor was also leased to a tenant. A fire destroyed the building. Sumitomo (D) denied the claim on the basis that the warranty regarding the third floor being occupied by the janitor had been breached. Vlastos (P) sued. The court instructed the jury that the policy language meant that the janitor's occupancy was to be exclusive. The jury returned a defense verdict, and Vlastos (P) appealed.

ISSUE: Will a warranty in a policy of property insurance that a certain area is occupied by a certain person void the policy if the occupancy is not exclusive?

HOLDING AND DECISION: (Adams, J.) No. A warranty in a policy of property insurance that a certain area is occupied by a certain person will not void the policy if the occupancy is not exclusive. Absent language to the effect that the occupancy must be exclusive, which was not the case here, the language is ambiguous. This being the case, under Pennsylvania law, which the district court must apply in this diversity action, the construction favoring Vlastos (P) must be adopted. The case must therefore be remanded. If a question exists as to whether the janitor lived on the third floor, a jury must decide this issue. If no such issue exists, judgment must be entered for Vlastos (P). Reversed.

▶ ANALYSIS

Vlastos (P) argued that the clause was a representation, not a warranty. The difference between the two is that a false representation, to void a policy, must be material. A false warranty, on the other hand, need not be material. The court found it unnecessary to decide this issue, as its ruling was based on the assumption that the clause was a warranty.

Quicknotes

DIVERSITY ACTION An action commenced by a citizen of one state against a citizen of another state or against an alien, involving an amount in controversy set by statute, over which the federal court has jurisdiction.

WARRANTY An assurance by one party that another may rely on a certain representation of fact.

■=■

Neill v. Nationwide Mutual Fire Insurance Company

Insured homeowner (D) v. Insurance company (P)

Ark. Ct. App., 81 Ark. App. 67; 98 S.W.3d 448 (2003).

NATURE OF CASE: Appeal from summary judgment for plaintiff in declaratory relief action.

FACT SUMMARY: After Neill (D) made a claim for fire loss under his policy with Nationwide Mutual Fire Insurance Company (Nationwide) (P), Nationwide (P) sought to void Neill's (D) insurance policy because Neill (D) had failed to disclose previous fire losses in his policy application. Neill (D) counterclaimed for breach of contract and bad faith.

RULE OF LAW
Summary judgment is not appropriate where: an application for insurance contains a misrepresentation; it is possible the misrepresentation occurred inadvertently through an agent's mistake or negligence; the applicant attests that the facts in the application are true; but the applicant does not read the application.

FACTS: Neill's (D) home was damaged by fire, and he filed a claim with his homeowner's insurance company, Nationwide Mutual Fire Insurance Company (Nationwide) (P). Nationwide (P) denied his claim and brought suit seeking to void *ab initio* Neill's (D) insurance policy because Neill (D) had failed to disclose three previous fire losses in his policy application. Neill (D) counterclaimed for breach of contract and bad faith. Neill (D) had met with Nationwide agent Anderson, to apply for the homeowner's insurance. According to Neill (D), Anderson asked him several questions and typed in Neill's (D) answers on the computer. Neill (D) testified that Anderson did not ask him about any previous fire losses, or if he did ask him, Neill (D) stated that he must not have understood the question because he would not have replied that he had no prior losses. After Anderson finished asking the questions, the application for insurance was printed out, and Neill (D) testified that he signed it without reading it, as he assumed that it contained the answers he had given to Anderson. Above his signature, the application contained a clause that Neill (D) declared that the facts in the application were true and that he was requesting the company to issue the policy in reliance thereon. The trial granted summary judgment to Nationwide (P), finding that Neill's (D) failure to inform Nationwide (P) of his prior fire losses amounted to material misrepresentation. The appellate court granted review.

ISSUE: Is summary judgment appropriate where: an application for insurance contains a misrepresentation; it is possible the misrepresentation occurred inadvertently through an agent's mistake or negligence; the applicant attests that the facts in the application are true; but the applicant does not read the application?

HOLDING AND DECISION: (Roaf, J.) No. Summary judgment is not appropriate where: an application for insurance contains a misrepresentation; it is possible the misrepresentation occurred inadvertently through an agent's mistake or negligence; the applicant attests that the facts in the application are true; but the applicant does not read the application. It is a well-settled proposition that where the facts have been truthfully stated by an insured to the soliciting agent, but by fraud, negligence, or mistake the facts are misstated in the application to the insurer, the insurer cannot rely on the misstatements in avoidance of liability, if the agent was acting within his real or apparent authority, and there is no fraud or collusion on the part of the insured. However, it is equally well-settled that a person is bound under the law to know the contents of the papers he signs and that he cannot excuse himself by saying that he did not know what the papers contained. Here, Neill (D) is able to testify and has testified that he was not asked about prior losses by the agent. In contrast, Nationwide (P) has not presented evidence by its agent that the question was asked and answered incorrectly by Neill (D). Therefore, there is a fact question as to whether Nationwide (P) asked and correctly recorded Neill's (D) answer about previous losses. The fact that Neill (D) signed the certification that the information was true is merely probative evidence of his misrepresentation and not dispositive of the case. Reversed and remanded.

ANALYSIS

Had Anderson (the agent) not been an intermediary in this case, and if Neill (D) had filled out the application on his own, summary judgment would have been appropriate, as the failure to disclose the previous fire losses would have been considered a material misrepresentation, and Neill (D) would have had no possible excuse that he did not know the contents of the application.

Quicknotes

AB INITIO From its inception or beginning.

BAD FAITH Conduct that is intentionally misleading or deceptive.

BREACH OF CONTRACT Unlawful failure by a party to perform its obligations pursuant to contract.

HOMEOWNER'S INSURANCE An insurance policy protecting persons against all or a portion of potential damage to, and liability for, real or personal property.

Continued on next page.

MISREPRESENTATION A statement or conduct by one party to another that constitutes a false representation of fact.

SUMMARY JUDGMENT Judgment rendered by a court in response to a motion made by one of the parties, claiming that the lack of a question of material fact in respect to an issue warrants disposition of the issue without consideration by the jury.

■══■

MacKenzie v. Prudential Insurance Company of America

Beneficiary (P) v. Insurance company (D)

411 F.2d 781 (6th Cir. 1969).

NATURE OF CASE: Appeal from summary judgment for defendant in an action to recover payments under an insurance policy.

FACT SUMMARY: Prudential Insurance Company of America (D) refused to make payments to MacKenzie's beneficiary (P) of his life insurance policy on the basis that MacKenzie made material misrepresentations regarding his health when he accepted delivery of the policy.

🏛 RULE OF LAW
In order to prevent recovery on an insurance policy, material misrepresentations made by the insured must either be sufficiently material to the risk or fraudulently made.

FACTS: MacKenzie applied with Prudential Insurance Company of America (Prudential) (D) for a $40,000 decreasing term life insurance policy. The application required him to disclose whether he had ever been treated for or had any indication of heart problems or high blood pressure, to which he answered in the negative. The application also stated that no insurance would take effect unless all answers to these questions continued to be true and complete as of the date of delivery of the policy. Sometime before the date the policy was delivered MacKenzie suffered a chest bruise. After examination a doctor found his blood pressure to be above normal so he prescribed medication. When the policy was delivered, MacKenzie said nothing regarding the recent developments. MacKenzie died and Prudential (D) refused to disburse payments to his beneficiary (P) under the policy on the basis that MacKenzie made material misrepresentations regarding his health when he accepted delivery of the policy. Prudential (D) stated in its responses to interrogatories that if the change in his condition had been revealed, Prudential (D) either would have refused to issue the policy or increased the premiums. The district court granted summary judgment for Prudential (D) and the beneficiary (P) appealed.

ISSUE: In order to prevent recovery on an insurance policy, must material misrepresentations made by the insured either be sufficiently material to the risk or fraudulently made?

HOLDING AND DECISION: (Combs, J.) Yes. In order to prevent recovery on an insurance policy, material misrepresentations made by the insured must either be sufficiently material to the risk or fraudulently made. Prudential (D) claimed that since MacKenzie's misrepresentation with respect to his blood pressure was material, no fraud need be shown. Materiality is measured in accordance with the standard which the insurance company would have taken on the application, if the truth were told. Here the issue is whether MacKenzie had a duty to divulge his change in health, and whether breach of that duty amounted to a material misrepresentation. The Supreme Court has held that when a potential insured learns any additional information while an insurance company is in deliberation of whether to issue him a policy, that would make parts of his application therefore untrue, the duty of good faith and fair dealing would require him to disclose such new information. If he fails to do so, the insurance company may refuse to issue him a policy or have a valid defense to a suit for recovery. Here MacKenzie's failure to divulge the new information relating to his blood pressure constituted a material misrepresentation sufficient to render the policy void. Affirmed.

▶ ANALYSIS

Other courts have held that an insurance policy applicant has no duty to disclose a change in health unless specifically asked. In *Seidler v. Georgetown Life Insurance Company*, 82 Ill. App. 3d 361 (1980), the court held that the applicant's failure to disclose the fact that he suffered a heart attack between the time he submitted to a physical examination and the time the policy was delivered did not preclude recovery since he was not asked to disclose the information, even though the company customarily required applicants to fill out a form at time of delivery requesting disclosure of any such changes in the applicant's health.

━■━

Quicknotes

BENEFICIARY A third party who is the recipient of the benefit of a transaction undertaken by another.

DELIVERY The transfer of title or possession of property.

DUTY OF GOOD FAITH AND FAIR DEALINGS An implied duty in a contract that the parties will deal honestly in the satisfaction of their obligations and without intent to defraud.

MATERIAL FALSE REPRESENTATIONS A statement or conduct by one party to another that constitutes a false representation of a material fact.

SUMMARY JUDGMENT Judgment rendered by a court in response to a motion made by one of the parties, claiming that the lack of a question of material fact in respect to an issue warrants disposition of the issue without consideration by the jury.

━■━

CHAPTER 2

Formation of the Insurance Contract and Its Meaning

AU ✓

Quick Reference Rules of Law

Vargas v. Insurance Company of North America

Estate of deceased family (P) v. Insurance company (D)

651 F.2d 838 (2d Cir. 1981).

NATURE OF CASE: Appeal from summary judgment for defendant in an action for declaratory judgment on insurance liability.

FACT SUMMARY: Khurey and his family died when their private plane crashed going to Puerto Rico and Insurance Company of North America (D) denied coverage based on a territorial limit of the policy.

RULE OF LAW

An ambiguous provision in an insurance policy is construed most favorably to the insured and strictly against the insurer.

FACTS: Khurey had aviation insurance from Insurance Company of North America (INA) (D) that provided for coverage for occurrences and accidents which happened in the United States, its territories, Canada and Mexico. An endorsement extended the territorial limits to include the Bahama Islands. On December 23, 1977, Khurey and his family were killed when their plane crashed into the sea about 25 miles west of Puerto Rico, where they were flying from Miami, via Haiti. INA (D) denied coverage on the ground that the crash did not occur within the policy territory limits because it was not within the territorial waters of Puerto Rico. The district court granted summary judgment to INA (D).

ISSUE: Is an ambiguous provision in an insurance policy construed most favorably to the insured and strictly against the insurer?

HOLDING AND DECISION: (Sofaer, J.) Yes. An ambiguous provision in an insurance policy is construed most favorably to the insured and strictly against the insurer. The insurer bears a heavy burden of proof to establish that the words and expressions used in the policy are susceptible for only one fair construction. Thus, the insurer must show that it would be unreasonable for the average man reading the policy to construe it only as the insurer does. In the present case, the policy at issue is readily susceptible of a fair interpretation that would cover the Khurey's flight. The parties both knew that the plane was covered for flights between territories that brought it outside the territorial waters boundaries. As long as the plane was on a reasonably direct course from and to geographic areas covered by the policy, it could be said to be within the contemplated limits. Furthermore, looking at the addition of the Bahamas endorsement, the extension of the limits addressed flights to the Bahamas, not the entire flight path. Accordingly, it is clear that the policy was intended to cover reasonable routes to the locations covered by the policy's territory clause.

Given this ambiguity in the policy, it must be construed against INA (D) and in favor of coverage. Summary judgment is reversed.

ANALYSIS

The court also noted that the intent of the parties could have provided grounds for coverage. There was evidence that Khurey indicated that the plane would be outside the continental United States for vacations on the application. Given this factual possibility, summary judgment was inappropriate.

Quicknotes

AMBIGUITY Language that is capable of being understood to have more than one interpretation.

DECLARATORY JUDGMENT A judgment of the court establishing the rights of the parties.

SUMMARY JUDGMENT Judgment rendered by a court in response to a motion made by one of the parties, claiming that the lack of a question of material fact in respect to an issue warrants disposition of the issue without consideration by the jury.

World Trade Center Properties, L.L.C. v. Hartford Fire Insurance Company

Insured property owners (P) v. Insurance companies (D)

345 F.3d 154 (2d Cir. 2003).

NATURE OF CASE: Appeals by insured from grant of summary judgment to insurers and from denial of summary judgment to insured.

FACT SUMMARY: Insured owners (P) of various property interests in the World Trade Center, which was destroyed by terrorist attacks involving two airplanes on September 11, 2001, had insurance on a "per occurrence" basis. The insureds (P) argued that the insurance binders of three of four insurers (D) were intended to include the specimen policy form of the fourth insurer—a form that did not define "occurrence"—and they also argued that the events of September 11, 2001, under the form, could be interpreted as two separate "occurrences."

🏛 RULE OF LAW
(1) Where an insurer issues a binder on the basis of a specimen form provided by a broker, the terms of that form govern any losses pending issuance of a final policy.
(2) The undefined term "occurrence" when used in a first-party property damage insurance binder is ambiguous.

FACTS: Insured owners (P) of various property interests in the World Trade Center (WTC), which was destroyed by terrorist attacks involving two airplanes on September 11, 2001, had obtained insurance on a "per occurrence" basis. Silverstein Properties, Inc. and related entities (Silverstein Parties) (P), who held a 99-year lease on the property, had engaged Willis of New York (Willis), an insurance broker, to set up a multi-layered insurance program, providing $3.5 billion insurance on the "per occurrence" basis. In soliciting insurers, Willis circulated information regarding the proposed placement that included a "broker" form (the "WilProp form"). That form defined "occurrence" as "all losses or damages that are attributable directly or indirectly to one cause or to one series of similar causes. All such losses will be added together and the total amount of such losses will be treated as one occurrence irrespective of the period of time or area over which such losses occur." Of four insurers (D) involved, Travelers (D) was the only insurer to submit its own specimen policy form (the "Travelers form") during the course of negotiating the terms of coverage. The Travelers form did not define the term "occurrence." Each of the insurers (D) negotiated separately with Willis. The insurance coverage issue was whether the events of September 11, 2001, constituted one or two "occurrences" for the purpose of determining policy limits. The district court granted partial summary judgment to the three insurers (D) other than

Travelers (D) on the grounds that each of the insurers had issued a binder that incorporated the terms of the WilProp form and that under the WilProp form's definition of "occurrence" there was only one occurrence on September 11, 2001. Thus, the Silverstein Parties (P) were entitled to no more than a single policy limit on each of the insurers' (D) policies. The district court also denied summary judgment to the Silverstein Parties (P) against Travelers (D), because it found that contrary to the Siverstein Parties' (P) assertion, the term "occurrence" in the Travelers (D) form was not free from ambiguity. The court of appeals granted review.

ISSUE:
(1) Where an insurer issues a binder on the basis of a specimen form provided by a broker, do the terms of that form govern any losses pending issuance of a final policy?
(2) Is the undefined term "occurrence" when used in a first-party property damage insurance binder ambiguous?

HOLDING AND DECISION: (Walker, C.J.)
(1) Yes. Where an insurer issues a binder on the basis of a specimen form provided by a broker, the terms of that form govern any losses pending issuance of a final policy. Here, the binders issued by the three insurers (D) other than Travelers (D) were issued on the basis of negotiations involving the WilProp form, a copy of which had been provided to each insurer by Willis. The parties intended and understood the binders to incorporate the terms of the form except as expressly modified. Therefore, the obligations of the insurers (D) were governed by the terms included in the binders, which means that "occurrence" was defined by the WilProp form. Under the definition in that form, the events of September 11, 2001, constituted a single occurrence as a matter of law.
(2) Yes. The undefined term "occurrence" when used in a first-party property damage insurance binder is ambiguous. As with all contracts, the intention of the parties to an insurance contract should control the meaning of terms therein. If a court finds that a contract is ambiguous, it may look to extrinsic evidence to determine the parties' intent. While state (New York) law is clear that extrinsic evidence may not be used to contradict clearly unambiguous language contained in an insurance binder, it is just as well settled that extrinsic evidence is admissible to determine the parties' intentions with respect to the incomplete and unintegrated terms of a binder. Therefore, extrinsic evidence would be permitted here. Considering such evidence, the custom and usage of the insurance

Continued on next page.

industry is not consistent on whether to define "occur-rence" or not. Next, state law also does not provide a uniform meaning of "occurrence." Because there is not a well settled definition of the term under state law, the district court was correct in finding that the Travelers (D) binder was sufficiently ambiguous to preclude summary judgment and to permit the factfinder to consider extrin-sic evidence of the parties' intent. Affirmed.

▌▶ ANALYSIS

The principle of contract interpretation most frequently used with insurance contracts is the principle known as contra proferentem. This principle states that an ambiguous provi-sion in an insurance policy is interpreted against the drafter. Here, the insured (Silverstein Parties) (P) was not claiming that the term "occurrence" was ambiguous (ordinarily, it is the policyholder who asserts ambiguity of the policy). None-theless, it seems that the court, having determined on its own that the term, as a matter of law, was ambiguous, should have applied contra proferentem against Travelers (D) to find that the term favored the insured. Of course, the court is not obligated to use this principle of contract interpretation, and, in fact, on remand, the district court made no reference to this principle in its jury instructions—it merely instructed the jury to determine the parties' intent (the jury found that there were two occurrences).

■▬■

Quicknotes

AMBIGUOUS Vague; unclear; capable of being under-stood to have more than one meaning.

EXTRINSIC EVIDENCE Evidence that is not contained within the text of a document or contract, but which is derived from the parties' statements or the circumstances under which the agreement was made.

■▬■

Atwood v. Hartford Accident & Indemnity Co.

Insured electrician (P) v. Insurance company (D)

N.H. Sup. Ct., 365 A.2d 744 (1976).

NATURE OF CASE: Appeal from judgment in an action for insurance liability.

FACT SUMMARY: Atwood (P), an electrician, sought coverage for a negligence claim against him for completed work.

🏛 RULE OF LAW
The objectively reasonable expectations of the insured will be honored even though the technical provisions of the insurance policy would have negated those expectations.

FACTS: Atwood (P) was a self-employed electrician who had an insurance policy with Hartford Accident & Indemnity Co. (Hartford) (D). The policy included a completed operations exclusion provision which stated that coverage did not apply to bodily injury or property damage for work done by Atwood (P) that was completed. This provision was contained in a section with thirteen other clauses, none of which were applicable. Atwood (P) repaired a thermostat in an apartment in 1972 and subsequently a child died from heat prostration. The child's estate brought suit against Atwood (P), who notified Hartford (D) of the claim. Hartford (D) denied coverage on the basis of the completed operations exclusion.

ISSUE: Will the objectively reasonable expectations of the insured be honored even though the technical provisions of the insurance policy would have negated those expectations?

HOLDING AND DECISION: (Kenison, C.J.) Yes. The objectively reasonable expectations of the insured will be honored even though the technical provisions of the insurance policy would have negated those expectations. An insured must be able to read an insurance policy and have reasonable expectations of coverage. There must be fair notice to the insured about what will be covered and what will not be covered by the insurer. In the present case, a reasonable person reading the policy in question could conclude that it would cover the type of claim against Atwood (P). The exclusion clause was both unclear and buried within an irrelevant section. Therefore, Atwood (P) had reasonable expectations that his work was covered against claims after he left a job site. Despite the fact that the policy expressly provided against such coverage, Atwood (P) is entitled to coverage. Exceptions overruled.

▶ ANALYSIS

The court also noted that there was evidence that Atwood's (P) insurance agent believed Atwood (P) was covered for completed operations. The court stated that if an agent did

not realize the extent of coverage, a lay person such as Atwood (P) couldn't be expected to. The granting of coverage in such situations is based on both misrepresentation and estoppel theories.

Quicknotes

ESTOPPEL An equitable doctrine precluding a party from asserting a right to the detriment of another who justifiably relied on the conduct.

LIABILITY Any obligation or responsibility.

MISREPRESENTATION A statement or conduct by one party to another that constitutes a false representation of fact.

NEGLIGENCE Conduct falling below the standard of care that a reasonable person would demonstrate under similar conditions.

Atwater Creamery Company v. Western National Mutual Insurance Company

Creamery supply company (P) v. Insurance company (D)

Minn. Sup. Ct., 366 N.W.2d 271 (1985).

NATURE OF CASE: Appeal from directed verdict in an action for declaratory judgment on insurance coverage.

FACT SUMMARY: Western National Mutual Insurance Company (D) denied Atwater Creamery Company's (P) theft insurance claim because there were no visible marks of forced entry.

RULE OF LAW
Ambiguity in an insurance policy is not required for application of the reasonable expectations doctrine.

FACTS: Atwater Creamery Company (Atwater) (P), a creamery and supplier of farm chemicals, had burglary insurance from Western National Mutual Insurance Company (Western) (D) that contained an "evidence of forcible entry" requirement in its definition of burglary. In April 1977, Atwater (P) was robbed of $15,587 of chemicals when unknown persons loosened turnbuckles on a door. A plant manager had secured the building prior to the robbery and an investigation determined that the robbery was not committed by an Atwater (P) employee. Western (D) denied Atwater's (P) insurance claim because there were no visible marks of physical damage to the exterior or interior at the point of the burglar's entrance and exit. Atwater (P) brought suit against Western (D) and the trial court granted a directed verdict to Western (D).

ISSUE: Is ambiguity in an insurance policy required for application of the reasonable expectations doctrine?

HOLDING AND DECISION: (Wahl, J.) No. Ambiguity in an insurance policy is not required for application of the reasonable expectations doctrine. Some courts have found that enforcing the visible marks burglary definition literally does not serve the purpose of the provision. It is designed to protect insurers from fraud by way of "inside jobs" and encourage insureds to reasonably secure their premises. This approach merely substitutes the court's own definition of burglary and is not proper. Other courts have found the definition to act as a hidden exclusion. Under this approach, it is seen as defeating the reasonable expectations of the insured. Where there is unequal bargaining power between contracting parties, the contract will be construed against the drafting party. There is this type of disparity in bargaining position in most insurance policies. Thus, the reasonable expectations of the insured should be honored even if the policy does not technically provide for coverage. Some courts have applied this doctrine only where there is some ambiguity in the policy. However, the better approach is to apply it even where there is no ambiguity. The burglary definition contained in Western's (D) policy is a classic example of a provision that should be interpreted according to the reasonable expectations of the insured. A business that purchases burglary insurance is seeking coverage for losses that occur whether the thieves are highly skilled and leave no marks at all or if they are inept and cause much damage. Accordingly, in the present case, Atwater (P) reasonably expected that coverage would be available for the type of theft that occurred and the directed verdict for Western (D) must be reversed.

ANALYSIS

The court pointed out that ambiguity in the policy is not irrelevant using this approach. Rather, it becomes a factor in determining the reasonable expectations. The court also noted that it places a burden on insurers to communicate coverage and exclusions accurately and clearly.

Quicknotes

BURGLARY Unlawful entry of a building at night with the intent to commit a felony therein.

DIRECTED VERDICT A verdict ordered by the court in a jury trial.

Elmer Tallant Agency, Inc. v. Bailey Wood Products, Inc.

Insurance agent (D) v. Insured client (P)

Ala. Sup. Ct., 374 So. 2d 1312 (1979).

NATURE OF CASE: Appeal from judgment in action for declaratory judgment on insurance coverage.

FACT SUMMARY: Elmer Tallant Agency, Inc (D), an insurance agent for Zurich American Insurance Company (Zurich) (D), bound coverage for Bailey Wood Products, Inc. (P), although Zurich's (D) rules required prior approval.

🏛 RULE OF LAW
An insurance agent acting with apparent authority can bind coverage although there were private, undisclosed limitations on the authority.

FACTS: Bailey Wood Products, Inc. (Bailey Wood) (P) sought to obtain workers compensation insurance but was declined by several insurers, including Zurich American Insurance Company (Zurich) (D) through their agent, Elmer Tallant Agency, Inc. (D). Zurich's (D) rules for agents included a requirement of prior approval for coverage if there had been prior denial of a risk. Subsequently, Bailey Wood (P) again sought coverage through Tallant (D) and Tallant bound the coverage and forwarded it to Zurich (D), despite the rules for prior approval. Tallant (D) never indicated to Bailey Wood (P) that Zurich would be the insurer. Soon after, Coleman, a Bailey Wood (P) employee was injured in the course and scope of employment. However, Zurich (D) refused to accept the claim. Bailey Wood (P) filed suit against both Tallant (D) and Zurich (D).

ISSUE: Can an insurance agent acting with apparent authority bind coverage although there were private, undisclosed limitations on the authority?

HOLDING AND DECISION: (Bloodworth, J.) Yes. An insurance agent acting with apparent authority can bind coverage although there were private, undisclosed limitations on the authority. Generally, a contract of insurance is valid if made by an agent within the actual or apparent scope of his authority. Even where there is no agreement between the applicant and agent as to the insurer, if the agent has authority and designates the insurer through some act, the insurer is liable. Thus, the mere fact that Bailey Wood (P) was not informed that Zurich (D) was the designated insurer does not release Zurich (D) from liability because Tallant (D), a general agent for Zurich (D), had already submitted the risk. In the present case, Tallant (D) had no actual authority to bind Zurich (D) to the Bailey Wood (P) risk because coverage would not have been bound if Zurich's (D) rules had been followed. Accordingly, while Zurich (D) is liable to Bailey Wood (P), it is also entitled to indemnity from Tallant (D) for losses sustained due to Tallant's (D) exceeding the scope of its actual authority. The portions of the judgment in accordance with this position are affirmed, the portion that held Tallant (D) directly liable to Bailey Wood (P) is reversed.

▶ ANALYSIS

Zurich (D) conferred apparent authority in the present case by allowing Tallant (D) to act as a general agent. The construction of liability in this case protects the insureds, who rely upon agents for their insurance needs. If Tallant (D) had told Bailey Wood (P) that there was coverage, but hadn't sent on the application to Zurich (D), it would have been directly liable to Bailey Wood (P) for breach of contract.

Quicknotes

AGENCY A fiduciary relationship whereby authority is granted to an agent to act on behalf of the principal in order to effectuate the principal's objective.

AGENT An individual who has the authority to act on behalf of another.

APPARENT AUTHORITY The authority granted to an agent to act on behalf of the principal in order to effectuate the principal's objective, which may not be expressly granted, but which is inferred from the conduct of the principal and the agent.

INDEMNITY The duty of a party to compensate another for damages sustained.

Roseth v. St. Paul Property & Liability Insurance Company

Cattle transporter (P) v. Insurance company (D)

S.D. Sup. Ct., 374 N.W.2d 105 (1985).

NATURE OF CASE: Appeal from judgment in action for insurance coverage.

FACT SUMMARY: Roseth (P), a transporter of livestock, alleged that wrong information about the scope of his policy's coverage from a St. Paul Property & Liability Insurance Company (D) adjuster after an accident led to additional financial loss.

🏛 RULE OF LAW
Estoppel for a misrepresentation by an insurer after the inception of the policy is not available to bring within coverage those risks not covered by the policy terms.

FACTS: Roseth (P), a transporter of livestock, had a cargo insurance policy with St. Paul Property & Liability Insurance Company (St. Paul) (D). The policy, which provided the maximum coverage then available, insured against livestock deaths but specifically excluded injuries to cattle that could still walk away from an accident. Subsequently, a livestock trailer owned by Roseth (D) had an accident in which 14 of the 109 cattle died or ended up missing and the others were injured. Roseth (P) called St. Paul (D) and talked to an adjuster about the situation. The adjuster mistakenly assumed that Roseth (P) was covered for the injured cattle and recommended that the loss be minimized by immediately selling the remaining cattle at a price approximately $8,800 below their value before the accident. After St. Paul (D) paid out only for the cattle who were killed or missing, Roseth (P) filed suit to recover the amount lost on the injured cattle, based on the adjuster's representations. The trial court ruled that St. Paul (D) was estopped from using the exclusion and ruled for Roseth (P).

ISSUE: Is estoppel for a misrepresentation by an insurer after the inception of the policy available to bring within coverage those risks not covered by the policy terms?

HOLDING AND DECISION: (Wollman, J.) No. Estoppel for a misrepresentation by an insurer after the inception of the policy is not available to bring within coverage those risks not covered by the policy terms. Some jurisdictions have held that an insurance company may be estopped to defend liability on the basis of an exclusionary clause when the insured was led to believe that coverage would be available. However, this minority rule is based on circumstances when the misrepresentation by the insurer occurs before or at the inception of the insurance contract. In such a situation, the insured has relied to his detriment on the insurer's superior knowledge about the scope of insurance and is deprived of the ability to find coverage elsewhere. In the present case, Roseth (P) was not told that the coverage would be available for injured cattle at the time he obtained the policy. Rather, the St. Paul (D) adjuster merely perpetuated a misconception regarding the nature of the coverage. Accordingly, there was no conduct that required estopping. The judgment for Roseth (P) is reversed.

▶ ANALYSIS

This decision isn't wholly satisfactory. Roseth (P) did rely on the St. Paul (D) adjuster for advice that led to an action that might have increased his loss. The adjuster certainly should have checked the policy before offering suggestions.

■━■

Quicknotes

ESTOPPEL An equitable doctrine precluding a party from asserting a right to the detriment of another whom justifiably relied on the conduct.

MISREPRESENTATION A statement or conduct by one party to another that constitutes a false representation of fact.

■━■

Richard C. Gossett and Margaret D. Gossett v. Farmers Insurance Company of Washington

Would-be homeowners (P) v. Insurance company (D)

Wash. Sup. Ct., 948 P.2d 1264 (1997).

NATURE OF CASE: Appeal from summary judgment for plaintiffs in action to collect insurance benefits.

FACT SUMMARY: The Gossetts (P) obtained homeowner's insurance from Farmers Insurance Co. of Washington (D) on a home that they intended to buy but were not yet legal owners.

RULE OF LAW
A party must have an ownership interest in property in order to collect insurance benefits on its loss.

FACTS: The Gossetts (P) made an offer on a home in Tacoma that was accepted. The Gossetts (P) represented to Farmers Insurance Co. of Washington (Farmers) (D) that they would be legal owners of the property and obtained a homeowner's insurance policy. Actually, the Gossetts (P) assigned all their interest in the purchase and sale agreement to Trusty Deed, who was also to take title to the home. After the sale closed, the Gossetts (P) began to work on the house and planned to move in, but a fire destroyed the home and the improvements made before the Gossetts (P) could obtain long-term financing and actually buy the property. Farmers (D) denied coverage on the basis that the Gossetts (P) did not have legal title and an insurable interest in the property. The trial court ruled that the Gossetts (P) were entitled only to recover the value of the improvements they made to the property.

ISSUE: Must a party have an ownership interest in property in order to collect insurance benefits on its loss?

HOLDING AND DECISION: (Madsen, J.) Yes. A party must have an ownership interest in property in order to collect insurance benefits on its loss. A fundamental premise of insurance law is that insureds may not have an opportunity to gain more through insurance proceeds than the loss they suffered. Thus, insurance is intended only to restore an insured to a condition equivalent to that which existed before the loss occurred. This is referred to as the principle of indemnity. This prevents insurance contracts from acting as a gambling arrangement and protects against the intentional destruction of property. In the present case, although the Gossetts (P) apparently intended to buy the property, they had no security interest in the home at the time of the fire. They had absolutely no obligation or debt with regard to the property. If they recovered the value of the home, they would be in a far better position than they were before the fire. Moreover, the Gossetts' (P) expectations and payment of insurance premiums do not constitute an insurable interest. It is true that a party with a partial interest in property can recover to that extent. In the present case, the improvements made represent an actual pecuniary loss to the Gossetts (P) that may be recovered. Thus, the trial court acted properly in awarding those benefits only. Affirmed.

ANALYSIS

The insurable interest requirement is essentially the modern version of the principle of indemnity. This principle goes back to the 1700s. In the United States it began as a common law rule but has since been codified in most states.

Quicknotes

SECURITY INTEREST An interest in property that may be sold upon a default in payment of the debt.

Ryan v. Tickle

Estate executrix (P) v. Decedent's former business partner (D)

Neb. Sup. Ct., 316 N.W.2d 580 (1982).

NATURE OF CASE: Appeal from dismissal of action to recover life insurance proceeds.

FACT SUMMARY: The decedent's widow (P) claimed that she was entitled to life insurance that named the decedent's business partner as the beneficiary.

🏛 RULE OF LAW
Only insurers have standing to object to a beneficiary's lack of insurable interest.

FACTS: Ryan and Tickle (D) were morticians who went into business together. Their ultimate business goal was to acquire full ownership of two funeral homes. They decided to purchase life insurance policies on each other's lives to provide a fund by which the survivor could fulfill this goal. After Ryan died, the insurance benefits were paid to Tickle (D), who bought out Ryan's interest and acquired the funeral homes completely. Ryan's widow (P) then filed suit to recover the insurance proceeds from Tickle (D) claiming that Tickle (D) did not have an insurable interest in the life of Ryan. The trial court dismissed the action and Ryan's widow (P) appealed.

ISSUE: Do some third parties have standing to object to a beneficiary's lack of insurable interest?

HOLDING AND DECISION: (Brodkey, J.) No. Only insurers have standing to object to a beneficiary's lack of insurable interest. The rule is well established in virtually all jurisdictions that only an insurer can raise the objection of want of an insurable interest. Adverse claimants and the heirs of the insured have no cause of action. Therefore, Ryan's widow (P) has no standing to bring suit against Tickle (D) on the allegation that Tickle (D) had no insurable interest in Ryan's life. The dismissal is affirmed.

▶ ANALYSIS

The court appeared to indicate that it would have found an insurable interest for Tickle (D) in any case. As partners, it seems that Tickle (D) was benefitting from the continued life of Ryan at the time the policy was issued. The insurer in this case did not raise any objection with regard to the insurable interest issue.

■▬■

Quicknotes

CAUSE OF ACTION A fact or set of facts the occurrence of which entitles a party to seek judicial relief.

STANDING The right to commence suit against another party because of a personal stake in the resolution of the controversy.

■▬■

→ didn't own the funeral home, but evidence suggests they had an agreement to do this. Shows another type of insurable interest.

Mayo v. Hartford Life Insurance Company

Decedent's estate (P) v. Insurance company (D)

354 F.3d 400 (5th Cir. 2004).

NATURE OF CASE:
Appeal from grant of partial summary judgment to plaintiff and from denial of summary judgment to defendant, in life insurance case.

FACT SUMMARY:
The estate (P) of a Wal-Mart Stores, Inc. (D) employee contended that a company-owned life insurance (COLI) policy on the life of the employee violated Texas's insurable interest doctrine because, it argued, an employer has no insurable interest in an ordinary employee under Texas law.

🏛 RULE OF LAW
A company-owned life insurance (COLI) policy on the life of an ordinary employee violates the insurable interest doctrine.

FACTS:
Acting in pursuit of tax benefits related to the deductibility of premium payments, Wal-Mart Stores, Inc. (Wal-Mart) (D) took out life insurance on its employees and made itself the beneficiary. Wal-Mart (D) established a trust to hold these company-owned life insurance (COLI) policies, and the instrument establishing the trust provided that Georgia law would govern the trust's construction, validity, and administration. Sims, a Wal-Mart (D) employee was covered by a COLI policy. After Sims died, his estate (P) sued Wal-Mart (D) on the ground that the COLI violated the Texas insurable interest doctrine. The estate sought, in relevant part, a declaratory judgment of its rights under Sims' COLI policy, the imposition of a constructive trust on the policy benefits, and disgorgement of the money it claimed Wal-Mart (D) unjustly received. The district court denied summary judgment for Wal-Mart (D) and granted partial summary judgment for the estate (P). The court of appeals granted an interlocutory appeal.

ISSUE:
Does a company-owned life insurance (COLI) policy on the life of an ordinary employee violate the insurable interest doctrine?

HOLDING AND DECISION:
(Jolly, J.) Yes. A company-owned life insurance (COLI) policy on the life of an ordinary employee violates the insurable interest doctrine. Here, Texas law applies. Texas has an insurable interest doctrine, which requires a person insuring the life of another to have an insurable interest in the insured person's life. Texas courts have recognized three categories of individuals having an adequate interest: 1) close relatives; 2) creditors; and 3) those having an expectation of financial gain from the insured's continued life. Texas courts have also held that employment alone does not give an employer an insurable interest. Wal-Mart (D) contends that, in addition to the bare employer/employee relationship, it possesses an expectation of financial gain from the continued lives of its employees by virtue of the costs associated with the death of an employee, such as productivity losses, hiring and training a replacement, and payment of death benefits. These are costs that are associated with the loss of any employee, however. And, as the estate (P) points out, Wal-Mart (D) does not claim that Sims was of any special importance to the company, much less that Wal-Mart's success or failure was dependent upon Sims. Additionally, no legislative amendments to the insurable interest doctrine are applicable here, and case law precedents show that Texas courts have held fast to the common law insurable interest doctrine. Therefore, applying that doctrine, Wal-Mart's (D) COLI on Sims violated Texas law. Affirmed.

▶ ANALYSIS
At the time Wal-Mart (D) and other like companies were using COLIs, federal tax law permitted the companies to deduct the interest on loans funding the premiums for COLIs on all employees. Since premiums equal losses plus minor administrative expenses, and since it was certain that employees would eventually die, the companies were able to obtain a tax deduction for essentially transferring money from one account to another. Congress and the IRS eliminated these tax advantages, except for interest deductions for policies taken out on the lives of "key" employees.

Quicknotes

CONSTRUCTIVE TRUST A trust that arises by operation of law whereby the court imposes a trust upon property lawfully held by one party for the benefit of another, as a result of some wrongdoing by the party in possession so as to avoid unjust enrichment.

INTERLOCUTORY APPEAL The appeal of an issue that does not resolve the disposition of the case, but is essential to a determination of the parties' legal rights.

KEY MAN INSURANCE POLICY A type of life insurance policy pursuant to which the insured is an officer or employee of a business entity and the beneficiary of the policy is that entity.

Hartford Casualty Insurance Company v. Powell

Insurance company (P) v. Insured drunk driver (D)

19 F. Supp. 2d 678 (N.D. Tex. 1998).

NATURE OF CASE: Motion for summary judgment in a declaratory judgment action on insurance coverage.

FACT SUMMARY: Hartford Casualty Insurance Co. (P) claimed that it couldn't be held liable for punitive damages assessed against Powell (D).

🏛 RULE OF LAW
Insurance contracts may not provide for punitive damages coverage in Texas because of public policy considerations.

FACTS: Hartford Casualty Insurance Co. (Hartford) (P) provided auto insurance to Powell's (D) employer. Powell (D) was involved in an auto accident driving a vehicle covered by Hartford (P) in which Gann was injured. Gann filed suit, alleging that Powell (D) was drunk and seeking punitive damages for gross negligence. Hartford (P) sought a declaratory judgment that it was not responsible for covering any punitive damages award against Powell (D). It claimed that the policy excluded expected and intended injuries and that the coverage of punitive damages violated the public policy of Texas.

ISSUE: Do public policy considerations prohibit the inclusion in Texas insurance contracts of punitive damages coverage?

HOLDING AND DECISION: (McBryde, J.) No. Insurance contracts may not provide for punitive damages coverage in Texas because of public policy considerations. Punitive damages may only be awarded in Texas after a finding of malice against the defendant. Thus, there must be some intention to cause harm. The purpose of punitive damages in the state is to punish the wrongdoer. Punishment and deterrence is the only public purpose of such awards. Contracts against public policy are void and will not be enforced by courts. The public policy of a state can be found in the statutes and judicial decisions. In the present situation, an insurance contract that provides coverage for punitive damages would prevent the strong public purpose of punishment and deterrence from taking effect. Accordingly, these contracts violate public policy and are void. Therefore, Hartford's (P) motion for summary judgment is granted.

▶ ANALYSIS

Since the court found that coverage of punitive damages violated public policy, it declined to reach the question of whether it was excluded by the Hartford (P) policy. Some jurisdictions do not follow the rule expressed here. The district court did not have a definitive Texas Supreme Court case to guide it so it had to make an "*Erie* guess."

■■■

Quicknotes

PUBLIC POLICY Policy administered by the state with respect to the health, safety and morals of its people in accordance with common notions of fairness and decency.

PUNITIVE DAMAGES Damages exceeding the actual injury suffered for the purposes of punishment of the defendant, deterrence of the wrongful behavior or comfort to the plaintiff.

■■■

First Bank (N.A.)—Billings v. Transamerica Insurance Company

Insured bank (D) v. Insurance company (P)

Mont. Sup. Ct., 209 Mont. 93 (1984).

NATURE OF CASE: Certified question to state supreme court from federal district court.

FACT SUMMARY: Transamerica Insurance Company (P) asserted that it should not be liable for coverage of punitive damages against its insured.

▥ RULE OF LAW
Providing insurance coverage of punitive damages is not contrary to public policy.

FACTS: First Bank (N.A.)—Billings (First Bank) (D) was sued for wrongful repossession in three cases. Its insurer, Transamerica Insurance Company (Transamerica) (P), defended First Bank (D) but denied coverage for any potential punitive damages. The federal district court hearing the case certified the question to the Montana Supreme Court.

ISSUE: Is providing insurance coverage of punitive damages contrary to public policy?

HOLDING AND DECISION: (Gulbrandson, J.) No. Providing insurance coverage of punitive damages is not contrary to public policy. Montana law provides that insurers are not liable for losses caused by the willful act of the insured. A similar provision in California has been held to bar coverage of punitive damages. However, this court finds no express policy by the legislature on the subject of insurance coverage for punitive damages. Thus, the court must look to other sources of public policy such as judicial decisions. Several courts have found insurance coverage of punitive damages is inconsistent with the purpose of punitive damages to punish wrongdoers. While such a deductive conclusion may be accurate, it is not enough to determine public policy. In the present case, Transamerica (P) provides First Bank (D) with coverage against several types of intentional torts, including false arrest and malicious prosecution. All of these torts can give rise to punitive damages. The awarding of punitive damages in these cases can be very uncertain. First Bank (D) cannot be expected to know what type of conduct will be penalized with punitive damages given the fact that juries are wrestling the ambiguous concepts of recklessness and reasonableness. The law is still in a state of flux with regard to punitive damages. Accordingly, although there are strong reasons for not allowing coverage of punitive damages, there is no clear public policy in Montana for adopting the position.

the law of punitive damages is more certain and predictable, it may make more sense to follow other jurisdictions on this issue. This Montana decision is not in accord with the majority of states.

Quicknotes

PUBLIC POLICY Policy administered by the state with respect to the health, safety and morals of its people in accordance with common notions of fairness and decency.

PUNITIVE DAMAGES Damages exceeding the actual injury suffered for the purposes of punishment of the defendant, deterrence of the wrongful behavior or comfort to the plaintiff.

▶ ANALYSIS

The decision left open the possibility that this ruling could change under different circumstances. It stated that when

Strickland v. Gulf Life Insurance Company

Insured amputee (P) v. Insurance company (D)

Ga. Sup. Ct., 242 S.E.2d 148 (1978).

NATURE OF CASE: Appeal from summary judgment for defendant in action to collect on insurance policy.

FACT SUMMARY: Gulf Life Insurance Company (D) denied coverage to Strickland (P) for the loss of his leg based on a time limitation in the policy.

RULE OF LAW
An insurance limitation requiring the insured to choose between continued treatment of an injury and eligibility for coverage may be unreasonable and void as against public policy.

FACTS: Gulf Life Insurance Company (Gulf) (D) provided insurance coverage to Strickland (P) for personal injuries. One provision of the policy stated that there was coverage if within 90 days of an injury there is dismemberment by severance of a limb. Strickland injured his leg and medical efforts to save the leg continued for 118 days. Finally, the leg had to be amputated. Gulf (D) denied coverage based on the time limitation. Strickland (P) filed suit but Gulf (D) was granted summary judgment.

ISSUE: May an insurance limitation requiring the insured to choose between continued treatment of an injury and eligibility for coverage be unreasonable and void as against public policy?

HOLDING AND DECISION: (Undercofler, J.) Yes. An insurance limitation requiring the insured to choose between continued treatment of an injury and eligibility for coverage may be unreasonable and void as against public policy. Standardized contracts such as insurance policies that are submitted to potential insureds on a take it or leave it basis must be carefully scrutinized by courts for unconscionable clauses. A time limitation clause on coverage for injuries has been found unreasonable and void in other jurisdictions. Such time limitations seem to be designed to prevent disputes over the causal connection between an accident and an injury. Courts have found that causation was not a serious enough concern to arbitrarily deny benefits to those who die or suffer serious injuries after a time limitation. Although the liberty to contract is very important, it is not an unlimited freedom. Courts must take into account public policy when asked to enforce contracts. In the present case, the time limitation that denied coverage to Strickland (P) may have been unreasonable. Accordingly, the issue should be remanded and the summary judgment for Gulf (D) is reversed.

DISSENT: (Bowles, J.) Only a couple of jurisdictions have found time limitations to violate public policy. This court should continue to follow earlier precedent that follows the majority view allowing such limitations.

ANALYSIS

The dissent also complained that the trial court did not have to hear evidence on the clause to determine that it wasn't unreasonable. The dissent maintained that the majority decision seemed to overrule previous decisions. However, the majority declined to go that far, preferring to remand the case for the development of a better factual record.

Quicknotes

PUBLIC POLICY Policy administered by the state with respect to the health, safety and morals of its people in accordance with common notions of fairness and decency.

UNCONSCIONABILITY A situation in which a contract, or a particular contract term, is unenforceable if the court determines that such terms are unduly oppressive or unfair to one party to the contract.

Insurance Regulation

None

Quick Reference Rules of Law

Commissioner of Insurance v. North Carolina Rate Bureau

Government agency (D) v. Rate-proposing organization (P)

N.C. Ct. App., 478 S.E.2d 794 (1996).

NATURE OF CASE: Appeal from agency order on insurance rates.

FACT SUMMARY: The North Carolina Rate Bureau (Bureau) (P) complained that the Insurance Commissioner (Commissioner) (D) had used improper methods in calculating insurance rate changes.

RULE OF LAW

Insurance agencies must make specific findings of fact with regard to evidence submitted supporting rate increases.

FACTS: In 1994, the North Carolina Rate Bureau (Bureau) (P) filed a request for rate increases for auto and motorcycle insurance. The Insurance Commissioner (Commissioner) (D) held extensive hearings over several months. The transcript was more than 3,500 pages and included 120 exhibits. The Bureau (P) based some of its request for the increases on calculations of profits using one type of accounting system. The Insurance Commissioner (D) based its calculations on a different method. Also, the parties differed on what evidence was better with regard to trend provisions. Finally, the Insurance Commissioner (D) did not grant the requested increases when setting the new rates. The Bureau (P) appealed.

ISSUE: Must insurance agencies make specific findings of fact with regard to evidence submitted supporting rate increases?

HOLDING AND DECISION: (McGee, J.) Yes. Insurance agencies must make specific findings of fact with regard to evidence submitted supporting rate increases. In reviewing orders of an Insurance Commissioner, the test is whether the conclusions of law are supported by material and substantial evidence in light of the whole record. The weight and sufficiency of the evidence, and the credibility of the witnesses, are to be determined by the agency. In the present case, there is no reason that the Commissioner (D) could not choose the accounting method it did. There was expert testimony that this accounting system was the logical choice for making the necessary calculations. Accordingly, that portion of the order is affirmed. With regard to the trend provisions, the Commissioner (D) acted properly in crediting certain expert testimony. However, the Commissioner (D) made conclusory statements about the Bureau's (P) evidence on this issue without specific evidentiary findings. The Commissioner (D) is not required to disprove the Bureau's (P) filing evidence, but must precisely and in detail resolve, the conflicts in evidence. It must be shown that the Commissioner (D) considered the evidence before rejecting it. Therefore, this issue must be remanded for more specific findings.

ANALYSIS

The standard of review used here is the majority position. However, there are not many states which have judicial decisions on ratemaking issues. In a case like this, the insurance commission can easily make more specific factual findings without actually changing its substantive ruling.

Allstate Insurance Company v. Schmidt

Insurance company (D) v. Insurance commissioner (P)

Haw. Sup. Ct., 104 Haw. 261, 88 P.3d 196 (2004).

NATURE OF CASE: Appeal from affirmance of insurance Commissioner's order.

FACT SUMMARY: The state's Insurance Commissioner (P) instructed Allstate Insurance Company (D) that it could not use the length of an applicant's driving experience as a basis for rejecting an automobile insurance application.

🏛 RULE OF LAW
An issuer of automobile insurance may not discriminate on the length of driving experience in underwriting.

FACTS: An applicant for automobile insurance with Allstate Insurance Company (Allstate) (D) filed a complaint with the state's insurance division regarding the calculation of her insurance premium. Allstate (D) initially rejected her application because it required an insured to hold a driver's license for more than one year, but she had held a driver's license for less than one year. The state's Insurance Commissioner (P) issued a cease and desist order, instructing Allstate (D) that it was not permitted to use the length of driving experience as a basis for rejection, and also ordered it pay a $3,000 penalty. The trial court affirmed the Commissioner's (P) final order in the case, and the state's highest court granted review.

ISSUE: May an issuer of automobile insurance discriminate on the length of driving experience in underwriting?

HOLDING AND DECISION: (Duffy, J.) No. An issuer of automobile insurance may not discriminate on the length of driving experience in underwriting. Here, the Commissioner's (P) decision carries a presumption of validity and Allstate (D) has a heavy burden of making a convincing showing that the decision is invalid because it is unjust and unreasonable. Allstate (D) argues that the relevant statute is inapplicable to underwriting, but applies only to rate making. The Commissioner (P) concluded that the plain language of the statute's reference to "any standard or rating plan" included underwriting guidelines and standards: "Otherwise, insurers would be able to discriminate, via underwriting guidelines and standards, against a person applying for insurance on the basis of race, creed, ethnic extraction, age, sex, length of driving experience, credit bureau rating, marital status, or physical handicap." The Commissioner (P) is correct. The statute is not entirely clear on its face as to whether "standard" includes underwriting standards, or means only "rating plan." Because no clause, sentence, or word in a statute shall be construed as superfluous, void, or insignificant if a construction can be

legitimately found which will give force to and preserve all words of the statute, the statute here applies to both rating plans and standards, including underwriting standards. Thus, the Commissioner (P), contrary to Allstate's (D) argument, neither engaged in impromptu rule making, nor abused his discretion, and, instead, applied existing law. As the statute provides for a mandatory penalty for its violation, the Commissioner (P) also did not abuse his discretion in issuing a penalty. Affirmed.

▶ ANALYSIS

The regulation of insurers' risk classifications to eliminate unfair discrimination necessarily raises complex issues of social policy and economics, raising such questions as what the social benefits of the regulation are, and who will bear the cost of increasing the insurer's risk. Although the state has the general authority to regulate classifications that are unfairly discriminatory, typically states enact legislation that is specifically directed at particular forms of classification. At the federal level, Title VII of the Civil Rights Act of 1964 applies to insurance indirectly through its application to discrimination in employment, and, therefore, employer-sponsored insurance plans.

■=■

Quicknotes

CEASE AND DESIST ORDER An order from a court or administrative agency prohibiting a person or business from continuing a particular course of conduct.

DISCRIMINATION Unequal treatment of a class of persons.

RISK Danger of damage to or loss of property.

Union Labor Life Insurance Co. v. Pireno

Professional association and insurance company (D) v. Chiropractor (P)

458 U.S. 119 (1982).

NATURE OF CASE: Appeal from reversal of summary judgment dismissing suit for declaratory and injunctive relief alleging violation of the Sherman Antitrust Act.

FACT SUMMARY: Pireno (P), a chiropractor, claimed that the practices of the Peer Review Committee that reviewed chiropractors' services and charges for purposes of determining insurance coverage, constituted a conspiracy to fix prices in restraint of trade in violation of the Sherman Antitrust Act.

🏛 RULE OF LAW
Section 2(b) of the McCarran-Ferguson Act expressly exempts from the effects of the antitrust law those practices that constitute the "business of insurance" where the practice has the effect of transferring or spreading a policyholder's risk, is an integral part of the relationship between the insurer and the insured, and is limited to entities within the insurance industry.

FACTS: Union Labor Life Insurance (ULL) (D), an insurance company, had policies that covered chiropractic treatments. Certain policies, however, limited the company's liability to reasonable charges for necessary medical care and services, requiring ULL (D) to determine whether the chiropractic treatments were necessary and the charges for them reasonable. ULL (D) arranged with the New York State Chiropractic Association (NYSCA) (D) to use the advice of its Peer Review Committee. The Committee was established in order to help insurers evaluate claims for chiropractic treatments. Pireno (P), a chiropractor, had several of his charges referred to the Committee, which concluded the treatments were unnecessary or charges unreasonable. Pireno (P) brought suit claiming the peer review practices of the Committee constituted a violation of the Sherman Antitrust Act as a conspiracy to fix prices that chiropractors would be permitted to charge, and constituted a restraint of trade. The district court dismissed, the court of appeals reversed, and the United States Supreme Court granted certiorari.

ISSUE: Does § 2(b) of the McCarran-Ferguson Act expressly exempt from the effects of the antitrust law those practices that constitute the "business of insurance" where the practice has the effect of transferring or spreading a policyholder's risk, is an integral part of the relationship between the insurer and the insured, and is limited to entities within the insurance industry?

HOLDING AND DECISION: (Brennan, J.) Yes. Section 2(b) of the McCarran-Ferguson Act expressly exempts from the effects of the antitrust law those practices that constitute the "business of insurance" where the

practice has the effect of transferring or spreading a policyholder's risk, is an integral part of the relationship between the insurer and the insured, and is limited to entities within the insurance industry. The issue here is whether the peer review practices are exempt from antitrust law as part of the "business of insurance." In *Group Life & Health Ins. Co. v. Royal Drug Co.*, 440 U.S. 205 (1979), the Court re-examined the scope of the express antitrust exemption under § 2(b) of the McCarran Ferguson Act for the "business of insurance." That decision is controlling here. The Court examined three characteristics of the business of insurance that Congress intended to exempt through § 2(b). First is whether the practice had the effect of spreading and transferring a policyholder's risk. Second was whether the practice is an integral part of the relationship between the insurer and the insured. Third was whether the practice was limited to entities within the insurance industry. Congress intended that cooperative ratemaking efforts be exempt from antitrust laws. This was based on the view that it would be difficult to underwrite risks in an informed manner without cooperation. The Court did not extend that exemption to the *Royal Drug* case because the agreements involved parties wholly outside the insurance industry. Here the ULL's (D) use of the peer review committee does not constitute the "business of insurance" within the meaning of § 2(b) of the Act. The ULL's (D) use of the Peer Review Committee does not have the effect of spreading and underwriting the policyholder's risk. Nor is it an integral part of the relationship between the insurer and the insured. Last, the peer review practices are not limited to entities within the insurance industry, but third parties wholly outside the industry: practicing chiropractors. Affirmed.

DISSENT: (Rehnquist, J.) The Peer Review Committee is the type of claims adjustment activity within the insurance industry that § 2(b) of the Act intended to protect from the effect of antitrust law as part of the business of insurance. Here, the Peer Review Committee assumes the role and function of a claims adjustor, since it in effect makes the determination of whether the policyholder's claims will be paid. The legislative history of the Act demonstrates that such a claims settlement function was intended to be shielded from the antitrust laws, especially given the insurance companies' needs to consult with outside experts, such as the Committee here, to determine whether a host of medical ailments are covered risks.

▶ ANALYSIS

While the insurance industry is primarily regulated by State law, federal law also provides for some regulation. Section 2

Continued on next page.

of the McCarran-Ferguson Act states that "No Act of Congress shall be construed to invalidate, impair or supersede any law enacted by any State for the purpose of regulating the business of insurance." This federal statute has the effect of exempting from antitrust law the "business of insurance" to the extent that it is not regulated by state law. Nonetheless, the Sherman Act still applies to agreements or acts intended to boycott, coerce or intimidate.

■═■

Quicknotes

CERTIORARI A discretionary writ issued by a superior court to an inferior court in order to review the lower court's decisions; the Supreme Court's writ ordering such review.

■═■

St. Paul Fire & Marine Insurance Co. v. Barry

Insurance company (D) v. Doctors' group (P)

438 U.S. 531 (1978).

NATURE OF CASE: Appeal from reversal of dismissal of a class action for antitrust violations.

FACT SUMMARY: Doctors (P) claimed that insurers (D) conspired to alter the terms of medical malpractice insurance by refusing to sell certain policies.

🏛 RULE OF LAW
The Sherman Act prohibits insurers from agreeing together to stop selling insurance to particular customers.

FACTS: A small number of insurers (D), including the largest, St. Paul Fire & Marine Insurance Co. (St. Paul) (D), sold medical malpractice insurance in Rhode Island. St. Paul (D) announced that it would not renew coverage on an "occurrence" basis, but would write only "claims made" coverage. The state's doctors (P) claimed that all the other insurers (D) thereafter refused to accept applications from St. Paul (D) policyholders. They allege that the insurers were attempting to compel them to purchase "claims made" coverage. They filed suit, including counts for antitrust violations involving an illegal boycott. The district court dismissed these claims. However, the court of appeals reversed, holding that the Sherman Act applied to agreements to boycott. The United States Supreme Court granted certiorari.

ISSUE: Doe the Sherman Act prohibit insurers from agreeing together to stop selling insurance to particular customers?

HOLDING AND DECISION: (Powell, J.) Yes. The Sherman Act prohibits insurers from agreeing together to stop selling insurance to particular customers. The applicability of the Sherman Act to illegal boycotts is clear, but the meaning of a boycott is less so. The generic concept of boycott refers to a method of pressuring a party by withholding patronage or services from the target. The insurers (D) argue that boycotts only deal with actions that target competitors of the boycotters as the ultimate objects of a concerted refusal to deal. However, this Court has consistently held that boycotts include attempts by businesses to agree among themselves to stop selling to particular customers. The allegations in the present case maintain that St. Paul (D) induced its competitors to refuse to deal on any terms with its customers. This alleged pact served as a tactical weapon in support of its dispute with policyholders. The enlistment of third parties in an agreement not to trade has long been viewed as conduct supporting a finding of an unlawful boycott. Therefore, the court of appeals reversal of dismissal was proper and is affirmed.

▶ ANALYSIS

This case involved an intersection of the McCarran-Ferguson Act and the Sherman Act. The McCarran Act ordinarily governs insurance disputes, but a provision provides an exception where the Sherman Act applies to boycotts. While McCarran usually protects state regulatory laws on insurance, the Sherman Act exception applies federal antitrust law to complaints such as the present case.

■=■

Quicknotes

BOYCOTT A concerted effort to refrain from doing business with a particular person or entity, usually to achieve a particular result.

CERTIORARI A discretionary writ issued by a superior court to an inferior court in order to review the lower court's decisions; the Supreme Court's writ ordering such review.

SHERMAN ACT Prohibits unreasonable restraint of trade.

■=■

Hartford Fire Insurance Company v. California

Insurer (D) v. State (P)

509 U.S. 764 (1993).

NATURE OF CASE: Appeal from reversal of dismissal of antitrust action.

FACT SUMMARY: California (P) and other states (P) claimed that insurers (D) illegally conspired to force changes to standard commercial general liability policies.

🏛 RULE OF LAW
Illegal boycotts do not include all concerted refusals to deal.

FACTS: Commercial general liability (CGL) policies were traditionally sold on an "occurrence" basis, which obligated insurers to pay for claims based on accidents that happened within the policy period. Certain primary insurers, including Hartford Fire Insurance Company (Hartford) (D), sought to change these CGL policies to "claims made" coverage where insurers only pay and defend claims made during the policy period. Many states, including California (P), alleged that Hartford (D) pressured other primary insurers to make this change by a variety of means. Among the allegations were charges that Hartford (D) and others manipulated the Insurance Service Office (ISO), the group in charge of drafting standard policies and collecting actuarial data on risks. Also, Hartford (D) is alleged to have conspired with foreign reinsurers to have reinsurance refused to primary insurers who continued to use occurrence CGL policies. The federal district court dismissed the antitrust claims on the basis of the immunity granted in the McCarran-Ferguson Act. However, the Ninth Circuit reversed, on the ground that the allegations constituted a boycott that is an exception to the immunity. The Supreme Court granted certiorari.

ISSUE: Do illegal boycotts include all concerted refusals to deal?

HOLDING AND DECISION: (Scalia, J.) No. Illegal boycotts do not include all concerted refusals to deal. Boycotts have not been precisely defined in the applicable acts. It is clear that it does not ordinarily require an absolute refusal to deal on any terms. The refusal may be imposed to punish the target for the position he has taken or to coerce him into abandoning it. Thus, a boycott's refusal may be conditional. However, it is important to distinguish between a conditional boycott and a concerted agreement to terms. The latter is a way of obtaining and exercising market power by concertedly exacting terms like a monopolist would. While the Sherman Act prohibits both, the exemption to McCarran-Ferguson immunity applies only to boycotts. In the present case, it was not a boycott, but a concerted action to change terms, for reinsurers to refuse reinsurance coverage of CGL

occurrence policies. This is because the reinsurers may have been trying to avoid the particular risk of occurrence policies and dealt directly with that issue. However, where the reinsurers refused to provide any type of coverage to primary insurers who used occurrence policies, this entered into boycott territory. Therefore, the allegations in the complaint which claim boycott allegations under this standard must be allowed to go forward. Affirmed in part, reversed in part.

▶ ANALYSIS

Other issues in this dispute included Hartford's (D) desire to completely eliminate coverage of pollution costs. They also sought to have defense costs included within policy limits. These sought-after changes came after an explosion of pollution claims in the 1980s and 1990s and resulting coverage disputes where it was extremely difficult to pinpoint the timing of pollution occurrences.

━━■

Quicknotes

BOYCOTT A concerted effort to refrain from doing business with a particular person or entity, usually to achieve a particular result.

CERTIORARI A discretionary writ issued by a superior court to an inferior court in order to review the lower court's decisions; the Supreme Court's writ ordering such review.

REINSURANCE A contract between an insurer and a third party to insure the insurer against potential loss or liability resulting from a previous insurance contract.

SHERMAN ACT Prohibits unreasonable restraint of trade.

━━■

Fire and Property Insurance

Quick Reference Rules of Law

Port Authority of New York and New Jersey v. Affiliated FM Insurance Company

Insured property owner (P) v. Insurer (D)

311 F.3d 226 (3d Cir. 2002).

NATURE OF CASE: Appeal from summary judgment for defendant insurers in action for insurance coverage.

FACT SUMMARY: The Port Authority of New York and New Jersey (P) contended that required asbestos abatement in various properties it owned was covered by "physical loss or damage" clauses in first-party insurance policies it had with several insurers (D). The insurers (D) argued that this coverage was only triggered when the quantity and condition of asbestos in a given property made the property unusable or uninhabitable.

🏛 RULE OF LAW
"Physical loss or damage" coverage is triggered with regard to asbestos in a covered structure only where the quantity and condition of the asbestos make the structure unusable or uninhabitable.

FACTS: The Port Authority of New York and New Jersey (Port Authority) (P) owned various properties throughout New York and New Jersey that were insured under first-party policies with various insurers (D). The policies, which had been negotiated by Port Authority's (P) attorneys, contained coverage for "ALL RISKS of physical loss or damage . . . ." Many of Port Authority's (P) properties, including airport terminals and public buildings, contained asbestos, some of which Port Authority (P) abated, to prevent the asbestos from becoming friable and dangerous to human health. However, air levels of asbestos in the structures never exceeded EPA standards and Port Authority (P) assured the public that its buildings were safe. Port Authority (P) sought recovery under its policies for its abatement efforts, claiming it had suffered "physical loss or damage" by the mere presence of the asbestos and the anticipation that the asbestos would eventually deteriorate and become dangerous. The insurers (D) denied coverage, and Port Authority (P) brought suit for coverage, which was removed to federal district court because the covered properties were in two states. Port Authority (P) argued that the mere presence of the asbestos and the general threat of its future release, and hence the need to abate it, came within the policies. The district court, finding the policies' language unambiguous, ruled that the expense of abating the asbestos was not within the scope of the "physical loss or damage" coverage and that Port Authority (P) had failed to present sufficient evidence of such loss or damage to survive summary judgment. The court of appeals granted review.

ISSUE: Is "physical loss or damage" coverage triggered with regard to asbestos in a covered structure only where the

quantity and condition of the asbestos make the structure unusable or uninhabitable?

HOLDING AND DECISION: (Weis, J.) Yes. "Physical loss or damage" coverage is triggered with regard to asbestos in a covered structure only where the quantity and condition of the asbestos make the structure unusable or uninhabitable. The issue is one of state law, on which there is no substantive differences between the states involved here. Case law on third-party asbestos personal injury suits is unhelpful here, since third-party policies are concerned with insuring against liability claims of others. Therefore, case law on first-party policies is apposite. Cases cited by Port Authority (P) from other jurisdictions treating first-party coverage for asbestos are minimally helpful, as those cases relate to actual releases of asbestos fibers and resulting contamination, or relied on the definition of physical loss in a general liability policy rather than a first-party policy. The cases cited by the insurers (D) support the notion that all risks first-party insurance coverage does not protect against losses that are certain to happen, but have not yet occurred. In ordinary parlance and widely accepted definition for insurance purposes, physical damage to property means a distinct, demonstrable, and physical alteration of its structure. Fire, water, smoke and impact from another object are typical examples of physical damage from an outside source that may demonstrably alter the components of a building and trigger coverage. However, physical damage to a building as an entity by sources unnoticeable to the naked eye must meet a higher threshold. Such a threshold is met where, even though a building or its elements are not demonstrably altered, its function is eliminated. Routine maintenance to seal asbestos does not meet this threshold. Here, Port Authority's (P) structures never violated EPA standards, and Port Authority (P) assured the public that its buildings were safe. Thus, the buildings were never rendered unusable or uninhabitable and coverage was not triggered. To hold otherwise would transform the "all risks" insurance policy into a maintenance contract. Affirmed.

▌ ANALYSIS

While the result of this case would seem to discourage property owners from regularly abating asbestos or other known latent defects or risks, and encouraging owners to wait until such defects or risks have become imminent—at which point coverage under a first-party policy would be triggered—other insurance policies, as well as public policy

Continued on next page.

and regulations, work to encourage such abatement and concomitant reduction of potential liability for injury to third parties. In sum, as the court concludes, the purpose of first-party "all risks" insurance is not to protect against certain maintenance requirements, but against unanticipated risks that occur despite such regular maintenance.

■■■

Quicknotes

AMBIGUOUS Vague; unclear; capable of being understood to have more than one meaning.

■■■

Duane Reade, Inc. v. St. Paul Fire & Marine Insurance Company

Insured property owner (P) v. Insurance company (D)

279 F. Supp. 2d 235 (S.D.N.Y. 2003).

NATURE OF CASE: Cross-motions for summary judgment in declaratory action involving business interruption insurance coverage.

FACT SUMMARY: After one of Duane Reade Inc.'s (Duane Reade) (P) stores was destroyed in the World Trade Center (WTC), it claimed that under its business interruption coverage with St. Paul Fire & Marine Insurance Company (St. Paul) (D), the applicable restoration period was the time necessary to rebuild the entire WTC, whereas St. Paul (D) claimed the applicable period was the time when Duane Reade (P) could have restored operations at a location other than the WTC.

> ## RULE OF LAW
> (1) Where multiple business properties are covered by one insurance policy, and one of the properties, located in a retail center, is destroyed along with the retail center, the restoration period for business interruption coverage is neither the period that it takes to restore the entire retail center nor the period in which the chain could have restored operations at a location other than the retail center.
> (2) A loss of market exclusion in an insurance policy does not bar recovery for business interruption losses occasioned by physical destruction of the insured property.

FACTS: Duane Reade, Inc. (Duane Reade) (P) operated a drug store (one of many that it owned) in the retail concourse of the World Trade Center (WTC) prior to September 11, 2001. After the WTC was destroyed, Duane Reade (P) sought to recover under an insurance policy issued by St. Paul Fire & Marine Insurance Company (St. Paul) (D). The policy covered losses at all Duane Reade (P) stores. When the parties were unable to resolve a dispute concerning the scope of the policy's coverage for business interruption losses, Duane Reade (P) filed suit for, *inter alia*, declaratory judgment. The parties' submissions showed that St. Paul (D) did not dispute that the destruction of the store was caused by a covered peril. In fact, it had already satisfied Duane Reade's (P) property loss claims. Although St. Paul (D) disputed that any monies were due for business interruption losses, it had already paid close to $10 million for what it previously perceived as business interruption losses. The principal coverage issue was how the policy should be interpreted in determining the length of the restoration period applicable to the WTC store. The policy provided in pertinent part that: "The measure of recovery or period of indemnity shall not exceed such length of time as would be

required with the exercise of due diligence and dispatch to rebuild, repair, or replace such property that has been destroyed or damaged ...." The policy also specifically excluded coverage for losses caused by "loss of market." Duane Reade (P) argued the applicable restoration period was the time necessary to rebuild the entire WTC, whereas St. Paul (D) claimed the applicable period was the time when Duane Reade (P) could have restored operations at a location other than the WTC. St. Paul (D) also argued that the loss of market exclusion barred recovery in any event. The parties each moved for summary judgment.

ISSUE:
(1) Where multiple business properties are covered by one insurance policy, and one of the properties, located in a retail center, is destroyed along with the retail center, is the restoration period for business interruption coverage either the period that it takes to restore the entire retail center or the period in which the chain could have restored operations at a location other than the retail center?
(2) Does a loss of market exclusion in an insurance policy bar recovery for business interruption losses occasioned by physical destruction of the insured property?

HOLDING AND DECISION: (Rakoff, J.)
(1) No. Where multiple business properties are covered by one insurance policy, and one of the properties, located in a retail center, is destroyed along with the retail center, the restoration period for business interruption coverage is neither the period that it takes to restore the entire retail center nor the period in which the chain could have restored operations at a location other than the retail center. The plain language of the policy governs as a matter of law. Duane Reade's (P) contention that the restoration period must be coterminous with the time actually required to rebuild the entire complex that will replace the WTC is untenable. On their face, the restoration period clauses envision a hypothetical or constructive (as opposed to actual) time frame for rebuilding, as evidenced, for example, by their use of the subjunctive "would." Moreover, what is to be hypothesized is the time it would take to rebuild, repair, or replace the WTC store itself, not the entire complex that once surrounded it. Once Duane Reade (P) could resume functionally equivalent operations in the location where its WTC store once stood, the restoration period would be at an end. A further limitation to the hypothesized period of reconstruction results from the provision in the policy mandating that losses be calculated with "due consideration" both to the experience of

Continued on next page.

the WTC store prior to the loss as well as the "probable experience thereafter had no loss occurred." "Probable experience" includes, *inter alia*, the likelihood *vel non* that Duane Reade's (P) lease for the WTC store would have been renewed. Thus, if Duane Reade (P) is unable to prove at trial that its lease of the WTC store would likely have been renewed absent the events of September 11, 2001, then the period of restoration cannot extend beyond Duane Reade's (P) present lease term. St. Paul (D) contended that the word "property" refers not to a store in any particular location, but to the "business" of the entire Duane Reade (P) chain. This argument finds no support in the text of the policy and, indeed, is manifestly unreasonable. As St. Paul (D) would have it, either Duane Reade (P) never suffered any business interruption at all because the chain was able to "stay open for business," or the period of restoration ended when Duane Reade's (P) chain-wide sales attained pre-peril levels. This, however, would mean that Duane Reade purchased coverage that either (1) only applies when every last one of its stores is destroyed, or (2) unlike all other business interruption insurance, does not protect against lost profits. Neither alternative makes sense. Summary judgment denied to both parties on this issue.

(2) No. A loss of market exclusion in an insurance policy does not bar recovery for business interruption losses occasioned by physical destruction of the insured property. St. Paul (D) argues that the loss of market exclusion contained in the policy bars coverage for Duane Reade's (P) business interruption losses, since the terrorist attack destroyed not just the WTC but the entire downtown market. The argument lacks substance. The loss of market exclusion relates to losses resulting from economic changes occasioned by, e.g., competition, shifts in demand, or the like; it does not bar recovery for loss of ordinary business caused by a physical destruction or other covered peril. Here, St. Paul (D) admitted that interruption was caused by a covered peril. Summary judgment granted to Duane Reade (P) on this issue.

▎ *ANALYSIS*

As the court in this case indicates, where a policy contains a loss of market exclusion, business interruption coverage does not insure against the risk of pure economic loss. However, the mere showing that there has been a covered peril is itself not enough to trigger the business interruption coverage; there must also be a showing that the peril caused a loss of business. Another form of related insurance, known as contingent business interruption coverage, covers the risk of a business suffering economic loss from damage to non-covered property, such as that of suppliers or customers.

Quicknotes

INTER ALIA Among other things.

SUMMARY JUDGMENT Judgment rendered by a court in response to a motion made by one of the parties, claiming that the lack of a question of material fact in respect to an issue warrants disposition of the issue without consideration by the jury.

■━■

Chute v. North River Insurance Company

Insured jewelry owner (P) v. Insurance company (D)

Minn. Sup. Ct., 172 Minn. 13, 214 N.W. 473 (1927).

NATURE OF CASE: Appeal from order sustaining a general demurrer to the complaint in an insurance coverage action.

FACT SUMMARY: Chute (P) claimed that the insurance policy she had with North River Insurance Company (D), which covered jewelry against all risks of loss and damage, covered the cracking that occurred naturally in her fire opal.

RULE OF LAW
An insurance policy that covers property against "all risks of loss or damage" does not cover loss that occurs from inherent flaws in the property.

FACTS: Chute (P) purchased an insurance policy from North River Insurance Company (D), which covered jewelry and fur against all risks of loss and damage during transportation or otherwise. Chute (P) filed a claim when her fire opal valued at $2,000 became cracked. The crack developed after the policy became effective but during the time it was in force. Chute (P) alleged that the crack was due to an inherent vice (flaw) in the opal and was not the result of outside force. The trial court ruled in the insurance company's (D) favor, and the state's highest court granted review.

ISSUE: Does an insurance policy that covers property against "all risks of loss or damage" cover loss that occurs from inherent flaws in the property?

HOLDING AND DECISION: (Stone, J.) No. An insurance policy that covers property against "all risks of loss or damage" does not cover loss that occurs from inherent flaws in the property. Unless the policy expressly provides coverage for loss occurring from inherent flaws in property, there cannot be recovery for such loss that does not arise from an "extraneous and fortuitous cause." Although a literal reading of an "all risk" policy could be read to cover inherent flaws that would ignore the purpose of the insurance contract. Here, Chute (P) purchased insurance that covered against loss or damage from fortuitous and extraneous circumstances rather than a warranty of the quality and durability of her property. Express language would be needed to indicate that the insurance covered loss from "automatic deterioration alone." To apply any other rule here would make the policy cover natural disintegration, something clearly not intended. Affirmed.

ANALYSIS

The issue raised by this case is known as the "intrinsic-loss" issue, and illustrates the principle, regarding all-risk policies, that even when a policy is sold on an all-risk or open-peril basis, loss must be caused by an extraneous force rather than by an inherent flaw in the property.

Quicknotes

DEMURRER The assertion that the opposing party's pleadings are insufficient and that the demurring party should not be made to answer.

Rosen v. State Farm General Insurance Company

Insured homeowner (P) v. Insurance company (D)

Cal. Sup. Ct., 30 Cal. 4th 1070, 135 Cal. Rptr. 2d 361, 70 P.3d 351 (2003).

NATURE OF CASE: Appeal from affirmance of judgment for insured in insurance coverage action.

FACT SUMMARY: Rosen (P) contended that the homeowner insurance policy he had with State Farm General Insurance Company (D), which provided coverage only for "actual collapse," should be interpreted to provide coverage for "imminent" collapse.

RULE OF LAW
Where the language of an insurance policy is clear, courts may not rewrite the coverage to conform it to public policy or the insured's expectations.

FACTS: Rosen (P) submitted a claim to State Farm General Insurance Company (State Farm) (D), his homeowner insurance carrier, for the cost of repairing two decks attached to his home. Rosen (P) repaired the decks upon the recommendation of a contractor who had discovered severe deterioration of the framing members supporting the decks. Rosen (P) believed his decks were in a state of imminent collapse, entitling him to policy benefits. State Farm (D) denied Rosen's (P) claim on the ground, among others, that there had been no collapse of his decks within the meaning of the policy, in that its coverage was expressly restricted to actual collapse. State Farm (D) moved for summary judgment, which the trial court denied because it found that there were triable issues of material fact as to whether the collapse had been imminent. At trial, the trial court held that public policy required that "policyholders are entitled to coverage for collapse as long as the collapse is imminent, irrespective of policy language." The trial court declined to honor the policy's restriction of coverage because it would, in the court's view, "encourage property owners to place lives in danger in order to allow insurance carriers to delay payment of claims until the structure actually collapses . . . ." The intermediate appellate court affirmed, and the state's highest court granted review.

ISSUE: Where the language of an insurance policy is clear may courts rewrite the coverage to conform it to public policy or the insured's expectations?

HOLDING AND DECISION: (Brown, J.) No. Where the language of an insurance policy is clear, courts may not rewrite the coverage to conform it to public policy or the insured's expectations. The policy language here was clear and explicit; under no stretch of the imagination does "actually" mean "imminently." Applying the logic of the lower courts, in allowing public policy to dictate the terms of an unambiguous insurance policy, courts could convert life insurance into health insurance. In rewriting the coverage provision to conform to their notions of sound public

policy, the trial court and the appellate court exceeded their authority. Reversed and remanded.

▶ ANALYSIS

In this case, the court discussed at some length, and distinguished, cases involving collapse where the policy language was found to be unclear. The court emphasized that, in those cases, the courts were merely construing ambiguous policy language, and were neither holding that an unambiguous collapse provision expressly limiting recovery to actual collapse must nevertheless be construed to provide coverage for imminent collapse, nor purporting to discern a public policy establishing a contractual entitlement to coverage for imminent collapse in all cases.

◼◼◼

Quicknotes

AMBIGUITY Language that is capable of being understood to have more than one interpretation.

PUBLIC POLICY Policy administered by the state with respect to the health, safety and morals of its people in accordance with common notions of fairness and decency.

◼◼◼

State Farm Fire and Casualty Company v. Bongen

Insurer (D) v. Insured home owner (P)

Alaska Sup. Ct., 925 P.2d 1042 (1996).

NATURE OF CASE: Appeal from summary judgment in action on insurance contract.

FACT SUMMARY: State Farm Fire and Casualty Company's (D) homeowner's policy excluded damages caused by earth movements although the cause of the movement was covered.

RULE OF LAW
An exclusion of coverage is enforceable even if a concurrent cause of the event is covered under the policy.

FACTS: Bongen (P) had a home insured by State Farm Fire and Casualty Company (State Farm) (D). The policy contained a provision that excluded coverage for a loss caused by earth movements such as earthquakes and landslides. Subsequently, construction activity above the Bongen (P) home caused a mudslide that damaged the home. State Farm (D) denied the claim based on the exclusion. However, Bongen (P) filed suit, arguing that the negligence that caused the slide was a covered event under the policy. On cross motions for summary judgment, the trial court ruled for Bongen (P), holding that the exclusion was unenforceable because of the efficient proximate cause rule. State Farm (D) appealed.

ISSUE: Is an exclusion of coverage enforceable even if a concurrent cause of the event is covered under the policy?

HOLDING AND DECISION: (Compton, C.J.) Yes. An exclusion of coverage is enforceable even if a concurrent cause of the event is covered under the policy. Other jurisdictions have applied the so-called efficient proximate cause rule in cases such as this one. Under the rule, an insurer is required to pay for damages resulting from a combination of covered and excluded perils if the efficient proximate cause is a covered peril. This rule operates even if there is a policy exclusion stating the opposite. Thus, in the present case, if the proximate cause of the mudslide was negligence by construction workers and this was a covered event, the State Farm (D) exclusion would not be enforceable. However, a majority of jurisdictions allow for enforcement of an exclusion found in the State Farm (D) policy. The court favors the majority rule because the parties should be free to contract for the exact terms of obligations. The restriction in the State Farm (D) policy is in plain language and was agreed to by Bongen (P). There is no sound policy reason for preventing enforcement. Reversed.

DISSENT: (Matthews, J.) The minority approach, which denies exclusion of coverage where an excluded secondary peril is also present in the chain of causation, is far better at meeting the reasonable expectations of the insured. The efficient proximate cause rule comports with those expectations, since the insured has sought protection from a given peril, and the insurer should not be able to avoid coverage because an excluded peril happens to be in the chain of causation if the covered peril is the dominant cause of the loss.

ANALYSIS

The court also found that the earth movement exclusion was not ambiguous. Additionally, it held that it did not violate the reasonable expectations of the insured. Some states such as California provide that there can be only one proximate cause of a loss.

━━■

Quicknotes

PROXIMATE CAUSE The natural sequence of events without which an injury would not have been sustained.

━━■

[handwritten margin note: Efficient proximate cause is opposite of test that this court used]

Liristis v. American Family Mutual Insurance Company

Insured homeowner (P) v. Insurance company (D)

Ariz. App. Div., 204 Ariz. 140, 61 P.3d 22 (2002).

NATURE OF CASE: Appeal from summary judgment in favor of defendant insurer in insurance coverage action.

FACT SUMMARY: Although the insurance policy that Liristis (P) had with American Family Mutual Insurance Company (D) excluded loss resulting from mold, Liristis (P) argued that the policy covered damage from mold that occurred as the result of eliminating a covered peril (fire).

🏛 RULE OF LAW
An insurance policy that excludes coverage for loss to property from a certain cause, but does not exclude coverage for the cause itself, provides coverage for damage by that cause, which has been occasioned by a covered event.

FACTS: Liristis (P) had an insurance policy with American Family Mutual Insurance Company (American Family) (D) that excluded loss resulting from mold. Liristis (P) had a fire in his home that resulted in fire and water damage. A contractor performed repairs and American Family (D) paid for the claims related to the fire. Within a few months of the fire, Liristis (P) noticed mold growth in the home. Liristis (P) suffered allergic reactions and respiratory and other unexplained illnesses. Additionally, following the repairs, the roof leaked each time it rained and caused water damage to the home. An expert confirmed the presence of mold in the home, and Liristis (P) made a claim for contamination caused by the mold. American Family (D) denied the claim based on the policy exclusion for mold, which said, "We do not cover loss to the property . . . resulting directly or indirectly from or caused by . . . mold." The trial granted summary judgment to American Family (D) on the ground that there was no coverage for mold damage. The appellate court granted review.

ISSUE: Does an insurance policy that excludes coverage for loss to property from a certain cause, but does not exclude coverage for the cause itself, provide coverage for damage by that cause, which has been occasioned a covered event?

HOLDING AND DECISION: (Gemmill, J.) Yes. An insurance policy that excludes coverage for loss to property from a certain cause, but does not exclude coverage for the cause itself, provides coverage for damage by that cause, which has been occasioned a covered event. Mold can be a loss and a cause of loss. Liristis (P) argues that the loss to the property was not caused by mold but was mold, and that the losses-not-covered provisions do not apply. The language of the policy supports this interpretation, which does not exclude all mold. If American Family (D) had intended to exclude not only losses caused by mold but also mold itself, it could have easily expressed that intention by adding the words "either consisting of, or . . ." to its exclusionary language. Then, loss "consisting of" mold as well as loss caused by mold would be subject to this restrictive language. In the policy, mold is listed as a cause of loss. But mold that is the loss is not mentioned. To express the intention to exclude all mold, the company could have chosen "Other Excluded Losses" or "Other Losses Not Covered" as the title of its exclusionary paragraph, rather than "Other Causes of Loss." Thus, if Liristis (P) proves that the mold resulted from the fire, then the cost of removing the mold is not a "loss" separate from or caused by the mold itself, but rather is simply the implementation of the mold damage coverage provided under the policy. Phrased differently, when a covered event causes mold, the mold damage includes the cost of removal. The purpose of the policy supports this conclusion. Fire insurance, which was part of the policy, "is intended to cover every loss, damage, or injury proximately caused by fire, and every loss necessarily following directly and immediately from such peril or from the surrounding circumstances, the operation and influence of which could not be avoided." Since the policy does not exclude mold damage caused by a covered event, Liristis (P) is entitled to coverage for the mold damage caused by the fire and the water used to extinguish the fire, including the cost of removal or repair of the damage. Because a fact question is presented as to whether the mold damage was caused by the fire, summary judgment was inappropriate. Reversed and remanded.

▶ ANALYSIS

This case illustrates how insurance policy interpretation can turn on a single word included—or omitted—by the insurer. Claims involving mold coverage are being increasingly litigated, and, as in this case, the claims often turn on the precise language used in the policy.

■=■

Quicknotes

SUMMARY JUDGMENT Judgment rendered by a court in response to a motion made by one of the parties, claiming that the lack of a question of material fact in respect to an issue warrants disposition of the issue without consideration by the jury.

■=■

Broussard v. State Farm Fire and Casualty Company

Insured homeowner (P) v. Insurer (D)

523 F.3d 618 (5th Cir. 2008).

NATURE OF CASE: Appeal from judgment as a matter of law for plaintiff in action for insurance coverage.

FACT SUMMARY: State Farm Fire and Casualty Company (D) contended that it was not obligated to cover losses of the Broussards' (P) personal property and residence occasioned by Hurricane Katrina because its homeowner's policy excluded losses caused by water damage and coverage was subject to an Anti-Concurrent Cause (ACC) clause.

🏛 RULE OF LAW

(1) A finding that property was destroyed during a hurricane does not entitle an insured to judgment as a matter of law that the property was destroyed by "windstorm" rather than flooding.

(2) An insured is not entitled to judgment as a matter of law on a claim for insurance coverage where the insurer has presented evidence sufficient to permit a reasonable jury to find in its favor on the issue.

(3) Where an "open peril" policy is involved, once an insurer has presented evidence to establish an affirmative policy exclusion defense, the burden of proof does not shift back to the insured to prove that there is an exception to the defense or to segregate covered from non-covered damages.

FACTS: The Broussards' (P) home and personal property were destroyed by Hurricane Katrina. They had a homeowner insurance policy with State Farm Fire and Casualty Company (State Farm) (D) that contained "named peril" coverage for their personal property and "open peril" coverage for their dwelling. Both coverages excluded losses caused by water damage, and were subject to an Anti-Concurrent Cause (ACC) clause. The Broussards' (P) losses met or exceeded the policy limits for these coverages. State Farm (D) denied the Broussards' (P) claims for coverage because it found that their losses were caused principally by water damage. The Broussards (P) brought suit for coverage, which was removed to federal district court and tried before a jury. However, the district court granted judgment as a matter of law (JMOL) to the Broussards (P) on both claims. With regard to the personal property claim, the district court found that the property had been destroyed during Hurricane Katrina, and therefore had been destroyed by a "windstorm," which was a covered, named peril. As to the dwelling claim, the district court found that State Farm (D) bore the burden of proving that the Broussards' (P) loss resulted from the excluded peril of

flooding, and that State Farm (D) had failed to meet this burden because its expert admitted that he could not distinguish between the wind and water damage to the dwelling with any reasonable degree of probability. The court also granted punitive damages to the Broussards (P). The court of appeals granted review.

ISSUE:

(1) Does a finding that property was destroyed during a hurricane entitle an insured to judgment as a matter of law that the property was destroyed by "windstorm" rather than flooding?

(2) Is an insured entitled to judgment as a matter of law on a claim for insurance coverage where the insurer has presented evidence sufficient to permit a reasonable jury to find in its favor on the issue?

(3) Where an "open peril" policy is involved, once an insurer has presented evidence to establish an affirmative policy exclusion defense, does the burden of proof shift back to the insured to prove that there is an exception to the defense or to segregate covered from non-covered damages?

HOLDING AND DECISION: (Clement, J.)

(1) No. A finding that property was destroyed during a hurricane does not entitle an insured to judgment as a matter of law that the property was destroyed by "windstorm" rather than flooding. The insured bears the burden of establishing that damages sustained by property were inflicted by the peril insured against. The fact that insured property was destroyed during a hurricane does not automatically establish that the damage was caused by wind rather than water. Because Hurricane Katrina unleashed both wind and water forces, it was error for the district court to grant JMOL to the Broussards (P) on this issue. Reversed and remanded to permit the Broussards (P) to carry their burden of proving that their personal property was destroyed by wind.

(2) No. An insured is not entitled to judgment as a matter of law on a claim for insurance coverage where the insurer has presented evidence sufficient to permit a reasonable jury to find in its favor on the issue. Whether a party has met its burden of proof is reviewed under the clearly erroneous standard. Here, the district court found that a finder of fact could not rationally determine that State Farm (D) had met its burden of proof to show that the Broussards' (P) home was destroyed by an excluded peril. This finding was clearly erroneous because State Farm (D) presented sufficient evidence to permit a reasonable jury to find in its favor, since it presented

Continued on next page.

evidence that the dwelling's structural damage was brought about by the storm surge (water) and that it was "75% likely" that wind caused a relatively small amount of damage. Such evidence was more than sufficient to withstand a motion for JMOL, given that a rational jury could conclude, based on this evidence, that the Broussards' (P) home and personal property were destroyed by water. Reversed and remanded.

(3) Where an "open peril" policy is involved, once an insurer has presented evidence to establish an affirmative policy exclusion defense, the burden of proof does not shift back to the insured to prove that there is an exception to the defense or to segregate covered from non-covered damages. This issue is a matter of state law, upon which the state's courts have not ruled. Therefore, this federal court must guess what the state's highest court would hold, if presented with this issue. State Farm (D) points to cases from other jurisdictions that have held that once an insurer has pled an exception to the insurance policy, the burden is on the insured to prove that the occurrence in question did not come within the exclusion. The state's highest court here has rejected a similar rule in cases involving "named peril" policies. In those cases, the court ruled that the insured carried the burden of showing that the named peril caused the loss, but not of also showing that the loss was not caused by an excluded peril. Given that the court has rejected State Farm's (D) proposed "shifting back" rule in "named peril" cases, it is unlikely that it would accept the rule in "open peril" situations since the court seems to favor giving the issue of causation to the jury, and the "shifting back" rule would take that issue away from the jury. Therefore, on remand, the parties will bear their burdens of proof without application of the "shifting back" rule.

[The award of punitive damages is reversed because such damages are recoverable only where the insurer has no arguable basis for its position in fact or law.]

▌ ANALYSIS

After Hurricane Katrina, there was widespread litigation over the applicability of flood exclusions and anti-concurrent causation (ACC) clauses in homeowner policies. The ACC clause provides that: "We do not insure under any coverage for any loss which would not have occurred in the absence of one or more of the following excluded events. We do not insure for such loss regardless of: (a) the cause of the excluded event; or (b) other causes of the loss; or (c) whether other causes acted concurrently or in any sequence with the excluded event to produce the loss . . . ." Some courts held that the ACC clause precluded coverage of damage caused by a storm-surge (tidal wave of water) brought ashore by the hurricane, because the storm-surge constituted "flood" even if it itself was produced by hurricane winds, regardless of whether the damage was concurrent or sequential. Other courts, e.g., the Supreme Court of Mississippi, held that ACCs

were inapplicable to damage caused sequentially, reasoning that coverage vests at the time of loss.

■━■

Quicknotes

BURDEN OF PROOF The duty of a party to introduce evidence to support a fact that is in dispute in an action.

CAUSATION The aggregate effect of preceding events that bring about a tortious result; the causal connection between the actions of a tortfeasor and the injury that follows.

PUNITIVE DAMAGES Damages exceeding the actual injury suffered for the purposes of punishment of the defendant, deterrence of the wrongful behavior or comfort to the plaintiff.

■━■

Dynasty, Inc. v. Princeton Insurance Company

Insured business (P) v. Insurance company (D)

N.J. Sup. Ct., 165 N.J. 1, 754 A.2d 1137 (2000).

NATURE OF CASE: Appeal from affirmance of judgment for insured in insurance coverage action.

FACT SUMMARY: Princeton Insurance Company (D), which had issued a fire insurance policy to Dynasty, Inc. (Dynasty) (P), contended that because there was evidence of arson in the burning of Dynasty's (P) commercial premises, and evidence that its sprinkler system had been tampered with to ensure that it stayed off during a fire, the jury should have been given an increase-of-hazard instruction.

RULE OF LAW

It is reversible error for a trial court to refuse to give an increase-of-hazard jury instruction where a fire has destroyed insured commercial premises and there is evidence that the sprinkler system was intentionally turned off, possibly by the business's owner.

FACTS: Dynasty, Inc. (Dynasty) (P), owned by Esposito, operated a nightclub, the premises of which had a sprinkler system. The business had fire insurance through Princeton Insurance Company (Princeton) (D). The insurance policy contained a provision that Princeton (D) would not be liable for loss occurring "while the hazard is increased by any means within the control or knowledge of the insured." One night, the nightclub was destroyed by fire. There was evidence of arson and that the sprinkler system had been chain-locked in the "off" position at the time of the fire, thus preventing it from activating. There was also evidence that the nightclub and Esposito were experiencing financial difficulty; that in the weeks immediately prior to the fire, Esposito changed the front door locks to the building, installed a new tile floor, repainted the inside and outside of the building, and restocked the liquor inventory; that Esposito was at the movies at the time the fire started; and that the key for the sprinkler control valve was kept near the valve. Esposito denied any complicity or knowledge in the setting of the fire. Dynasty (P) made a claim to Princeton (D) for the full amount of the policy ($150,000), as the damages totaled about $244,000. Princeton (D) denied the claim on the basis of its belief that Esposito ordered or acquiesced in the setting of the fire. Thereafter, Dynasty (P) sued Princeton (D), and the action was tried before a jury. At trial, Princeton (D) requested that the jury be given an increase-of-hazard instruction, which would have indicated to the jury that Princeton (D) would not be liable if the jury found that Esposito had unjustifiably turned off the sprinkler system. The trial court refused to give the requested instruction. The jury returned a verdict for Dynasty (P), the intermediate appellate court upheld the verdict, and the state's highest court granted review.

ISSUE: Is it reversible error for a trial court to refuse to give an increase-of-hazard jury instruction where a fire has destroyed insured commercial premises and there is evidence that the sprinkler system was intentionally turned off, possibly by the business's owner?

HOLDING AND DECISION: (Verniero, J.) Yes. It is reversible error for a trial court to refuse to give an increase-of-hazard jury instruction where a fire has destroyed insured commercial premises and there is evidence that the sprinkler system was intentionally turned off, possibly by the business's owner. A sub-issue that must be decided in resolving this issue is whether an intentionally disabled sprinkler system constitutes an increase of hazard. This is a question of fact. Ordinarily, an increase of hazard will generally not be found if there has been merely a casual change of a temporary character. However, an increase-of-hazard clause is stated in general terms because parties to an insurance contract cannot with certainty spell out every possible scenario that may lead to an increase of hazard. The clause essentially means that an insured may not do anything to materially increase the risk during the policy's term without forfeiting coverage. Therefore, an insured's unjustified disabling of a sprinkler system falls within the realm of an increase-of-hazard clause. Accordingly, coverage will be suspended pursuant to that clause provided the insurer proves the insured's conduct to the satisfaction of the jury. The trial court found that the increase-of-hazard instruction would have been duplicative of an instruction that if the jury found that Esposito had engaged in arson, Princeton (D) would not be liable. However, the acts necessary to accomplish arson may be different from the steps that one would take to disable a sprinkler system. Both forms of conduct could increase the risk of hazard and each might result in the same loss; however, they are factually distinct, and thus give rise to separate jury determinations. Moreover, there was a sufficient basis, viewing the record in its entirety, to support the increase-of-hazard instruction. Princeton's (D) theory was that Dynasty (P) or its agents participated in the arson and that Esposito or someone on his behalf disengaged the sprinkler system, thereby increasing the risk of hazard. There was sufficient evidence in the record to support this theory and to give it to the jury to decide. Therefore, the trial court erred in instructing the jury solely on arson. The trial court's rejection of Princeton's (D) charge constituted plain error. Because Princeton's (D) increase-of-hazard instruction represented an entirely separate defense, its omission by the trial judge unjustly denied it an alternative basis on which to defend the action. Reversed and remanded.

Continued on next page.

ANALYSIS

The standard fire insurance policy and many other kinds of property insurance policies include an increase-of-hazard clause. Some commentators view this clause as a modern-day warranty. Robert Jerry, for instance, has said that "[i]nstead of including a laundry-list of situations in which insureds would forfeit coverage if they failed to take certain risk-reducing measures, insurers now state that insureds lose coverage in the event the hazard is increased. Such a condition is eminently reasonable; even if this provision were not set forth in an insurance policy in express terms, it would be an implied term in the policy that the insured could not do anything to materially increase the risk during the policy's term without forfeiting the coverage." The increase-of-hazard clause is usually not, however, included in the standard homeowner insurance policy or in commercial property insurance policies.

Quicknotes

JURY INSTRUCTIONS A communication made by the court to a jury regarding the applicable law involved in a proceeding.

Zochert v. National Farmers Union Property & Casualty Company

Insured silo owner (P) v. Insurance company (D)

S.D. Sup. Ct., 576 N.W.2d 531 (1998).

NATURE OF CASE: Appeal from summary judgment in action to recover insurance proceeds.

FACT SUMMARY: Zochert (P) claimed that it was entitled to the replacement costs of its damaged silos rather than their depreciated value.

▥ RULE OF LAW
Depreciation must be considered in assessing the actual cash value of property for purposes of insurance loss claims.

FACTS: Zochert (P) owned two silos that were insured by National Farmers Union Property & Casualty Company (National) (D) under a farmowner's policy. The silos, about 20 years old, suffered wind damage. National's (D) adjuster estimated the total cost of repair and replacement cost and deducted the estimated depreciation of the silos before issuing a check for the loss. Zochert (P) filed suit to recover the deducted depreciation cost, claiming that National (D) should have reimbursed the full replacement cost. Both parties moved for summary judgment, which was granted to Zochert (P). National (D) appealed.

ISSUE: Must depreciation be considered in assessing the actual cash value of property for purposes of insurance loss claims?

HOLDING AND DECISION: (Per curiam) Yes. Depreciation must be considered in assessing the actual cash value of property for purposes of insurance loss claims. There are two types of loss settlements, depending on the coverage obtained. Insurers sometimes are required to pay the cost of repair or replacement. Other times they must pay the actual cash value of the loss. Actual cash value is a lesser amount that reflects consideration of depreciation. If an insured recovered the original value of property that had depreciated, it would violate the principle of indemnity by providing a windfall. Actual cash value is typically figured by taking either the market value, the replacement cost less depreciation, or using the broad evidence test. The latter, looking at all the relevant considerations, should be used. The trial court held that the purpose of the insurance was to allow Zochert (P) to rebuild after a loss. However, this position would allow Zochert (P) more coverage than is allowed under the policy and would disregard the contractual language providing for actual cash value. Accordingly, the trial court is reversed.

▶ *ANALYSIS*

The broad evidence test is used by the majority of jurisdictions when figuring actual cash value. Some believe that the principle of indemnity operates differently for commercial operations than for homeowners. While Zochert (P) would be benefitting by damage to the silo (getting a new silo to replace an old one) if replacement costs were used, a typical homeowner is far worse off if a home is severely damaged and the cash value does not provide enough for rebuilding.

◼◼◼

Quicknotes

REPLACEMENT COST The monetary amount necessary in order to replace property or improvements.

◼◼◼

Great Northern Oil Company v. St. Paul Fire and Marine Insurance Company

Insured oil refinery (P) v. Insurance company (D)

Minn. Sup. Ct., 189 N.W.2d 404 (1971).

NATURE OF CASE: Appeal from judgment in action to recover on insurance policy.

FACT SUMMARY: Great Northern Oil Company (P) sought to recover for a business-interruption although a contract it had made with a third party had released all possible claims and defeated the insurer's (D) subrogation rights.

🏛 RULE OF LAW
A release of all claims for damages against a potential wrongdoer does not preclude recovery under a policy even though it defeats the insurer's subrogation rights.

FACTS: Great Northern Oil Company (Great Northern) (P) operated an oil refinery and obtained all-risk insurance from St. Paul Fire and Marine Insurance Company (St. Paul) (D). The policy covered losses due to interruption of the business. It also contained a subrogation clause that gave it the right to recover from responsible third parties if it had to pay Great Northern (P) for losses under the policy. Subsequently, Great Northern (P) contracted with Litwin for the construction of catalytic cracking expansion facilities. The construction agreement released Litwin from any potential liability for business interruption losses. A crane accident ended up causing a business interruption and Great Northern (P) ended up filing suit to recover the losses from St. Paul (D). However, St. Paul (D) argued that the release of Litwin (P) had defeated their subrogation rights and denied the insurance proceeds. The trial court ruled that the release did not preclude recovery and St. Paul (D) appealed.

ISSUE: Does a release of all claims for damages against a potential wrongdoer preclude recovery under a policy if it defeats the insurer's subrogation rights?

HOLDING AND DECISION: (Rogosheske, J.) No. A release of all claims for damages against a potential wrongdoer does not preclude recovery under a policy even though it defeats the insurer's subrogation rights. Upon payment of a loss, the insurer is entitled to pursue those rights which the insured party may have against a third party whose negligence or wrongful act caused the loss. However, the insurer is entitled to no greater rights than that of the insured. The insurer-subrogee steps into the shoes of the insured-subrogor. Thus, it is well established that an insured may defeat the insurance company's subrogation rights by settling with a wrongdoer after a loss but before or after payment under the policy or entering into an agreement of release prior to issuance of the policy. The present situation is slightly different in that the release was provided after the policy was issued. Some cases have ruled that an insured is precluded from recovery on a policy where a pre-loss release was given. However, in those cases, the policies expressly provided that a release would render the policy void. The balance of equities in the present situation are nearly equal, but shift slightly toward the insured. The insurer can protect itself by expressly prohibiting an insured from entering into release agreements. Accordingly, the trial court's ruling that recovery was not precluded is affirmed.

⏵ ANALYSIS

The court correctly observed that insurers are not helpless in these cases. They can either include provisions that expressly hold a policy void if the subrogation rights are released or they could require advance notification so that additional premiums could be assessed. The reason that construction agreements often include such releases is that it eliminates disputes and reduces costs.

━━

Quicknotes

SUBROGATION The substitution of one party for another in assuming the first party's rights or obligations.

SUBROGEE A party who is substituted for another in assuming the first party's rights or obligations for purposes of subrogation.

━━

Northwest Farm Bureau Insurance Company v. Althauser

Insurer (P) v. Insured mortgage holder (D)

Or. Ct. App., 750 P.2d 1166 (1988).

NATURE OF CASE: Appeal from summary judgment in a foreclosure action.

FACT SUMMARY: Northwest Farm Bureau Insurance Company (P) paid insurance benefits to Althauser's (D) mortgagee after a fire and sought to foreclose when Althauser (D) failed to make further payments.

🏛 RULE OF LAW
A party compelled to pay another's debt is entitled to exercise all the remedies that the creditor possessed.

FACTS: Althauser (D) owned a house that was subject to two mortgages. Northwest Farm Bureau Insurance Company (Northwest) (P), insured the home on a homeowners policy, which provided that any fire loss would be payable to the mortgagees. Subsequently, a fire severely damaged the house and Northwest (P) paid the mortgagees the values of their mortgages. The mortgage was then assigned to Northwest (P). Althauser (D), after losing a suit to recover personal property losses because of material misrepresentations, failed to make any mortgage payments after the fire. Northwest (P) brought a foreclosure action.

ISSUE: Is a party compelled to pay another's debt entitled to exercise all the remedies that the creditor possessed?

HOLDING AND DECISION: (Joseph, C.J.) A party compelled to pay another's debt is entitled to exercise all the remedies that the creditor possessed. In the instant action, prior to the fire, Althauser (D) was primarily responsible for the mortgage debt. The insurance contract required that Northwest (P) pay the mortgagees after the fire and acquire the mortgage. Thus, Northwest (P) was subrogated to the rights of the mortgagees because it paid debts that Althauser (D) was primarily responsible for. Because Althauser's (D) misrepresentations voided the insurance policy, Northwest's (P) payments to the mortgagees did not satisfy Althauser's (D) obligations on the mortgage. Rather, Northwest (P) had satisfied a separate and distinct duty that was owed to the mortgagees. Althauser (D) was responsible for the mortgage debts after the fire because the insurance was void and Northwest (P) was subrogated to the mortgagee's remedies by paying the debt. Affirmed.

▶ ANALYSIS

Althauser (D) had argued that insurance premiums were paid, but no benefits were obtained. The court laid the responsibility for this turn of events on Althauser (D) due

to the misrepresentations that voided the policy. In this case, the policy was voided only as to the homeowner but not as to the mortgagees.

■=■

Quicknotes

MISREPRESENTATION A statement or conduct by one party to another that constitutes a false representation of fact.

Alaska Insurance Company v. RCA Alaska Communications, Inc.

Landlord's insurer (P) v. Tenant (D)

Alaska Sup. Ct., 623 P.2d 1216 (1981).

NATURE OF CASE: Appeal from summary judgment in subrogation action.

FACT SUMMARY: Alaska Insurance Company (P) sought to recover money it paid to a landlord-insured from a tenant (D) it claimed caused the loss.

🏛 RULE OF LAW
If a landlord covenants to maintain fire insurance and the lease does not establish the tenant's liability for loss due to its negligence, the tenant is a co-insured for purposes of defeating the insurer's subrogation claim.

FACTS: Bachner owned a commercial warehouse that RCA Alaska Communications, Inc. (RCA) (D) leased. According to the terms of the lease, Bachner was required to have fire insurance coverage. Also, the lease provided that RCA (D) would hold harmless and indemnify Bachner for any losses caused by RCA's (D) negligence. Bachner had insurance coverage for the warehouse from Alaska Insurance Company (AIC) (P), but RCA (D) was not named in the policy. Later, a fire occurred in the warehouse and destroyed the building. AIC (P) paid Bachner for the loss and then commenced an action against RCA (D) as the subrogee of Bachner, contending that the fire was caused by RCA's (D) negligence. The trial court granted partial summary judgment to RCA (D) on the basis that they were an implied insured precluding subrogation. AIC (P) appealed.

ISSUE: If a landlord covenants to maintain fire insurance and the lease does not establish the tenant's liability for loss due to its negligence, is the tenant a co-insured for purposes of defeating the insurer's subrogation claim?

HOLDING AND DECISION: (Connor, J.) Yes. If a landlord covenants to maintain fire insurance and the lease does not establish the tenant's liability for loss due to its negligence, the tenant is a co-insured for purposes of defeating the insurer's subrogation claim. It is a well established rule that an insurer cannot recover by means of subrogation against its own insured. Therefore, if a tenant is a co-insured of the landlord, the insurer has no right of subrogation against the tenant. Other jurisdictions have found that unless there is an express provision in the lease establishing the tenant's liability for loss from negligence, the insurance obtained by the landlord was for the mutual benefit of both parties. Thus, the tenant stands in the shoes of the landlord for the limited purpose of subrogation claims. In the present case, the lease provisions for indemnity do not demonstrate a clear intent that RCA (D) be held liable for fire losses it negligently caused. Furthermore, given the requirement that Bachner carry fire insurance, it would contradict the reasonable expectations of RCA (D) to allow AIC (P) to proceed against it. It could have been expected to be treated as a co-insured. Thus, the judgment for RCA (D) is affirmed.

DISSENT: (Rabinowitz, C.J.) The general principle enunciated by the majority is correct. However, the express provisions of the lease in this case seem to indicate that RCA (D) would be liable for its negligence, especially since there was no disparity in bargaining between the tenant and landlord here, so public policy concerns are not implicated.

▶ ANALYSIS

The rule explained in this case is in accord with most jurisdictions. However, not all courts have been so generous with tenants who have lease provisions similar to those here. This court seemed to think that anything short of a clear and express clause holding the tenant liable was not adequate.

■■■

Quicknotes

SUBROGATION The substitution of one party for another in assuming the first party's rights or obligations.

SUBROGEE A party who is substituted for another in assuming the first party's rights or obligations for purposes of subrogation.

■■■

Paramount Fire Insurance Company v. Aetna Casualty and Surety Company

[Parties not identified.]

Tex. Sup. Ct., 353 S.W.2d 841 (1962).

NATURE OF CASE: Appeal from reversal of summary judgment in action to determine coverage liability.

FACT SUMMARY: Paramount Fire Insurance Company, the insurer of the property sellers, and Aetna Casualty and Surety Company, the buyer's insurer, disputed how liability should be apportioned after a fire on the property in the middle of the sale.

🏛 RULE OF LAW
A property vendor who collects the full purchase price despite fire damage has suffered no legal loss that requires insurance recovery.

FACTS: Cameron entered into a contract to sell real property to Holmes and Reece. Both parties were given the right of specific performance and the purchasers had the right to occupy the premises and make improvements from the inception of the contract. Cameron procured an insurance policy from Paramount Fire Insurance Company (Paramount) covering improvements and payable to only to Cameron. Subsequently, a fire occurred on the property. By that time, Cameron had prepared a warranty deed conveying the property but had not been fully signed. In the meantime, the purchasers had made their required payments and had procured a fire insurance policy from Aetna Casualty and Surety Company (Aetna). When the sale finally closed, the sellers assigned all their rights and claims under the Paramount policy to the purchasers. The purchasers then filed suit against both Aetna and Paramount for a property loss claim. This action was settled when the insurers contributed a prorata share. However, they reserved their rights to recover against the other. On motions for summary judgment in the subsequent action between the insurers, the trial court ruled that Aetna should pay the entire loss. The court of appeals reversed.

ISSUE: Has a property vendor who collects the full purchase price despite fire damage suffered legal loss that requires insurance recovery?

HOLDING AND DECISION: (Greenhill, J.) No. A property vendor who collects the full purchase price despite fire damage has suffered no legal loss that requires insurance recovery. Paramount, the insurer of the property seller argued that since the vendors suffered no pecuniary loss from the fire, the purchaser's insurer should incur the full liability. This is basically the position of the principle of indemnity, where recovery is limited to the extent of the loss. However, there is also a line of cases finding that compensation from third parties is an entirely separate matter and that

an insured is entitled to compensation even if it produces a windfall. Some jurisdictions have held that the vendor is allowed to collect on the insurance policy subject to a constructive trust for the vendee's benefit. This position works well where the vendee has not obtained its own insurance policy. However, where the vendee has coverage it does not make sense to follow this rule. In the instant case and circumstances, it is better to follow the basic principle of indemnity. The only true interest that the vendors had in the property after the contract for sale was the unpaid purchase price. Since they suffered no loss of that interest in this case, there can be no liability that the Paramount policy is required to indemnify. Thus, the court of appeals is reversed and the trial court's ruling against Aetna is affirmed.

DISSENT: (Griffin, J.) The rule applied by the majority does not make sense in a situation where there are monthly installments paid by a purchaser to a seller. Following the majority's reasoning, the seller's insurer would not know its liability until after the last payment was made.

▶ ANALYSIS

The majority seemed very concerned with avoiding the situation of double recovery. However, in the instant case, there was no chance of that happening. The purchaser of the property had already received only one payment for the fire loss. All that remained to be decided was how the insurers should apportion the loss.

■══■

Quicknotes

INDEMNITY The duty of a party to compensate another for damages sustained.

■══■

Home Insurance Company v. Adler

Insurer (D) v. Insured's executor (P)

Md. Ct. App., 309 A.2d 751 (1973).

NATURE OF CASE: Appeal from judgment in action to collect insurance benefits.

FACT SUMMARY: Home Insurance Company (D) refused to pay a claim on Becker's fire insurance policy on the basis that Becker had only a life estate interest and died immediately following the fire.

🏛 RULE OF LAW
Life tenants who insure property in their own name are not precluded from recovering the full amount of the policy proceeds.

FACTS: Becker conveyed to herself a life tenant interest in property and conveyed the remainder to Scheinberg. Becker insured the property with Home Insurance Company (Home) (D). The policy provided that it would pay to the insured the actual cash value of the property in the event of loss by fire. Subsequently, a fire damaged the house and critically injured Becker. She survived only 19 minutes after the fire. Home (D) refused to pay for the fire damage to the house, maintaining that Becker's insurable interest was terminated at her death and thus there was no pecuniary loss to be compensated. Adler (P), the executor of Becker's estate, filed suit against Home and the trial court ruled for Adler (P). Home (D) appealed.

ISSUE: Are life tenants who insure property in their own name precluded from recovering the full amount of the policy proceeds?

HOLDING AND DECISION: (Murphy, C.J.) No. Life tenants who insure property in their own name are not precluded from recovering the full amount of the policy proceeds. Generally, fire insurance is a contract of personal indemnity requiring proof of actual loss as a prerequisite to recovery of insurance proceeds. However, the insurer's liability attaches at the moment a fire begins. Becker had insured the property against loss by fire during her lifetime. That contingent event occurred prior to her death, resulting in property damage to the house. That loss necessarily accrued prior to her death, no matter how long she lived after the fire began. Accordingly, Home (D) is liable for the fire loss. Affirmed.

▌ *ANALYSIS*

The net effect of the decision is that the insured only has to be alive at the beginning of the fire for the insurer to be liable. The court noted that testimony from counsel indicated that premiums were based on the building and risk, regardless of the insured's interest. Given that fire insurance actually seems to be more attached to the property than the insured, the indemnity principle doesn't necessarily work well in this context.

■══■

Quicknotes

LIFE TENANT An individual whose estate in real property is measured either by his own life or by that of another.

■══■

Folger Coffee Company, Inc. v. Great American Insurance Company

Insured's bailor (P) v. Insurer (D)

333 F. Supp. 1272 (W.D. Mo. 1971).

NATURE OF CASE: Action to recover insurance benefits.

FACT SUMMARY: Folger Coffee Company, Inc.'s (P) property was destroyed while in Ar-Ka-Mo's possession, but Great American Insurance Company (D), Ar-Ka-Mo's insurer, refused to pay the claim.

🏛 RULE OF LAW
Insurance covers property in the bailee's possession rather than only the bailee's legal liability to respond in damages.

FACTS: Ar-Ka-Mo Sporting Goods had a property insurance policy with Great American Insurance Company (Great American) (D). The policy covered property of others held by Ar-Ka-Mo "for which the insured is liable." Ar-Ka-Mo was holding Folger Coffee Company, Inc.'s (Folger) (P) property when it was destroyed. Folger (P) sought to recover the value of the property from Great American (D). However, Great American (D) asserted that Folger (P) had to show that Ar-Ka-Mo was negligent and legally liable for the damage. Folger (P) brought suit against Great American (D) for recovery of the insurance benefits.

ISSUE: Does insurance cover property in the bailee's possession rather than only the bailee's legal liability to respond in damages?

HOLDING AND DECISION: (Becker, C.J.) Yes. Insurance covers property in the bailee's possession rather than only the bailee's legal liability to respond in damages. In similar cases to the present one, courts have uniformly found that "liable" as used in the policy of the bailor-insured does not refer to any fixed legal liability, but should be construed more broadly to mean "responsible." There is no doubt from looking at the policy in its entirety that this is the fairest interpretation. The Great American (D) policy was intended to insure Ar-Ka-Mo for property for which it was responsible. It repeatedly used the word "property" to define the subject matter of the insurance. Thus, it is clear it was intended to cover property, not legal liability. Accordingly, summary judgment on the issue of Great American's (D) liability on the policy is granted to Folger (P).

▶ ANALYSIS

Other jurisdictions have not definitively ruled on this issue. However, given this decision and other similar ones, insurers now know for sure that "legally liable" can be interpreted as meaning "responsible." Often, bailors like Folger (P) have

their own coverage of property that is left in a bailee's possession. However, policy provisions usually prevent any double recovery by an insured.

◼═◼

Quicknotes

BAILEE Person holding property in trust for another party.

◼═◼

Life, Health, and Disability Insurance

Quick Reference Rules of Law

Gaunt v. John Hancock Mutual Life Insurance Company

Alleged insured (P) v. Insurer (D)

160 F.2d 599, *cert. denied*, 331 U.S. 849 (1947).

NATURE OF CASE: Appeal from dismissal of an action to collect life insurance benefits.

FACT SUMMARY: Gaunt applied for insurance, took a physical and paid his first premium, but died before John Hancock Mutual Life Insurance Company's (D) home office gave final approval to the policy.

RULE OF LAW
Applicants for insurance who pay premiums and successfully pass other conditions precedent, are entitled to immediate coverage despite the lack of final approval of the risk.

FACTS: Gaunt (P) applied for life insurance through Kelman, an agent, on August 3. He filled out the John Hancock Mutual Life Insurance Company (John Hancock) (D) application, which included a provision that stated the insurance was effective at the date of completion of Part B, if the insurer approved the risk at the home office. Gaunt (P) paid the full first premium and took a physical that same day. The physician found Gaunt (P) to be insurable. However, a week later the John Hancock home office requested that Gaunt (P) take another physical, which took place on August 17. This doctor also passed Gaunt (P), as did a medical examiner at the John Hancock (D) home office. Still, more information was requested and it was satisfactorily provided by Gaunt (P). However, although medically cleared, John Hancock (D) did not finally approve the application before Gaunt was shot days later. Gaunt's mother (P) filed suit to collect on the policy because John Hancock (D) denied that the insurance was in effect. The trial court dismissed the action.

ISSUE: Are applicants for insurance who pay premiums and successfully pass other conditions precedent, entitled to immediate coverage despite the lack of final approval of the risk?

HOLDING AND DECISION: (Hand, J.) Yes. Applicants for insurance who pay premiums and successfully pass other conditions precedent, are entitled to immediate coverage despite the lack of final approval of the risk. The policy at question here seems to make final approval by the home office a condition precedent to having the effective date of the insurance relate back to the time of the application. This provision is unclear and ambiguous to the applicant. An applicant could reasonably interpret this to mean that the insurance was effective as soon as the premiums were paid and applicant found to be insurable. If John Hancock (D) had intended another interpretation it should have done so clearly. Insurers who make policy language with esoteric significance must bear the burden of the resulting confusion. Thus, Gaunt (P), having paid the premiums and successfully passed the physical, could reasonably have expected that the insurance was then effective, and not when John Hancock (D) at its leisure approved the application. The dismissal is reversed and judgment is to be entered for Gaunt's mother (P).

CONCURRENCE: (Clark, J.) The majority decision is correct because of John Hancock's superior position in the negotiations. However, the contract language would not be ambiguous if the bargaining had occurred between parties of equal knowledge.

ANALYSIS
Typically, insureds are issued binders when an application is submitted. The binder acts as a receipt and is often a copy of the application. However, most binders do not make coverage effective immediately.

Quicknotes
AMBIGUOUS Vague; unclear; capable of being understood to have more than one meaning.

Engleman v. Connecticut General Life Insurance Company

Estate executor (P) v. Insurer (D)

Conn. Sup. Ct., 690 A.2d 882 (1997).

NATURE OF CASE: Appeal from judgment in a breach of insurance contract action.

FACT SUMMARY: Ryder sought to change the beneficiary of her life insurance policy but did not use an official Connecticut General Life Insurance Company (D) form.

RULE OF LAW
Life insurance policyholders effectively change their beneficiaries when they clearly intend a change, designate a new beneficiary and take a substantial affirmative action to effectuate the change.

FACTS: Ryder owned a life insurance policy through Connecticut General Life Insurance Company (Connecticut General) (D). The beneficiary was Zink, but Ryder subsequently decided to change the policy to make her estate the beneficiary. In 1978, Ryder's attorney wrote Connecticut General (D) asking it to prepare a change of beneficiary form naming the estate as the new beneficiary. However, nothing came of this request. The following year, Ryder sent a letter to Connecticut General (D), signed and witnessed, that requested the change once again. The letter was placed in the policy file. However, rather than make the change, Connecticut General (D) sent an official change of beneficiary form, but there was no evidence of what became of this form. When Ryder died in 1990, Engleman (P), the executor of the estate, demanded that Connecticut General (D) pay the policy proceeds. Connecticut General (D) refused on the basis that an official change was never made and instead paid the proceeds to Zink. Engleman (P) brought an action for breach of contract. The trial court ruled in favor of Connecticut General (D) and Engleman (P) appealed.

ISSUE: Do life insurance policyholders effectively change their beneficiaries when they clearly intend a change, designate a new beneficiary and take a substantial affirmative action to effectuate the change?

HOLDING AND DECISION: (Berdon, J.) Yes. Life insurance policyholders effectively change their beneficiaries when they clearly intend a change, designate a new beneficiary and take a substantial affirmative action to effectuate the change. The general rule is that a change of beneficiary must be effected by following the procedure prescribed in the policy. However, there is a narrow exception to this rule where the owner of the policy has substantially complied with the change requirements by doing all that is possible within the policyholder's control. The application of an exception seems appropriate in some situations, particularly where the insured has taken substantial affirmative action attempting to make the change. Thus, the technical requirements of the policy should not override the clear intentions of the insured in these circumstances. In the instant case, Ryder submitted a dated, signed, witnessed and unequivocal letter to Connecticut General (D) that properly referenced the policy by number and name. There is absolutely no doubt that Ryder intended to change the beneficiary from Zink to her estate. These actions are exactly the same as those required using the official company form. Accordingly, applying the substantial compliance doctrine in this case it is clear that Ryder effectively changed the beneficiary of the policy. Reversed.

ANALYSIS

This decision is in accord with the majority rule. The substantial compliance doctrine is sometimes applied only when the insured isn't able to technically comply for a reason beyond the insured's control. That wasn't the situation in the instant case.

Quicknotes

BENEFICIARY A third party who is the recipient of the benefit of a transaction undertaken by another.

Grigsby v. Russell

[Parties not identified.]

222 U.S. 149 (1911).

NATURE OF CASE: Bill of interpleader.

FACT SUMMARY: An insurance company brought a bill of interpleader requesting the Court to determine whether insurance policy proceeds should be paid to the deceased's estate administrators or to the assignee of the policy, Dr. Grigsby.

🏛 RULE OF LAW
The holder of a life insurance policy may validly assign his interest therein to a third party.

FACTS: Burchard, after having paid two insurance premiums and being overdue on the third, needed money for a surgical operation. He asked Grigsby to buy the policy and sold it to him for $100 and for Grigsby's acceptance to pay the premiums due. The court of appeals held that the assignment was valid only to the extent of the money actually paid for it and any premiums subsequently paid. The insurance company brought a bill of interpleader to determine whether the insurance policy should be paid to Burchard's administrators or the assignee, Grigsby. The United States Supreme Court granted certiorari.

ISSUE: May the holder of a life insurance policy validly assign his interest therein to a third party?

HOLDING AND DECISION: (Holmes, C.J.) Yes. The holder of a life insurance policy may validly assign his interest therein to a third party. Here the insurance policy was valid, the contract performed, and the money held by the court. Under the law, such insurance policies are typically given the same characteristics as property. Placing limitations on the right of the holder of the policy to sell diminishes the policy's value. Reversed.

▶ ANALYSIS

Public policy precludes third parties from being able to take out insurance policies on the lives of others in the first instance, since it would grant the holder of the policy an interest in having the insured's life ending. Here the Court makes an exception to this rule consistent with general property law principles.

■━■

Quicknotes

ASSIGNEE A party to whom another party assigns his interest or rights.

INTERPLEADER An equitable proceeding whereby a person holding property which is subject to the claims of

multiple parties may require such parties to resolve the matter through litigation.

■━■

State Mutual Life Assurance Company of America v. Hampton

Insurer (D) v. Policy beneficiary (P)

Okla. Sup. Ct., 696 P.2d 1027 (1985).

NATURE OF CASE: Appeal from judgment in interpleader action regarding insurance benefits.

FACT SUMMARY: Hampton (P), accused of killing her husband, claimed that her acquittal at trial automatically entitled her to the life insurance benefits.

RULE OF LAW

Where a beneficiary of a life insurance policy who has killed the insured has been acquitted of murder, the beneficiary may nevertheless be denied the proceeds of the policy.

FACTS: Tony Hampton had a life insurance policy with State Mutual Life Assurance Company of America (State Mutual) (D) that named Sawart Hampton (P), his wife, as beneficiary. Subsequently, Tony Hampton was killed as the result of injuries suffered in a family fight. Sawart (P) was arrested and charged with first-degree murder. State Mutual (D) filed an interpleader action in which it paid the $100,000 policy limit to the court to avoid potential conflicting claims given the circumstances of the death. Later, Sawart was acquitted of the criminal charges at trial and then filed a motion for summary judgment in the interpleader action. The trial court denied summary judgment and Sawart Hampton (P) appealed.

ISSUE: Where a beneficiary of a life insurance policy who has killed the insured has been acquitted of murder, may the beneficiary nevertheless be denied the proceeds of the policy?

HOLDING AND DECISION: (Simms, C.J.) Yes. Where a beneficiary of a life insurance policy who has killed the insured has been acquitted of murder, the beneficiary may nevertheless be denied the proceeds of the policy. Oklahoma Statute § 231 provides that no person who is convicted of murder or manslaughter is entitled to receive life insurance proceeds as the victim's beneficiary. This law is an extension of the old common law rule that a person should not benefit from his own wrongful conduct. However, there is no indication that the legislature wished to make conviction the only basis for denying insurance proceeds. There is no such limitation found in the statute. Thus, section 231 does not preclude application of the common law rule. Similarly, there is no indication that the law was intended to mean that an acquittal would have any effect on the beneficiary's right. Sawart Hampton (P) argues that the issue of her responsibility for Tony Hampton's death has been conclusively proven. However, a criminal trial has different standards with regard to burden of proof. Moreover, the estate administrator and Hampton's children, who could be entitled to the insurance benefits were not parties to the criminal case and shouldn't be bound by the results. Therefore, the issue of whether Sawart (P) unlawfully took her husband's life should be litigated in a civil proceeding to determine the rights to insurance benefits. Affirmed.

ANALYSIS

Other jurisdictions, but not all, are in accord with this decision. The Oklahoma law in question gives a conclusive effect to a criminal trial if there is a conviction, but not if the result is an acquittal. This is because the burden of proof in a criminal trial is the most exacting.

Quicknotes

BENEFICIARY A third party who is the recipient of the benefit of a transaction undertaken by another.

INTERPLEADER An equitable proceeding whereby a person holding property which is subject to the claims of multiple parties may require such parties to resolve the matter through litigation.

Silverstein v. Metropolitan Life Insurance Company

Beneficiary (P) v. Insurer (D)

N.Y. Ct. App., 171 N.E.2d 914 (1930).

NATURE OF CASE: Appeal from judgment in an action to collect insurance benefits.

FACT SUMMARY: Metropolitan Life Insurance Company (D) denied a claim for accidental death benefits because the insured's medical condition was a factor in the death.

🏛 RULE OF LAW
Where an insured suffers an accident that causes the insured injury or death because the insured has a medical condition, coverage for the accidental injury or death is not precluded if the condition's natural and probable development into a disease is remote, notwithstanding that the accident would not have injured or killed a healthy normal person.

FACTS: Metropolitan Life Insurance Company (Metropolitan) (D) issued a policy to the insured for bodily injuries and death caused by accidental means. The policy excluded coverage for injuries or death caused wholly or partly by disease or infirmity. The insured slipped and fell and caused a milk can to fall on his abdomen. This accident subsequently caused his death. A surgeon working on the insured's abdomen discovered that there was a perforation of the stomach where the can hit. Right at this spot was a previously unknown dormant ulcer. Although the ulcer was not growing and did not present any immediate problem to the insured, it had weakened the stomach wall at that point and had allowed the perforation that led to the insured's death. Metropolitan (D) denied Silverstein's (P) claim on the basis that the policy excluded death due to disease and infirmity. A lower court ruled for Silverstein (P).

ISSUE: Where an insured suffers an accident that causes the insured injury or death because the insured has a medical condition, is coverage for the accidental injury or death precluded if the condition's natural and probable development into a disease is remote, notwithstanding that the accident would not have injured or killed a healthy normal person?

HOLDING AND DECISION: (Cardozo, C.J.) No. Where an insured suffers an accident that causes the insured injury or death because the insured has a medical condition, coverage for the accidental injury or death is not precluded if the condition's natural and probable development into a disease is remote, notwithstanding that the accident would not have injured or killed a healthy normal person. The disease or infirmity referred to in the exclusion provision at issue here must be so considerable or significant that it would be characterized as disease in the common speech of men. The insured's ulcer was merely the size of a pea and left to itself would have been as harmless as a scratch. It was not the source of any pain or trouble to the insured. Therefore, it was not a disease or infirmity within the meaning of the policy. It is important to distinguish conditions of such quality or degree that their natural and probably development will be the source of mischief, and a condition that merely makes a person imperfect. The insured's ulcer falls into the latter category. Additionally, the rule is clear that recovery is allowed where an accident occurs to someone who is generally frail, even if the same accident would not have injured or killed a completely healthy person. The judgment for the insured's widow is affirmed.

▶ ANALYSIS

The court noted that it was impossible to segregate any single cause as operative and exclusive of all others. Thus, the chain of causation can only followed as far the parties intend by the policy. The court also provided the classic "egg-skull" example of a man who with abnormally thin skull who is seriously injured by a blow to the head which would not have affected a normal person.

Like eggshell rule in torts
↳ Take your victim as you find them.

Amex Life Assurance Company v. Superior Court

[Role of Superior Court not identified.]

Cal. Sup. Ct., 930 P.2d 1264 (1997).

NATURE OF CASE: [Lower court decisions not included in casebook.]

FACT SUMMARY: Amex Life Assurance Company refused to pay life insurance benefits because Morales, the insured, fraudulently obtained coverage, although the policy included an incontestability clause.

🏛 RULE OF LAW
Where an insurance policy contains an incontestability period, the insurer is barred from claiming fraud after the period has elapsed unless the insurer can demonstrate that the policy was void *ab initio*.

FACTS: Morales applied for life insurance from Amex Life Assurance Company (Amex) in January 1991. Morales knew that he had the HIV virus, but lied about it on the application and sent an impostor to the required medical examination. Although the medical examination showed indications that the man was not Morales, the examiner did not require that the man show proof of identity. Amex issued a life insurance policy to Morales effective May 1991. The policy contained an incontestability clause providing that the insurer would not contest coverage after it had been in force for two years and the premiums were paid in full. Morales died of AIDS in June 1993, but Amex denied payment on the policy on the basis of fraud in the application.

ISSUE: Where an insurance policy contains an incontestability period, is the insurer barred from claiming fraud after the period has elapsed unless the insurer can demonstrate that the policy was void *ab initio*?

HOLDING AND DECISION: (Chin, J.) Yes. Where an insurance policy contains an incontestability period, the insurer is barred from claiming fraud after the period has elapsed unless the insurer can demonstrate that the policy was void *ab initio*. Insurers initially offered the clause because of public distrust of insurance companies. They now protect insureds from allegations of pre-existing conditions and legal battles with large insurers. The incontestability clause prevents insurers from lulling insureds into security during the time when the facts are best ascertained and proven. There is one circumstance where the incontestability clause does not apply. When an impostor applies for insurance in the name of another, it has been held that no valid insurance policy ever existed. The invocation of the clause presupposes a valid contract. However, this impostor defense does not apply to the present case. Morales personally applied for the insurance on his life. There was no question about who the insurance was supposed to cover. The fraud perpetrated by Morales in this case could have been easily discovered by Amex at the outset. Amex merely had to require that applicants produce photo identification at the medical examination. Therefore, the incontestability clause applies to the present case and prevents Amex from denying the claim for fraud.

▶ ANALYSIS

The court noted that these clauses produce occasional inequities. The clauses are similar to statute of limitations. One important reason for their use is that fraud is much harder to discover, determine and defend years after it takes place.

Quicknotes

AB INITIO From its inception or beginning.

INCONTESTABILITY CLAUSE A clause in a life or health insurance policy providing that after the policy has been in force for a given length of time the insurer shall not be able to contest it as to statements contained in the application; and in the case of health insurance, that no claim shall be denied or reduced on the grounds that a condition not excluded by name at the time of issue existed prior to the effective date.

VOID Null; incapable of being enforced.

Void ab initio

Mauroner v. Massachusetts Indemnity and Life Insurance Company

Named beneficiary (P) v. Insurer (D)

La. Ct. App., 520 So. 2d 451 (1988).

NATURE OF CASE: Appeal from judgment in action to recover life insurance proceeds.

FACT SUMMARY: Mauroner's life insurance coverage was unduly delayed and he later committed suicide just prior to two years after the issue date, barring recovery. However, he had applied before the two years were up, and it was the negligence of Massachusetts Indemnity and Life Insurance Company (D) that delayed the inception of the policy.

🏛 RULE OF LAW
Insurers are liable for negligent delay in issuing a policy if it causes exclusion of coverage.

FACTS: Mauroner applied for life insurance through an agent of Massachusetts Indemnity and Life Insurance Company (MILICO) (D) on November 6, 1981 and included a check for the first premium. Marouner was given a conditional receipt that stated MILICO (D) would provide coverage as of November 6 if the application information was accurate and complete and Marouner was otherwise qualified. The processing period was to take four to eight weeks. However, partly due to an error by the agent MILICO (D) did not issue a policy until February 11, 1982. The policy included a suicide provision that excluded coverage for suicide within two years of the date of policy issue. Subsequently, Marouner killed himself on January 13, 1984, three weeks before the end of the policy exclusion. MILICO (D) tendered only the policy premiums and Marouner's wife (P) filed suit to recover the policy benefits. The trial court ruled that the policy date should have been November 6 but for MILICO's (D) negligence and granted judgment to Marouner's wife (P).

ISSUE: Are insurers liable for negligent delay in issuing a policy if it causes exclusion of coverage?

HOLDING AND DECISION: (Chehardy, C.J.) Yes. Insurers are liable for negligent delay in issuing a policy if it causes exclusion of coverage. In the present case, the suicide exclusion clause expressly provides that the two years runs from the date the policy is issued. However, the application and conditional receipt apparently provide retroactive coverage to the date of application. Still, this retroactive coverage is to be read in accordance with the policy's provisions and limitations. The suicide clause is just such a provision that must be given effect. Therefore, the trial court incorrectly substituted the application date for the issuance date. However, this does not necessarily negate liability. Mauroner's wife (P) alleged

damage due to MILICO's (D) negligence. This would require that MILICO (D) breached a duty and was the legal cause of damage. Insurers have a duty to act upon an insurance application within a reasonable time. Here, MILICO (D) normally processed applications within 56 days. Mauroner's policy was not issued for 92 days from the date of application, an unreasonable delay. Thus, MILICO (D) breached a duty. Since the evidence shows that had this breach not occurred, it was more likely than not that Mauroner's suicide would have happened after the two year exclusion period had expired, MILICO's (D) negligence was the cause of the injury. The damage was the amount of the policy benefits. The trial court's judgment is affirmed.

▶ ANALYSIS

Some jurisdictions would have found that MILICO's (D) negligence was not the proximate cause of the injury here. MILICO (D) had argued that Mauroner's suicidal act was the sole cause of the damage. The decision seems to leave open the policy that an insurer could simply promise less timely application processing as a means of avoiding the duty.

■==■

Quicknotes

BREACH The violation of an obligation imposed pursuant to contract or law, by acting or failing to act.

DUTY An obligation owed by one individual to another.

■==■

Lawson ex rel. Lawson v. Fortis Insurance Company

Insured medical patient (P) v. Insurance company (D)

301 F.3d 159 (3d Cir. 2002).

NATURE OF CASE: Appeal from summary judgment for plaintiff in health insurance action.

FACT SUMMARY: Lawson (P), who was treated for symptoms of an undiagnosed medical condition before coverage began, but then was diagnosed with, and treated for, leukemia after the effective date of the policy issued by Fortis Insurance Company (D), argued that coverage should not be denied on the ground that Lawson's condition was an excluded pre-existing condition.

RULE OF LAW
An insured who is treated for symptoms of an undiagnosed medical condition before the effective date of an insurance policy, but then is diagnosed with and treated for a known medical condition after the effective date of the policy, may not be denied coverage on the ground that the insured's condition is an excluded pre-existing condition.

FACTS: Lawson (P), a minor child, was covered under a health insurance policy that her father bought from Fortis Insurance Company (Fortis) (D). Two days prior to the effective date of the policy, Lawson (P) went to the emergency room for treatment of what was initially diagnosed as a respiratory tract infection, but which was discovered to be leukemia one week later, after the effective date of the policy. Fortis (D) denied coverage of medical expenses relating to the leukemia on the ground that it was a pre-existing condition for which Lawson (P) had received treatment prior to the effective date of the policy. The policy defined pre-existing condition as: "Sickness, Injury, disease or physical condition for which medical advice or treatment was recommended by a Physician or received from a Physician within the five (5) year period preceding that Covered Person's Effective Date of Coverage." Lawson's parents (P), acting on her behalf, sued for breach of contract, and the district court granted their motion for summary judgment. The court of appeals granted review.

ISSUE: May an insured who is treated for symptoms of an undiagnosed medical condition before the effective date of an insurance policy, but then is diagnosed with and treated for a known medical condition after the effective date of the policy, be denied coverage on the ground that the insured's condition is an excluded pre-existing condition?

HOLDING AND DECISION: (Alito, J.) No. An insured who is treated for symptoms of an undiagnosed medical condition before the effective date of an insurance policy, but then is diagnosed with and treated for a known medical condition after the effective date of the policy, may not be denied coverage on the ground that the insured's condition is an excluded pre-existing condition. Fortis (D) argues that the pre-existing condition language of the insurance policy does not require accurate diagnosis of the condition, but merely receipt of treatment or advice for the symptoms of it. Lawson (P) responds that the leukemia was not pre-existing because one cannot receive treatment "for" a condition without knowledge of what the condition is. State and federal courts have interpreted pre-existing condition clauses differently. Some have found ambiguous the lack of clarity regarding what constitutes treatment "for" a condition. Other courts, finding that the language of the clause is clear and unambiguous, have ruled that a pre-existing condition does not require a diagnosis of the condition. Some courts that find the clause ambiguous, have found that treatment for a condition requires some awareness on the part of the insured or physician that the insured is receiving treatment for the condition itself. Here, the contract language is either clear that there must be a diagnosis before treatment can be rendered for that diagnosed illness, or, at best is ambiguous and should be construed against Fortis (D). The key word is "for." Lawson (P) received treatment "for" what were initially diagnosed as symptoms of a respiratory tract infection. Therefore, the treatment she received was not "for" leukemia, but "for" a respiratory tract infection. The word "for" connotes intent, and, therefore, has an implicit intent requirement. In short, it is hard to see how a doctor can provide treatment "for" a condition without knowing what that condition is or that it even exists. In this case, the treatment Lawson (P) initially received for a respiratory tract infection was not the appropriate treatment for leukemia, and thus it does not make sense to say that she received treatment "for" leukemia when the actual condition was not suspected and the treatment was in any event wrong. In addition, considering treatment for symptoms of a not-yet-diagnosed condition as equivalent to treatment of the underlying condition ultimately diagnosed might open the door for insurance companies to deny coverage for any condition the symptoms of which were treated during the exclusionary period. "To permit such backward-looking reinterpretation of symptoms to support claims denials would so greatly expand the definition of pre-existing condition as to make that term meaningless: any prior symptom not inconsistent with the ultimate diagnosis would provide a basis for denial." At a minimum, the pre-existing condition language in Fortis's (D) insurance policy is susceptible to more than one reasonable interpretation and is therefore ambiguous. Therefore, the insurance policy is strictly construed against Fortis (D); either way, coverage is not excluded. Affirmed on this issue.

Continued on next page.

▶ *ANALYSIS*

Under the Health Insurance Portablility and Accountability Act of 1996 (HIPAA), pre-existing condition limitations in health insurance policies may not exceed 12 months. This provision addressed the concern that by changing jobs, an individual could lose coverage because of pre-existing condition exclusions in the new employer's health insurance policy. Accordingly, HIPAA also requires that most health insurance plans give an insured "credit" for the amount of time covered under another policy or plan. These provisions of HIPAA do not, however, cover the terms of coverage provided to first-time insureds who are not changing jobs.

■═■

Quicknotes

AMBIGUOUS Vague; unclear; capable of being understood to have more than one meaning.

■═■

Aetna Health, Inc. v. Davila

Health maintenance organization (D) v. Insured medical patients (P)

542 U.S. 200 (2004).

NATURE OF CASE: Appeal from reversal of judgment that claims were preempted by ERISA.

FACT SUMMARY: Insureds (P) brought state-court actions alleging that their health maintenance organizations (HMOs), Aetna Health, Inc. (D) and CIGNA Healthcare of Texas, Inc. (D), had violated duties "to exercise ordinary care" under state law. The HMOs (D) countered that the actions were preempted by the Employee Retirement Income Security Act of 1974.

RULE OF LAW

A state law that requires that health maintenance organizations (HMOs) exercise ordinary care in their administration of health insurance plans is preempted by Employee Retirement Income Security Act of 1974 § 502(a)(1)(B).

FACTS: Davila (P) and Calad (P) brought separate state-court suits, alleging that their health maintenance organizations (HMOs), Aetna Health, Inc. (Aetna) (D) and CIGNA Healthcare of Texas, Inc. (CIGNA) (D), had refused to cover certain medical services in violation of an HMO's duty "to exercise ordinary care" under the Texas Health Care Liability Act (THCLA), and that those refusals "proximately caused" their injuries. The HMOs (D) removed the cases to federal courts, claiming that the actions fit within the scope of, and were thus completely preempted by, § 502 of the Employee Retirement Income Security Act of 1974 (ERISA). The district courts agreed, declined to remand the cases to state court, and dismissed the complaints with prejudice after the insureds (P) refused to amend them to bring explicit ERISA claims. Consolidating these and other cases, the court of appeals reversed, finding that the insureds' claims could fall under two subsections of § 502(a): § 502(a)(1)(B), which provides a cause of action for the recovery of wrongfully denied benefits, and § 502(a)(2), which allows suit against a plan fiduciary for breaches of fiduciary duty to the plan. The Supreme Court granted certiorari.

ISSUE: Is a state law that requires that health maintenance organizations (HMOs) exercise ordinary care in their administration of health insurance plans preempted by ERISA § 502(a)(1)(B)?

HOLDING AND DECISION: (Thomas, J.) Yes. A state law that requires that health maintenance organizations (HMOs) exercise ordinary care in their administration of health insurance plans is preempted by ERISA § 502(a)(1)(B). Because ERISA's purpose is to provide a uniform regulatory regime, ERISA includes expansive preemption provisions, such as ERISA § 502(a)'s integrated

enforcement mechanism, which are intended to ensure employee benefit plan regulation is "exclusively a federal concern." Any state-law cause of action that duplicates, supplements, or supplants ERISA's civil enforcement remedy, conflicts with clear congressional intent to make that remedy exclusive, and is therefore, preempted. ERISA § 502(a)'s preemptive force is still stronger. Since ERISA § 502(a)(1)(B)'s preemptive force mirrors that of § 301 of the Labor Management Relations Act of 1947 (LMRA), and since § 301 converts state causes of actions into federal ones for purposes of determining the propriety of removal, so, too, does ERISA § 502(a)(1)(B). If an individual, at some point in time, could have brought his claim under ERISA § 502(a)(1)(B), and where no other independent legal duty is implicated by a defendant's actions, then the individual's cause of action is completely preempted by ERISA § 502(a)(1)(B). Here, the insureds (P) brought suit only to rectify wrongful benefits denials, and their only relationship with the HMOs (D) is the HMOs' (D) partial administration of their ERISA-regulated benefit plans; the insureds (P) therefore could have brought § 502(a)(1)(B) claims to recover the allegedly wrongfully denied benefits. The insureds (P) allege violations of the THCLA's duty of ordinary care, which they claim is entirely independent of any ERISA duty or the employee benefits plans at issue. However, the duties imposed by the THCLA in the context of these cases do not arise independently of ERISA or the plan terms. If a managed care entity correctly concluded that, under the relevant plan's terms, a particular treatment was not covered, the plan's failure to cover the requested treatment would be the proximate cause of any injury arising from the denial. More significantly, the THCLA provides that a managed care entity is not subject to THCLA liability if it denies coverage for a treatment not covered by the plan it administers. Thus, interpretation of the terms of the insureds' (P) benefit plans forms an essential part of their THCLA claim, and THCLA liability would exist here only because of the HMOs' (D) administration of ERISA-regulated benefit plans. The HMOs' (D) potential liability under the THCLA in these cases, then, derives entirely from the particular rights and obligations established by the benefit plans. For these reasons, the insureds' (P) state causes of action fall within the scope of § 502(a)(1)(B) and are completely preempted by ERISA and are removable to federal district court. Also unavailing is the insureds' (P) argument that the THCLA is a law regulating insurance that is saved from preemption by ERISA § 514(b)(2)(A). The Court's understanding of § 514(b)(2)(A) is informed by the overpowering federal policy embodied in ERISA § 502(a), which is intended to

Continued on next page.

create an exclusive federal remedy; allowing insureds (P) to proceed with their state-law suits would "pose an obstacle" to that objective. Reversed and remanded.

CONCURRENCE: (Ginsburg, J.) Although the Court's decision is correct under ERISA's preemptive scheme, and is consistent with prior case law, the decision highlights the need for Congress to revisit ERISA and rectify what has become an unjust and increasingly tangled ERIA regime. Because the Court has coupled an encompassing interpretation of ERISA's preemptive force with a cramped construction of the "equitable relief" allowable under § 502(a)(3), a "regulatory vacuum" exists: "[V]irtually all state law remedies are preempted but very few federal substitutes are provided." A series of the Court's decisions has yielded a host of situations in which persons adversely affected by ERISA-proscribed wrongdoing cannot gain make-whole relief. The current situation is untenable, and Congress should act quickly.

▶ *ANALYSIS*

The court of appeals found that the insureds' (P) claims did not fall under either ERISA § 502(a)(2), which allows suit against a plan fiduciary for breaches of fiduciary duty to the plan, because the HMOs (D) were being sued for mixed eligibility and treatment decisions that were not fiduciary in nature, or § 502(a)(1)(B), which provides a cause of action for the recovery of wrongfully denied benefits, because THCLA did not duplicate that cause of action. The crux of the Court's decision regarding preemption by § 502(a)(1)(B) is an explanation of why the duties imposed by THCLA could not arise independently of ERISA or the plan terms, thus distinguishing the court of appeals' reasoning.

■■■■

Quicknotes

CERTIORARI A discretionary writ issued by a superior court to an inferior court in order to review the lower court's decisions; the Supreme Court's writ ordering such review.

EMPLOYEE RETIREMENT INCOME SECURITY ACT OF 1974 (ERISA) Federal law of employee benefits which establishes minimum standards to protect employees from breach of benefit promises made by employers.

HMO Health Maintenance Organization; a group of physicians and other health practitioners who participate in providing medical services to members of a health insurance program.

PREEMPTION Doctrine holding that matters of national interest take precedence over matters of local interest; the federal law takes precedence over state law.

PROXIMATE CAUSE The natural sequence of events without which an injury would not have been sustained.

■■■■

McGann v. H & H Music Company

Insured employee (P) v. Employer-insurer (D)

946 F.2d 401 (5th Cir. 1991).

NATURE OF CASE: Appeal from summary judgment in Employee Retirement Income Security Act of 1974 discrimination action.

FACT SUMMARY: H & H Music Company (D) altered their medical insurance plan to exclude coverage for AIDS after McGann (P) disclosed he had the disease.

🏛 RULE OF LAW
The Employee Retirement Income Security Act of 1974 does not mandate that employers provide any particular benefits and does not prohibit discrimination against identifiable groups of employees.

FACTS: McGann (P) was an employee of H & H Music Company (H & H Music) (D) and was diagnosed with AIDS in December 1987. McGann (P) submitted claims for reimbursement of medical expenses under H & H Music's (D) group medical plan and informed them of his condition. At the time, the plan provided for lifetime medical benefits of up to $1 million for all employees. In July 1988, H & H Music (D) informed its employees that changes would be made to the plan. One of the new provisions limited benefits payable for AIDS-related claims to a lifetime maximum of $5,000. No limitation was placed on any other catastrophic illness. Shortly thereafter, McGann (P) exhausted the new coverage limit. McGann (P) then filed suit against H & H Music (D) for unlawful discrimination under the Employee Retirement Income Security Act of 1974 (ERISA), claiming that the AIDS provision was directed specifically at him in retaliation for exercising his rights under the plan. H & H Music (D) moved for summary judgment which was granted, the trial court ruling that they had an absolute right to alter the terms of the plan. McGann (P) appealed.

ISSUE: Does ERISA mandate that employers provide any particular benefits and prohibit discrimination against identifiable groups of employees?

HOLDING AND DECISION: (Garwood, J.) No. ERISA does not mandate that employers provide any particular benefits and does not prohibit discrimination against identifiable groups of employees. Section 510 of ERISA prohibits discrimination for exercising a right to which the beneficiary is entitled. However, the employer medical plan at issue here made no promised benefits to McGann (P). The H & H Music (D) plan expressly provided that it could be terminated or amended at any time. Thus, no promise with regard to benefits was ever made to McGann (P). ERISA does not provide for the vesting of rights in a medical plan. The only conduct that ERISA does not allow is the singling out of an individual for discriminatory treatment. Employers are free to treat groups of employees and categories of diseases differently. Plans may cover some illnesses and not others, even if it is because of a prejudice against a disease and its victims. In the present case, it is clear that the reason the H & H Music (D) plan was altered was to save expenses and allow for the continued viability of the plan as a whole. Therefore, summary judgment for H & H Music (D) was appropriate and is affirmed.

▶ ANALYSIS

The court also noted that McGann's (P) interpretation would prevent employers from reducing and/or terminating benefits once a covered person incurred the first expenses. This would not only change the express terms of the plan but would dramatically increase judicial involvement in ERISA plans. The courts are split whether the Americans with Disabilities Act prohibits discrimination as to the terms of health insurance.

Quicknotes

AMERICANS WITH DISABILITIES ACT Prohibits discrimination in employment, housing, transportation and other services on the basis of an individual's physical or mental disabilities.

DISCRIMINATION Unequal treatment of a class of persons.

EMPLOYEE RETIREMENT INCOME SECURITY ACT OF 1974 (ERISA) Federal law of employee benefits which establishes minimum standards to protect employees from breach of benefit promises made by employers.

Fuja v. Benefit Trust Life Insurance Company

Insured (P) v. Insurer (D)

18 F.3d 1405 (7th Cir. 1994).

NATURE OF CASE: Appeal from judgment in action to enjoin the denial of insurance coverage.

FACT SUMMARY: Fuja (P), a breast cancer patient, demanded that Benefit Trust Life Insurance Company (D) pay for bone marrow transplantation treatment, which it considered experimental.

🏛 RULE OF LAW
Insurers may exclude coverage for treatment that has uncertain medical efficacy and is subject to ongoing research.

FACTS: Fuja (P) had health insurance from Benefit Trust Life Insurance Company (Benefit Trust) (D). The insurance provided that treatment was medically necessary if it was not "furnished in connection with medical or other research." Fuja (P) was diagnosed with breast cancer in August 1989 and despite aggressive treatment the cancer was found to have spread to her lungs in February 1992. Fuja's (P) doctor concluded that ordinary chemotherapy offered Fuja (P) little chance of survival. The doctor prescribed a regimen of HDC/ABMT, which involves high dose chemotherapy in conjunction with bone marrow transplantation. Fuja (P) was informed that this treatment was part of a clinical trial. Benefit Trust (D) refused to cover the cost of this treatment on the basis that it was not medically necessary. Fuja (P) brought suit to enjoin the denial of coverage. The court issued a decision order Benefit Trust (D) to pay for treatment and Fuja (P) underwent the ADC/ABMT process but did not survive. Benefit Trust (D) appealed the district court order.

ISSUE: May insurers exclude coverage for treatment that has uncertain medical efficacy and is subject to ongoing research?

HOLDING AND DECISION: (Coffey, J.) Yes. Insurers may exclude coverage for treatment that has uncertain medical efficacy and is subject to ongoing research. The phrase in the policy at issue that denied coverage for treatment "in connection with medical or other research" does not seem to be ambiguous. The trial court held that insurers could use this phrase to deny any procedure that was merely being reported in a study. However, there is no evidence that Benefit Trust (D) ever exploited or expanded the use of this phrase. Courts should not artificially create ambiguities where none exists. The clause in question clearly excludes coverage of treatment that is unproven, has uncertain value and is subject to tests. Fuja's (P) own expert witness at trial acknowledged that the bone marrow transplantation was part of an investigative clinical trial. The treatment was in the middle of a clinical trial. In the first stage, there was excessive treatment-related mortality. Thus, it is obvious that the treatment was not yet proven to be effective. Fuja (P) was required to sign an informed consent that identified the treatment as experimental. Accordingly, the bone marrow transplantation treatment fit within the unambiguous excluding clause of the Benefit Trust (D) policy. The district court's judgment is reversed.

▶ ANALYSIS

The court went on to recommend that a committee be set up to prevent a duel of experts testifying differently on the nature of treatment. Other jurisdictions have ruled differently on this issue. The initial test results from clinical trial have suggested that the treatment received by Fuja (P) is not an effective treatment for her type of cancer.

■■■

Quicknotes

ENJOIN The ordering of a party to cease the conduct of a specific activity.

■■■

Harris Corporation v. Humana Health Insurance Company of Florida, Inc.

Insurer (P) v. Insurer (D)

253 F.3d 598 (11th Cir. 2001).

NATURE OF CASE: Appeal from summary judgment for defendant in action to determine priority among insurers.

FACT SUMMARY: Harris Corporation (Harris) (P), which paid disability claims for an employee covered by its insurance plan, claimed that the Medicare Payer Statute (MSP) operated to render Humana Health Insurance Company of Florida, Inc. (D), which also covered the employee, the primary insurer.

🏛 RULE OF LAW
The Medicare Secondary Payer (MSP) statute, 42 U.S.C. § 1395y(b), does not reorder priorities between private insurers once an individual covered by the private insurers becomes eligible for Medicare.

FACTS: Shallenberger was insured by Harris Corporation (Harris) (P), and by Humana Health Insurance Company of Florida, Inc. (Humana) (D). She became ill and became eligible for long-term disability benefits. She then became entitled to Medicare A and B coverage based upon her disability and illness. From the time Shallenberger became eligible for Medicare coverage through her death, Harris (P) paid approximately $780, 268 in benefits on her behalf. Harris (P) first submitted a claim for reimbursement of these expenditures to Medicare, which declined to pay and noted Shallenberger's dependent coverage through Humana (D). Thereafter, Harris (P) submitted a claim for reimbursement to Humana (D), which Humana (D) declined to pay, and Harris (P) sued Humana (D). The Humana (D) plan contained a "Coordination of Benefits Provision," but the Harris (P) plan did not. Accordingly, the district court held that the Harris (P) plan was primary and granted summary judgment to Humana (D). Harris (P) appealed, contending that the Medicare Secondary Payer (MSP) statute, 42 U.S.C. § 1395y(b), operated to reverse the priority of payment created by the provisions in the insurance plans and entitled Harris (P) to double damages. The court of appeals granted review.

ISSUE: Does the Medicare Secondary Payer (MSP) statute, 42 U.S.C. § 1395y(b), reorder priorities between private insurers once an individual covered by the private insurers becomes eligible for Medicare?

HOLDING AND DECISION: (Per curiam) No. The Medicare Secondary Payer (MSP) statute, 42 U.S.C. § 1395y(b), does not reorder priorities between private insurers once an individual covered by the private insurers becomes eligible for Medicare. In the MSP statute, Congress made Medicare coverage secondary to any coverage provided by private insurance programs in order to lower Medicare costs. To accomplish this, the MSP statute prohibits private insurers providing coverage as a result of an individual's current employment status from making Medicare primary to its coverage for that individual or that individual's spouse. Instead, Medicare is the "secondary payer" with respect to claims by an individual who is entitled to benefits under Medicare and also covered by private insurance as a result of the current employment status of that individual or that individual's spouse. The MSP statute contains no similar provision with respect to private insurance plans covering such individuals for reasons other than current employment status. Thus, private plans covering such individuals for reasons other than current employment status of that individual or that individual's spouse may make their coverage secondary to Medicare when those individuals are simultaneously eligible for Medicare. The MSP statute also provides a private cause of action for double damages against insurance carriers covering individuals by virtue of such current employment status that fail to provide for payment primary to Medicare consistent with the statute's mandate. There is no dispute between the parties that the MSP operated to make Humana's (D) coverage primary vis-à-vis Medicare, and that the statute did not prevent Harris (P) from making its coverage secondary to Medicare. However, Harris's (P) core argument is that Humana (D) became the primary payer as between the two private insurance carriers by virtue of the MSP statute because the statute required Humana (D) to pay in advance of Medicare, but allowed Harris (P) to pay after Medicare. Thus, Harris (P) argues that it may maintain a private cause of action for double damages against Humana (D) for its failure to reimburse Harris (P) according to its primary status under the MSP statute. The Sixth Circuit has held that the MSP statute has no impact on the priority as between solely private insurers and does not trump the plan language adopted by private insurers as to priority, reasoning that Congress manifested no interest whatever in who would pay first as between private insurance carriers. The analysis of the Sixth Circuit is persuasive. Here, as in the Sixth Circuit cases, Medicare is not a party to the suit, and the fiscal integrity of the Medicare program is not at risk. Humana (D) has never claimed that Medicare is the primary payer of Shallenberger's medical expenses in contravention of the priority created between it and Medicare under the MSP statute. Indeed, Humana (D) has denied coverage based upon legal and equitable defenses to Harris's (P)

Continued on next page.

claim for reimbursement unrelated to Shallenberger's Medicare eligibility. Because it is only the priority as between these two private insurance plans that is at issue in this case, the respective priority of the two insurers is not affected by the MSP statute. While Harris (P) was free to alter the coordination of benefits of its plan to align the priority of its liability vis-à-vis Medicare with the priority of its liability vis-à-vis other private insurance plans, the MSP statute was not enacted to address such private priorities and does not operate to reprioritize the obligations of private insurance plans where the liability of Medicare is not at issue. Thus, the plain language of the insurance plans governs the priority of payment as between the two insurers in this case. Affirmed.

▶ *ANALYSIS*

The decision in this case does not render superfluous the private cause of action in the MSP statute. Such a private right of action exists where an insurance plan fails to make its coverage primary to Medicare as required by the MSP statute. For example, if Humana (D) had been Shallenberger's only private insurer and had denied a timely claim for benefits based solely on her eligibility for Medicare, the MSP statute would afford Shallenberger a private cause of action for double damages against Humana (D). Further, Harris (P) could assert a private cause of action for double damages against Humana (D) acting on behalf of Shallenberger if Humana (D) was primary to Harris (P) under the private coordination of benefits provisions, Humana (D) asserted no coverage defenses to Shallenberger's claims, and Humana (D) refused to pay Shallenberger's medical expenses solely based on her eligibility for Medicare. A private cause of action for double damages in these contexts serves Congress's interest in the fiscal integrity of the Medicare program by deterring private-insurers primary to Medicare under the statute from attempting to lay medical costs at the government's doorstep.

■═■

Associated Hospital Service of Philadelphia v. Pustilnik

Insurer (P) v. Insured (D)

Pa. Sup. Ct., 396 A.2d 1332 (1979).

NATURE OF CASE: Appeal from adjudication of disbursement of escrow fund.

FACT SUMMARY: Associated Hospital Service of Philadelphia (P) claimed it was entitled to subrogation recovery of medical expenses after Pustilnik (D) was struck by a train and obtained a settlement.

🏛 RULE OF LAW
When a subrogor settles, he waives his right to a judicial determination of the loss and conclusively establishes the settlement amount as full compensation.

FACTS: Pustilnik (D) was hit by a SEPTA subway car in Philadelphia. Associated Hospital Service of Philadelphia (Blue Cross) (P), his insurer, provided a credit of $18,960 against his medical expenses. Pustilnik (D) sued SEPTA and Blue Cross (P) informed Pustilnik's (D) attorney that it had a subrogation interest in any recovery and invited the lawyer to represent this interest for a certain contingency percentage. However, the attorney and Blue Cross (P) could not agree on the percentage. In any event, the case settled in the middle of trial for $235,000. Blue Cross (P) and Pustilnik (D) could not agree on the amount that was owed Blue Cross (P) and a court eventually placed money in escrow awaiting a proper disbursement. After trial, the court ruled that Blue Cross (P) had not proved it paid the $18,960 and limited the subrogation recovery to $16,721. Next, the court ruled that Pustilnik's (D) settlement was less than the full value of the injury claim and reduced the subrogation 50 percent. Finally, it reduced recovery another 40 percent for the share of the attorney's fee. Both parties appealed the ruling.

ISSUE: When a subrogor settles, does he waive his right to a judicial determination of the loss and conclusively establish the settlement amount as full compensation?

HOLDING AND DECISION: (Spaeth, J.) Yes. When a subrogor settles, he waives his right to a judicial determination of the loss and conclusively establishes the settlement amount as full compensation. A subrogee is entitled to recovery in line with what the subrogor obtained in value. In the present case, Pustilnik (D), the subrogor, alleged to SEPTA that $18,960 was the value of the medical services provided to him. Since this was the figure that provided the basis for the settlement, Pustilnik (D) cannot turn around then and claim that his subrogee, Blue Cross (P), is not entitled to this amount because it is unproven. This would offend equity by unjustly enriching Pustilnik (D) through the taking of inconsistent positions. Additionally, a subrogor cannot defeat a subrogee's claim by asserting that a loss exceeded the settlement recovery. Allowing this would encourage unethical practice. Parties would claim that a case for liability was strong in the underlying suit and then turn around and claim it was weak in the subrogation claim. Liability should be determined in one proceeding and the settlement of a claim fixes the liability amount. The judgment is reversed and the case remanded for determination in light of this decision.

▶ ANALYSIS

The court also ruled that Pustilnik's (D) attorney was entitled to a reasonable fee from Blue Cross (P) for representing their interest and establishing the common fund. If the parties don't agree, the court will determine a reasonable fee. The 40 percent imposed by the trial court here was upheld.

■=■

Quicknotes

EQUITY Fairness; justice; the determination of a matter consistent with principles of fairness and not in strict compliance with rules of law.

ESCROW A written contract held by a third party until the conditions therein are satisfied, at which time it is delivered to the obligee.

SUBROGATION The substitution of one party for another in assuming the first party's rights or obligations.

SUBROGEE A party who is substituted for another in assuming the first party's rights or obligations for purposes of subrogation.

■=■

Mossa v. Provident Life and Casualty Insurance Company

Insured injured worker (P) v. Insurer (D)

36 F. Supp. 2d 524 (E.D.N.Y. 1999).

NATURE OF CASE: Motion for summary judgment in an action to recover disability benefits.

FACT SUMMARY: Mossa (P), injured while working, and Provident Life and Casualty Insurance Company (D), his disability insurer, disputed whether Mossa (P) was expected to take other employment positions given the resulting disability.

🏛 RULE OF LAW
An insured under a disability policy would expect that the insurance provided coverage against the inability to engage in a job paying a living wage and not merely any job.

FACTS: Mossa (P) worked for a plumbing contractor and had disability insurance through Provident Life and Casualty Insurance Company (Provident) (D). While working as a steamfitter at a construction site, Mossa (P) fell one story and fractured both knee caps. Mossa (P) submitted a claim for disability benefits, which Provident (D) paid for two years. Then, Provident (D) informed Mossa (P) that benefits would end because Mossa (P) was able to return to gainful occupation. The policy provided that after two years of benefits, continued payments were due if the insured was not able to engage in any gainful occupation in which one might reasonably be expected to engage because of education, training or experience. Provident (D) moved for summary judgment.

ISSUE: Would an insured under a disability policy expect that the insurance provided coverage against the inability to engage in a job paying a living wage and not merely any job?

HOLDING AND DECISION: (Dearie, J.) Yes. An insured under a disability policy would expect that the insurance provided coverage against the inability to engage in a job paying a living wage and not merely any job. The "other occupation" provision in a disability insurance policy has been interpreted differently in case law. Some prior cases have indicated a salary comparison and wage analysis are not proper considerations. However, the better rule is that such factors are entirely appropriate, especially given the expectations of the insured. The suitability of employment from a financial standpoint to the disabled insured should be considered when determining whether the insured is totally disabled and unable to work. This determination should also take into account the insured's education, training, age and any other relevant circumstance that affect employability. Thus, the severity of Mossa's (P) disability and the extent of Mossa's (P) prior education, training and experience as it relates to future employability are factual issues for a jury. Motion for summary judgment is denied.

▶ ANALYSIS

Many policies, such as the one in this case, are for total disability only. If the insured is only partially disabled, no benefits are paid. Apparently, this is mostly due to the problem assessing how disabled a person is.

■■■

Quicknotes

SUMMARY JUDGMENT Judgment rendered by a court in response to a motion made by one of the parties, claiming that the lack of a question of material fact in respect to an issue warrants disposition of the issue without consideration by the jury.

■■■

Heller v. The Equitable Life Assurance Society of the United States

Insured (P) v. Insurer (D)

833 F.2d 1253 (7th Cir. 1987).

NATURE OF CASE: Appeal from declaratory judgment in action to collect disability insurance benefits.

FACT SUMMARY: Heller (P) was disabled but refused to undergo surgery to correct his condition.

RULE OF LAW
In absence of an express contractual requirement, an insured is not required to undergo surgery to correct a disabling condition.

FACTS: Heller (P), a doctor, had disability insurance with The Equitable Life Assurance Society of the United States (Equitable) (D). The policy provided for benefits if the insured was completely unable to work and was under the regular care of a doctor. Heller (P) developed a painful and crippling condition in his left wrist diagnosed as carpal tunnel syndrome. The disability prevented him from working and he applied for total disability benefits. Equitable (D) initially paid the claim and then terminated the payments because Heller (P) refused to undergo surgery as recommended by two of his doctors. The trial court ruled for Heller (P) and Equitable (D) appealed.

ISSUE: In absence of an express contractual requirement, is an insured required to undergo surgery to correct a disabling condition?

HOLDING AND DECISION: (Coffey, J.) No. In absence of an express contractual requirement, an insured is not required to undergo surgery to correct a disabling condition. In the present case, the Equitable (D) policy provides only that the insured must be under the care of a doctor. This provision clearly does not include any mandate that the insured undergo a surgical procedure because the doctor recommends it. There is no suggestion that payment is conditioned on following a doctor's advice for surgery. Courts should not add requirements that are not part of the express language of a policy. The clause was not intended to allow insurers to scrutinize and determine the method of treatment that a claimant receives. Equitable's (D) argument that Heller (P) had a good faith duty to cure his disability is simply not applicable. There are significant risks to surgery that cannot be required of insureds absent an express contractual provision. Heller (P) was unable to work and was under the care of a doctor. Thus, he fulfilled the requirements of the policy and was entitled to payment from Equitable (D).

ANALYSIS

The court suggested that if Equitable (D) wanted to have its insured submit to surgery, it could incorporate a specific requirement in the policy and it would be enforced. Equitable (D) seemed to be arguing that there was some sort of duty of the insured to mitigate the loss. Had the treatment not been surgery, the court may have been more open to this suggestion. However, the risks attendant to surgery seemed to sway the court.

Quicknotes

DUTY OF GOOD FAITH AND FAIR DEALINGS An implied duty in a contract that the parties will deal honestly in the satisfaction of their obligations and without intent to defraud.

Silberg v. California Life Insurance Company

Insured (P) v. Insurer (D)

Cal. Sup. Ct., 521 P.2d 1103 (1974).

NATURE OF CASE: Appeal from an award of damages for failure to pay on an insurance contract.

FACT SUMMARY: California Life Insurance Company (D) refused to timely pay Silberg's (P) hospital bills when he was injured.

🏛 RULE OF LAW
An insurer's violation of the duty of good faith in paying benefits is a tort that can result in liability for mental distress damages and punitive damages.

FACTS: Silberg (P) owned a dry cleaning business. His landlord owned a laundromat located next door in which Silberg (P) performed services for a reduction in rent. One day, Silberg (P) noticed smoke in the laundromat and in trying to locate the source severely injured his foot. Silberg (P) was taken to the hospital for treatment and indicated that California Life Insurance Company (California Life) (D) was his insurer. California Life (D) did not pay the hospital bill, asserting that there was an issue over whether workers compensation coverage should pay. Silberg's (P) medical problems persisted, as did his financial problems when the hospital bills remained unpaid. As more surgeries were required, Silberg (P) was forced to seek new hospitals because of the unpaid bills, he lost his business and his credit record was destroyed. After California Life (D) forwarded the claim to the workers compensation board, a compromise was finally reached. California Life (D) then denied liability for Silberg's (P) claim on the basis of a workers compensation exclusion in the policy. Silberg (P) filed suit and a jury awarded him the unpaid medical expenses, mental distress damages and punitive damages. However, the trial court granted California Life's (D) motion for a new trial and Silberg (P) appealed.

ISSUE: Is an insurer's violation of the duty of good faith in paying benefits a tort that can result in liability for mental distress damages and punitive damages?

HOLDING AND DECISION: (Mosk, J.) Yes. An insurer's violation of the duty of good faith in paying benefits is a tort that can result in liability for mental distress damages and punitive damages. This jurisdiction has recognized that a duty of good faith and fair dealing exists in every insurance contract. Violation of this covenant by unreasonably withholding claim payments of an insured is a tort giving rise to tort-type damages. In the instant case, the California Life (D) application expressly declared that it would protect insureds against ruinous medical bills. Yet California Life (D), knowing that there was a serious question over whether Silberg's (P) bills would be paid by workers compensation, still delayed in paying the claim. California Life (D) could have paid the claim and asserted a lien against any possible workers compensation recovery, a typical process. California Life (D) did nothing to protect against Silberg's (P) ruinous medical bills. Such actions are clearly bad faith and entitled Silberg (P) to compensatory and punitive damages. The trial court had no basis for overturning the compensatory award of the jury. With respect to the punitive damages, the court's decision that the evidence didn't show oppressive conduct is not an abuse of discretion so a new trial should be held on that issue only.

▶ ANALYSIS

The court rejected California Life's (D) contention that its workers compensation exclusion provision was unambiguous. Both the trial and appellate courts found that the clause (as interpreted by California Life (D)) clearly conflicted with the insuring clause that benefits would be payable in full regardless of other insurance. Of course, the policy then has to be read in favor of the insured. The common law action for bad faith breach is a very recent development of the law.

■=■

Quicknotes

BAD FAITH Conduct that is intentionally misleading or deceptive.

COMPENSATORY DAMAGES Measure of damages necessary to compensate victim for actual injuries suffered.

DUTY OF GOOD FAITH AND FAIR DEALINGS An implied duty in a contract that the parties will deal honestly in the satisfaction of their obligations and without intent to defraud.

PUNITIVE DAMAGES Damages exceeding the actual injury suffered for the purposes of punishment of the defendant, deterrence of the wrongful behavior or comfort to the plaintiff.

■=■

Pilot Life Insurance Company v. Dedeaux

Insurance company (D) v. Injured worker (P)

481 U.S. 41 (1987).

NATURE OF CASE: Appeal from reversal of summary judgment for defendant in an action for breach of contract and duty.

FACT SUMMARY: Dedeaux (P) sought to bring state law breach of duty type claims with regard to a policy governed by the Employee Retirement Income Security Act of 1974 (ERISA).

🏛 RULE OF LAW
ERISA civil enforcement provisions preempt state law claims for bad faith and tortious breach of insurance contracts.

FACTS: Dedeaux (P) injured his back in an accident while working for Entex. The company had a benefit plan established by Pilot Life Insurance Company (Pilot Life) (D). Dedeaux (P) sought permanent disability benefits but they were terminated by Pilot Life (D). Dedeaux (P) then filed suit in federal district court alleging tortious breach of contract, breach of fiduciary duty and fraud. Pilot Life (D) moved for summary judgment on the basis that Employee Retirement Income Security Act (ERISA) preempted the common law claims and it was granted. However, the Fifth Circuit Court of Appeals reversed. The Supreme Court granted certiorari.

ISSUE: Do ERISA civil enforcement provisions preempt state law claims for bad faith and tortious breach of insurance contracts?

HOLDING AND DECISION: (O'Connor, J.) Yes. ERISA civil enforcement provisions preempt state law claims for bad faith and tortious breach of insurance contracts. ERISA comprehensively regulates employee benefit plans that provide insurance for disability. The law expressly states that it shall supersede all state laws as they relate to employee benefit plans. However, laws that regulate insurance are exempt from preemption. The common law causes of action in Dedeaux's (P) clearly relate to the employee benefit plan and thus fall under the ERISA preemption clause. Unless they fall under an exception, they are preempted. Dedeaux (P) argues that the state law concerning bad faith is a law that regulates insurance. However, this law is generally applicable and is not directed only at the insurance industry. Thus, it is not a law that can be considered to regulate insurance. Nor does the law have any direct connection to the insurer-insured relationship. Additionally, Congress clearly expressed intent that civil enforcement provisions of ERISA be the exclusive vehicle of ERISA beneficiaries asserting improper handling of a claim. Therefore, Dedeaux's (P) claims are preempted by ERISA. The court of appeals is reversed.

▌ ANALYSIS

The court also noted that ERISA does not provide expressly for punitive damages. Thus, the court reasoned that such damages were not available under ERISA. The court's decision left it unclear whether a claim based on a law that established bad faith for only insurance contracts would also be preempted.

Quicknotes

BAD FAITH Conduct that is intentionally misleading or deceptive.

BREACH OF CONTRACT Unlawful failure by a party to perform its obligations pursuant to contract.

BREACH OF FIDUCIARY DUTY The failure of a fiduciary to observe the standard of care exercised by professionals of similar education and experience.

EMPLOYEE RETIREMENT INCOME SECURITY ACT OF 1974 (ERISA) Federal law of employee benefits which establishes minimum standards to protect employees from breach of benefit promises made by employers.

PREEMPTION Doctrine holding that matters of national interest take precedence over matters of local interest; the federal law takes precedence over state law.

Liability Insurance

Quick Reference Rules of Law

A.Y. McDonald Industries, Inc. v. Insurance Company of North America

Insured manufacturer (P) v. Insurance company (D)

Iowa Sup. Ct., 475 N.W.2d 607 (1991).

NATURE OF CASE: Certified question from federal district court in action to recover insurance proceeds.

FACT SUMMARY: A.Y. McDonald Industries, Inc. (A.Y. McDonald) (P) was ordered by the EPA to clean up its manufacturing site and A.Y. McDonald (P) sought to recover the costs from its insurer.

🏛 RULE OF LAW
Response or cleanup costs are compensatory damages for injury to property and are covered by the property damage clause of the standard comprehensive general liability (CGL) policy.

FACTS: A.Y. McDonald Industries, Inc. (A.Y. McDonald) (P) manufactured brass valves at a site in Iowa. As a result of the manufacturing process, brass residue was dumped on the property. The Environmental Protection Agency (EPA) entered into a consent order with A.Y. McDonald (P) pursuant to the Comprehensive Environmental Response, Compensation, and Liability Act (CERCLA) that required A.Y. McDonald (P) to design a system for preventing any further pollution of the property. A.Y. McDonald (P) was insured by several companies including Insurance Company of North America (INA) (D), and the policies in question covered "all sums which the insured shall become legally obligated to pay as damages because of property damage." A.Y. McDonald (P) filed suit to recover the costs it would have to pay as a result of the consent order. The federal district court certified the question of whether such payments were covered under the policies to the Iowa Supreme court.

ISSUE: Are response or cleanup costs compensatory damages for injury to property and covered by the property damage clause of the standard comprehensive general liability (CGL) policy?

HOLDING AND DECISION: (Lavorato, J.) Yes. Response or cleanup costs are compensatory damages for injury to property and are covered by the property damage clause of the standard comprehensive general liability (CGL) policy. In the present case, the coverage dispute centers on whether the insuring clause for "damages" was intended to cover response costs. Nearly all state courts considering this issue have found that such costs are covered by this policy language. Most courts have also held that costs complying with injunctions are also covered. Some of these jurisdictions have found that these costs fit the ordinary meaning of damages. Others have ruled that holding otherwise would be unreasonable because coverage shouldn't depend on the exact EPA enforcement mechanism. On the other hand, several federal courts have found that only damages to natural resources are covered, and not response costs because "damages" has a more technical meaning that should be given effect. This court believes that the term is ambiguous. Therefore, it must be interpreted more broadly to provide coverage. The natural definition of damages makes no distinction between costs and losses due to the type of relief sought. Since these response costs are meant to restore property they clearly fit the policy requirement of "because of property damage." Accordingly, A.Y. McDonald (P) is entitled to coverage from INA (D) and the other insurers for the response costs imposed by the EPA consent order.

▶ ANALYSIS

The court also ruled that preventive measures are included within coverage under most circumstances. Only when such measures taken completely in advance of pollution are not covered. As long as the preventive measures are taken due to past property damage, they too are covered under the CGL policy.

■═■

Quicknotes

CERTIFIED QUESTION A question that is taken from federal court to the state supreme court so that the court may rule on the issue, or that is taken from a federal court of appeals to the United States Supreme Court.

■═■

F & H Construction v. ITT Hartford Insurance Company of the Midwest

Contractor (P) v. Insurance company (D)

Cal. Ct. App., 118 Cal. App. 4th 364, 12 Cal. Rptr. 3d 896 (2004).

NATURE OF CASE: Appeal from summary judgment for defendant insurer in commercial general liability insurance action.

FACT SUMMARY: F & H Construction (F & H) (P) claimed there was "property damage" under a commercial general liability insurance (CGLI) policy issued by ITT Hartford Insurance Group (D) to one of F & H's (P) subcontractors, O'Reilly & Son, Inc. (O'Reilly) where O'Reilly supplied non-specification pile caps that F & H (P) welded to driven piles, even though F & H (P) was able to modify the non-specification pile caps to meet design requirements.

> ## 🏛 RULE OF LAW
> Under a standard commercial general liability insurance policy, there is no "property damage" where inadequate pile caps are welded onto driven piles when there is no physical injury to the piles or to other property, and the defective pile caps are ultimately used as modified to meet design specifications.

FACTS: O'Reilly & Son, Inc. (O'Reilly), a manufacturer, supplied non-specification steel pile caps to F & H Construction (F & H) (P), a contractor, for use in the construction of a water facility pumping plant. F & H (P) did not discover that the caps (A-36 grade) did not meet its specifications (A-50 grade) until after it had welded the majority of them to driven piles. F & H (P) modified the caps to meet design requirements and was able to complete the project on time. F & H (P) then sought to recover damages under the property damage provisions of the commercial general liability insurance (CGLI) policy issued by ITT Hartford Insurance Group (Hartford) (D) to O'Reilly. That policy defines "property damage" in two ways: (1) "Physical injury to tangible property, including all resulting loss of use of that property. All such loss of use shall be deemed to occur at the time of the physical injury that caused it; or . . . [(2)] Loss of use of tangible property that is not physically injured. All such loss shall be deemed to occur at the time of the 'occurrence' that caused it." The trial court granted summary judgment to Hartford (D), and the appellate court granted review.

ISSUE: Under a standard commercial general liability insurance policy, is there "property damage" where inadequate pile caps are welded onto driven piles when there is no physical injury to the piles or to other property, and the

defective pile caps are ultimately used as modified to meet design specifications?

HOLDING AND DECISION: (Blease, J.) No. Under a standard commercial general liability insurance policy, there is no "property damage" where inadequate pile caps are welded onto driven piles when there is no physical injury to the piles or to other property, and the defective pile caps are ultimately used as modified to meet design specifications. Under the policy's first definition, physical injury to tangible property, the prevailing view is that the incorporation of a defective component or product into a larger structure does not constitute property damage unless and until the defective component causes physical injury to tangible property in at least some other part of the system. Some courts have applied this rule to reject property damage claims under policies that define "property damage" to mean "injury to tangible property." Under these cases, property damage is not established by the mere failure of a defective product to perform as intended, nor is it established by economic losses such as the diminution in value of the structure or the cost to repair a defective product or structure. Here, the only damages alleged by F & H (P) are the costs of modifying the pile caps and the lost bonus for early completion of the project. These are not recoverable as property damage because they are intangible economic damages rather than damages "to tangible property." Welding the inferior caps to the driven piles did not damage the piles or any other property; it merely rendered the piles inadequate for their intended purpose. However, commercial risk is not covered by liability insurance. Once modified, the caps served their intended purpose, further supporting the inference that the caps did not damage the piles or any other component of the piles. Cases cited by F & H (P) are inapposite because they relate to contamination by hazardous materials. The ordinary meaning of physical damage unambiguously connotes damage to tangible property causing an alteration in appearance, shape, color or in other material dimension. Therefore, there was no physical injury to tangible property here. As to the second definition of "property damage," loss of use of tangible property that is not physically injured," the measure of damages for the loss of use of personal property may be determined with reference to the rental value of similar property which the plaintiff can hire for use during the period when he is deprived of the use of his own property. F & H (P) does not seek damages for the rental value (or its equivalent) for the loss of the use of the facility during the time period modifications were made to the pile

Continued on next page.

caps, or even for a period of time caused by delay. The only costs claimed by F & H (P) are the costs for repairing and modifying the defective caps and for loss of an early completion bonus. Those costs are unrelated to rental value. F & H (P) has therefore failed to establish its damages are covered by the policy as "property damage." Affirmed.

▶ *ANALYSIS*

A liability insurance policy is not designed to serve as a performance bond or warranty of a contractor's product. CGLI policies are not designed to provide contractors and developers with coverage against claims their work is inferior or defective. The risk of replacing and repairing defective materials or poor workmanship has generally been considered a commercial risk that is not passed on to the liability insurer. Rather liability coverage comes into play when the insured's defective materials or work cause injury to property other than the insured's own work or products. As one commentator, MaCaulay, has explained, "This distinction is significant. Replacement and repair costs are to some degree within the control of the insured. They can be minimized by careful purchasing, inspection of material, quality control and hiring policies. If replacement and repair costs were covered, the incentive to exercise care or to make repairs at the least possible cost would be lessened since the insurance company would be footing the bill for all scrap. Replacement and repair losses tend to be more frequent than losses through injury to other property, but replacement and repair losses are limited in amount since the greatest loss cannot exceed the cost of total replacement."

Quicknotes

COMMERCIAL RISK Risk that arises from a company's commercial activities, as where a company will be unable to pay its debts because of a business bankruptcy, or where a company offers credit to customers with no collateral.

SUMMARY JUDGMENT Judgment rendered by a court in response to a motion made by one of the parties, claiming that the lack of a question of material fact in respect to an issue warrants disposition of the issue without consideration by the jury.

American Home Products Corporation v. Liberty Mutual Insurance Company

Insured drug manufacturer (P) v. Insurer (D)

565 F. Supp. 1485 (S.D.N.Y. 1983).

NATURE OF CASE: Motion for summary judgment in declaratory judgment action for insurance coverage.

FACT SUMMARY: Drugs manufactured by American Home Products (P) caused injuries sometimes years after exposure and after insurance policy periods had ended.

> ## 🏛 RULE OF LAW
> Occurrence-based liability coverage is triggered not by exposure or manifestation, but when a person suffers an injury-in-fact.

FACTS: American Home Products Corporation (AHP) (P) manufactured drugs including Ovral and DES. Exposure to these drugs caused physical harm to people and resulted in 54 product liability suits against AHP (P). Liberty Mutual Insurance Company (Liberty) (D) insured AHP (P) between 1944 and 1976, the time during which these drugs were used. However, the injuries suffered by the users did not become manifest until after 1976. The policies in question provided liability coverage for "occurrences" that result in "personal injury, sickness or disease including death resulting therefrom sustained by any person." Additionally, an "occurrence" was defined as when personal injury occurred during the policy period. AHP (P) demanded that Liberty (D) defend and indemnify it in the underlying lawsuits but Liberty (D) asserted that the injuries did not occur within the policy periods. Each party moved for summary judgment.

ISSUE: Is occurrence based liability coverage triggered not by exposure or manifestation, but when a person suffers an injury-in-fact?

HOLDING AND DECISION: (Sofaer, J.) Yes. Occurrence based liability coverage is triggered not by exposure or manifestation, but when a person suffers an injury-in-fact. Courts interpreting the terms of comprehensive general liability (CGL) coverage have not agreed on the scope and timing of coverage with respect to occurrences and injuries. Some have construed the policies to provide coverage upon exposure to a harmful substance that ultimately results in injury. Other courts have adopted a manifestation theory, finding that the injury must become manifest during the policy period. In the present case, AHP (P) has argued for the exposure theory and Liberty (D) has argued for the manifestation approach. However, neither theory can be wholly justified by the policy language. First, although courts have adopted different constructions, every court interpreting the provisions has reached a result that extended coverage to the insured. Thus, it seems that courts are finding this policy language to be ambiguous and resolving the ambiguities in favor of the insured. Additionally, the plain language of the policy terms supports a different approach. The policy demands that the insured prove the cause of the occurrence and that the result occurred in the policy period. An exposure that does not result in injury during the coverage period would not satisfy this. On the other hand, a real, but undiscovered, injury proved to have existed at the relevant time would establish coverage, regardless of when the manifestation happened. Thus, if injury existed at any time during the policy period, liability is insured against whether or not the injury coincides with exposure or manifestation.

▶ ANALYSIS

The injury-in-fact approach adopted here was affirmed on appeal. However, there is still some question as to when the injury occurs and whether it must be diagnosable to be considered an injury. The main problem with this approach is that many think it is unworkable in practice with large class actions such as asbestos litigation. It requires that medical testimony with regard to each and every exposed person attempt to establish exactly when the injury occurred. Obviously, both exposure and manifestation are much easier to determine.

▪═▪

Quicknotes

SUMMARY JUDGMENT Judgment rendered by a court in response to a motion made by one of the parties, claiming that the lack of a question of material fact in respect to an issue warrants disposition of the issue without consideration by the jury.

▪═▪

Could have either theory depending on policy language

In re Silicone Implant Insurance Coverage Litigation

[Parties not identified.]

Minn. Sup. Ct., 667 N.W.2d 405 (2003).

NATURE OF CASE: Appeal from affirmance of judgment in declaratory judgment action.

FACT SUMMARY: Excess insurers (P) in silicone gel breast implant mass tort litigation argued that their occurrence-based policies were not triggered upon implant, claiming that no injury occurred during the time the policies offered coverage, and that damages should not be allocated pro rata by time among the insurers (P).

🏛 RULE OF LAW
(1) Cellular injury can trigger occurrence-based insurance coverage where the injury occurs during the policy period.
(2) Under an actual-injury trigger theory of insurance coverage, losses should not be allocated pro rata by time among insurers on the risk where the origin of a continuing injury can be clearly identified.

FACTS:
Several of 3M's high-level, excess-layer, occurrence-based policy insurers (P) brought a declaratory action seeking to clarify their coverage obligations in 3M's ongoing silicone gel breast implant mass tort litigation. The insurance policies at issue were in place from 1977 to 1985 and covered claims arising from injuries occurring during that time period. The implant claims for which 3M sought reimbursement were brought in the early 1990s, but were based largely on implantations that occurred during the policy periods, which implants allegedly caused various systemic autoimmune diseases. The trial court determined that the actual-injury trigger, for purposes of determining coverage liability, began at or around the time of implantation when silicone first came in contact with body cells, and that the injury continued after implantation. The trial court also determined that 3M's losses should be allocated pro rata by time on the risk for the period from implantation through the end of the time period during which the policies were in place. The intermediate appellate court affirmed, and the state's highest court granted review.

ISSUE:
(1) Can cellular injury trigger occurrence-based insurance coverage where the injury occurs during the policy period?
(2) Under an actual-injury trigger theory of insurance coverage, should losses be allocated pro rata by time among insurers on the risk where the origin of a continuing injury can be clearly identified?

HOLDING AND DECISION: (Anderson, J.)
(1) Yes. Cellular injury can trigger occurrence-based insurance coverage where the injury occurs during the policy period. Under occurrence-based policies, coverage is determined by when the alleged bodily injury or property damage took place: all sums related to any such injury or damage that occurred during the policy period are covered by the policy, even if the claim is not asserted until after the end of the policy period. Both sides agree that the "actual-injury" or "injury-in-fact" trigger rule is the proper method of determining which policies are activated by an occurrence. Under such a rule, "the time of the occurrence is not the time the wrongful act was committed but the time the complaining party was actually damaged." Thus, under the actual-injury trigger rule, only those policies in effect when the bodily injury or property damage occurred are triggered. For purposes of the actual-injury trigger theory, an injury can occur even though the injury is not "diagnosable," "compensable," or manifest during the policy period as long as it can be determined, even retroactively, that some injury did occur during the policy period. Here, the trial court determined that the injury-causing event was the continuous leakage of silicone that came into contact with the body's cells on or about the time of implant, and that these injuries were continuous. The insurers (P) argued that the cellular injuries the trial court found were "fictional" and therefore those injuries could not trigger the policies because no injury actually took place during the policy period. They contended that in using a non-existent cellular injury to calculate when the policies were triggered, the court dispensed with the actual-injury trigger theory and erred as a matter of law. This argument, however, is unpersuasive. Because this litigation arose out of a settlement where it was assumed that the silicone implants caused auto-immune damage, the trial court did not err in holding that there was cellular injury since the experts agreed that if silicone caused autoimmune disease (which must now be assumed as a matter of law), then cellular injuries would occur sometime before the symptoms appeared. The trial court also weighed conflicting medical testimony as to when bodily injury occurs, and decided that injury is caused at or near the time of implant. A review of the record, therefore, reveals that the trial court was not clearly erroneous in this determination. Also

Continued on next page.

unpersuasive is the insurers' (P) argument that the district court dispensed with the actual-injury trigger rule when it determined that the policies were triggered at or about the time of implantation. This finding is consistent with the actual-injury trigger rule, which requires that bodily injury occur during the policy period, but does not require that the injury be diagnosable or even evident during the policy period. Affirmed as to this issue.

(2) No. Under an actual-injury trigger theory of insurance coverage, losses should not be allocated pro rata by time among insurers on the risk where the origin of a continuing injury can be clearly identified. Case law in the environmental contamination area is instructive, and a synthesis of that case law reveals that in "continuous and indivisible environmental contamination cases" (1) general liability policies are triggered when property damage occurred during the policy period; (2) insurer liability is consecutive, limited to property damage occurring during the insurer's policy period; and (3) one way to allocate loss among consecutively liable insurers, in the absence of applicable policy language, is pro rata by time on the risk. When environmental contamination arises from discrete and identifiable events, then the actual-injury trigger theory allows those policies on the risk at the point of initial contamination to pay for all property damage that follows. It is only in those "difficult" cases in which property damage is both continuous and so intermingled as to be practically indivisible that allocation properly applies. Applying these principles here, the time of implantation of the silicone gel breast implant is the discrete and identifiable event that is the onset of the continuing injury process. Since in the actual-injury trigger framework, allocation is meant to be the exception and not the rule because "it is only in those difficult cases" that allocation is appropriate, if a court can identify a discrete originating event that allows it to avoid allocation, it should do so. Here, the trial court labeled the time of implant as the beginning of the continuing injury process. The implantation, therefore, is a readily identifiable discrete event from which all of the alleged injuries arose. Such implantation is akin to a single spill that leads to continuing soil damage. Accordingly, this case is not one of the "difficult cases" in which allocation is appropriate and, therefore, the lower courts erred in allocating the damages among the insurers (P) in this case. Consistent with the actual-injury trigger theory, those insurers (P) on the risk at the time of implantation are liable up to the limits of their respective policies for 3M's losses arising from that implantation. Reversed on this issue.

addressed this issue. The primary alternative approach is to impose joint and several liability on all triggered policies, which leaves the insurers to work out an apportionment of liability and contribution among themselves.

Quicknotes

DECLARATORY JUDGMENT A judgment of the court establishing the rights of the parties.

▶ ANALYSIS

The approach to allocation taken by the court in this case is the approach preferred by a majority of the courts that have

Metropolitan Life Insurance Company v. Aetna Casualty & Surety Company

Insurance company (P) v. Excess insurers (D)

Conn. Sup. Ct., 255 Conn. 295, 765 A.2d 891 (2001).

NATURE OF CASE: Appeal from summary judgment for defendant excess insurers in insurance coverage action.

FACT SUMMARY: Metropolitan Life Insurance Company (P) contended that for the purposes of determining the scope and meaning of the "per occurrence" limit of liability under excess insurance policies, its failure to warn of the dangers of asbestos constituted one occurrence, rather than there having been multiple occurrences based on each claimant's exposure to asbestos.

🏛 RULE OF LAW
(1) Where an insurance policy limits liability "per occurrence," does not define the word "occurrence" and contains a continuous exposure clause, the clause does not limit "occurrence" to all related claims emanating from substantially the same conduct.
(2) Where an insurance policy limits liability "per occurrence" and does not define the word "occurrence," the number of insured occurrences is determined by the immediate event(s) triggering the insured's liability.

FACTS: Thousands of civil actions were brought against Metropolitan Life Insurance Company (Metropolitan) (P) for asbestos exposure that occurred over six decades in different locations on the tort theory that Metropolitan (P) failed to publicize adequately, or distorted, the health risks of asbestos exposure. Metropolitan (P) had purchased excess insurance through several excess insurers. None of the excess liability policies provided coverage for underlying claims unless and until an amount equal to $25 million was exhausted (this amount was covered by Travelers (D) in an umbrella policy). The policies also all provided a stated dollar amount of insurance on a "per occurrence" basis, in excess of $25 million per occurrence. Thus, the policies were not implicated until Metropolitan (P) exhausted underlying coverage of $25 million per occurrence. In addition, the policies contained, or incorporated by reference, a continuous exposure clause contained in the Travelers' umbrella insurance policies: "The total liability of the company for all damages . . . as the result of any one occurrence shall not exceed the limit of liability stated in the declarations as applicable to 'each occurrence.' For purposes of determining the limit of the company's liability and the retained limit, all bodily injury and property damage arising out of continuous or repeated exposure

to substantially the same general conditions shall be considered as arising out of one occurrence." The trial court concluded that each claimant's exposure constituted an occurrence, so that there were multiple occurrences. The state's highest court granted review.

ISSUE:
(1) Where an insurance policy limits liability "per occurrence," does not define the word "occurrence" and contains a continuous exposure clause, does the clause limit "occurrence" to all related claims emanating from substantially the same conduct?
(2) Where an insurance policy limits liability "per occurrence" and does not define the word "occurrence," is the number of insured occurrences determined by the immediate event(s) triggering the insured's liability?

HOLDING AND DECISION: (Katz, J.)
(1) No. Where an insurance policy limits liability "per occurrence," does not define the word "occurrence" and contains a continuous exposure clause, the clause does not limit "occurrence" to all related claims emanating from substantially the same conduct. Although "occurrence" is not defined, that term is not ambiguous. Metropolitan's (P) argument regarding the continuous exposure clause is essentially that all related claims emanating from substantially the same conduct, that is, Metropolitan's (P) alleged failure to warn, should be aggregated into a single occurrence. The policy, however, provides that "bodily injury and property damage arising out of continuous or repeated exposure to substantially the same general conditions shall be considered as arising out of one occurrence." The policy is silent as to aggregation of claims based solely on similar conduct. However, the purpose of the clause is simply to broaden "occurrence" beyond the word "accident" to include a situation where damage occurs (continuously or repeatedly) over a period of time, rather than instantly, as the word "accident" usually connotes. Thus, the continuous exposure clause has doubtful application here, wherein Metropolitan (P) claims that the occurrence was its alleged failure to warn, rather than the claimants' exposure to asbestos, and where it is attempting to combine hundreds of thousands of claims for bodily injury that have occurred in several locations, spanning six decades. An application of the continuous exposure clause to an allegation of negligent failure to warn, places "considerable strain on the

Continued on next page.

words 'exposure' and 'conditions.'" The proper interpretation of the continuous exposure clause is that it combines exposures to asbestos that occurred at the same place, at approximately the same time, which results, nonetheless, in multiple occurrences under the policy. The clause cannot be read plausibly, as Metropolitan (P) contends, to combine hundreds of thousands of exposures that occurred under different circumstances throughout the country over a period of sixty years, into one occurrence; such an interpretation is inconsistent with the plain language of the policy and with the purpose of a continuous exposure clause.

(2) Yes. Where an insurance policy limits liability "per occurrence" and does not define the word "occurrence," the number of insured occurrences is determined by the immediate event(s) triggering the insured's liability. Metropolitan (P) requested a finding that there was only one occurrence, namely, its negligent failure to warn, for which it was liable in the claimants' underlying suits. Under this view, the excess policies would be triggered. The excess insurers (D) requested a finding that each claimant's initial exposure to asbestos was a separate occurrence. Under this theory, the excess policies would not be implicated. Persuasive authority [from New York] has adopted the event test in determining the number of occurrences, whereby an occurrence is determined by the event or events triggering liability on the part of the insured. Cases using the event test in asbestos injury cases, such as this one, have concluded that the relevant event is exposure to asbestos, not a more remote cause, such as a failure to warn customers about dangers of asbestos. Here, the last link in the causal chain leading to Metropolitan's (P) liability was the claimants' exposure to asbestos. Metropolitan's (P) alleged failure to warn, while possibly a cause of the claimants' injuries, occurred earlier in the "causal chain," creating merely a "potential for future injury. . . ." Thus, if the claimants had never been exposed to the asbestos, there would have been no occurrence at all for which Metropolitan (P) could have been held liable. Even under the "cause" test (which this jurisdiction has rejected) the thousands of exposures to asbestos, occurring at different times and places, would not constitute one occurrence. Further, the court's holding would not, as Metropolitan (P) contends, eliminate excess coverage for almost all mass tort cases, because many such cases involve continuous exposure occurring at one place at the same time. Affirmed.

▶ ANALYSIS

In identifying the occurrence or occurrences for insurance purposes, courts have applied three tests. Some courts have concluded that an occurrence is determined by reference to the underlying cause or causes of the damage. The court in this case expressly rejected this approach.

Other courts have concluded that an occurrence is determined based on the effect of the accident. Finally, a third group of courts, such as the one in this case, have concluded that an occurrence is determined by reference to the event or events triggering liability on the part of the insured. Some version of this cause test is used by a majority of courts. The rationale underpinning that test is that the number of occurrences should be viewed from this viewpoint of the insured, not its claimants.

■■■

Quicknotes

SUMMARY JUDGMENT Judgment rendered by a court in response to a motion made by one of the parties, claiming that the lack of a question of material fact in respect to an issue warrants disposition of the issue without consideration by the jury.

■■■

[handwritten margin note:] Failure to warn only equals possible injuries + claims

Stonewall Insurance Company v. Asbestos Claims Management Corporation

[Parties not identified.]

73 F.3d 1178 (2d Cir. 1995).

NATURE OF CASE: Appeal from judgment in action for declaratory relief.

FACT SUMMARY: National Gypsum Company (P) was sued for exposing persons to asbestos and its insurers denied coverage for some claims on the basis that the injuries were known, expected and intended.

🏛 RULE OF LAW
The expected and intended clause excludes coverage only if the insured subjectively knew about or intended the harm.

FACTS: National Gypsum Company (NGC) (P) manufactured building materials that contained asbestos from 1930 to 1981. Since 1972, NGC (P) was sued by 100,000 claimants seeking damages for injury due to exposure to the asbestos. Since 1980, the owners of several thousand buildings have asserted claims against NGC (P). Many of the policies that insured NGC (P) during this period included coverage exclusion for damage that was expected or intended by the insured. NGC (P) filed suit for declaratory relief to clarify the extent to which it was entitled to indemnification for the claims. The trial court held that NGC (P) did not expect or intend the injuries underlying the claims. The insurers appealed.

ISSUE: Does the expected and intended clause exclude coverage only if the insured subjectively knew about or intended the harm?

HOLDING AND DECISION: (Newman, C.J.) Yes. The expected and intended clause excludes coverage only if the insured subjectively knew about or intended the harm. The exclusionary effect of policy language controls allocation of the burden of proof. Thus, even if the excluding language is not in a special exclusion clause, the insurer has the burden of proving the limitation applies. The language of the expected or intended clause does not indicate that there is any objective requirement. Therefore, it does not matter if the insured should have expected harm, only if they actually did from their subjective viewpoint. The insurer's argument with regard to the "known loss" defense is also lacking. It has been established that an insured's knowledge of a risk of loss does not bar indemnity coverage. The defense requires consideration of whether the insured knew about the loss at the time the policy was bought. In the present case, while NGC (P) had received many claims at the time of many of the policies, the degree that they would be successful and their amount was highly uncertain. It cannot be said that NGC (P) knew

about the loss to the extent that they could not insure against it. Affirmed as to this issue.

▶ ANALYSIS

Courts differ on whether expected and intended have different meanings. Some treat the terms as synonyms. The court in this decision treated the known loss defense separately from the expected and intended exclusion. However, some believe that there is no effective difference.

■ ■ ■

Unigard Mutual Life Insurance Company v. Argonaut Insurance Company

Insurer (P) v. Insurer (D)

Wash. Ct. App., 579 P.2d 1015 (1978).

NATURE OF CASE: Appeal from declaratory judgment for insurance coverage determination.

FACT SUMMARY: The Hensleys were sued after Winkler, their son, caused a fire. Their insurer, Unigard Mutual Life Insurance Company (P) contended it was not liable to the Hensleys or Winkler.

🏛 RULE OF LAW
The excluded act of one insured does not bar coverage for additional insureds who have not engaged in the excluded conduct.

FACTS: William Winkler, 11 years old, set a fire at the Wilson Elementary School that caused $250,000 in damages. He testified that he intended to light the fire but did not intend or expect to cause the damage to the school. Unigard Mutual Life Insurance Company (Unigard) (P) had issued a liability policy to the Hensleys, Winkler's parents. The policy covered both the parents and the child and excluded coverage of expected and intended injuries and damages. The school district sued the Hensleys and Winkler, but the trial court ruled that Unigard (P) was not obligated to defend or indemnify them. The school district's insurer (D) appealed this holding.

ISSUE: Does the excluded act of one insured bar coverage for additional insureds who have not engaged in the excluded conduct?

HOLDING AND DECISION: (McInturff, J.) No. The excluded act of one insured does not bar coverage for additional insureds who have not engaged in the excluded conduct. It is well established that an accident never occurs as the result of a deliberate act unless some additional unexpected, independent and unforeseen happening produces the injury or damage. The means as well as the result must be unforeseen. In the present case, it is unquestioned that the fire was the deliberate act of Winkler. The damage from the fire is the natural, expected and intended result of the fire. Thus, Unigard (P) has no duty to defend or indemnify Winkler. However, the trial court imputed Winkler's intentional act to his parents so as to exclude coverage for them all. In this case, it is not the intentional act of the parents that caused the damage. Given that the insurance contract between the insurer and several insureds is separable, rather than joint, exclusion to one, does not apply to all. Accordingly, the trial court is affirmed as to the denial of coverage to Winkler and reversed with respect to the Hensleys.

▶ ANALYSIS

The court seemed to suggest that it was possible that specific intent on the part of the insured was required for the exclusion to apply. It never really addressed the issue fully here though, holding that the evidence suggested Winkler knew damage would result, no matter how he testified. Some courts have held that an insured intends the natural results of a deliberate act.

Quicknotes

DECLARATORY JUDGMENT A judgment of the court establishing the rights of the parties.

Hakim v. Massachusetts Insurers' Insolvency Fund

Insured property owner (P) v. Insurer (D)

Mass. Sup. Jud. Ct., 675 N.E.2d 1161 (1997).

NATURE OF CASE: Appeal from summary judgment in action to determine insurance coverage.

FACT SUMMARY: Abington Mutual Fire Insurance Company (D) denied coverage to Hakim (P) for pollution cleanup costs based on the owned property exclusion.

🏛 RULE OF LAW

The costs of remedial efforts to prevent further contamination of property are not excluded from coverage by the owned property clause if there was contamination of adjacent property.

FACTS: Hakim (P), with a homeowners' insurance policy from Abington Mutual Fire Insurance Company (Abington) (D), had a ruptured underground fuel line from an oil storage tank in the basement of the home. About 100 gallons of heating oil leaked into the ground and contaminated the property and groundwater. The local fire department issued Hakim (P) an order of liability for necessary cleanup. An engineering firm took emergency measures to prevent any further contamination of the adjacent property and water. Later, the soil beneath the home was excavated and removed to achieve compliance with the order. Hakim (P) filed a notice of claim with Abington (D), which agreed to pay for the costs related to the containment and water cleanup. However, it denied coverage of the remedial efforts of the soil on the property. Abington (D) argued that the owned property exclusion in the policy applied. The trial court agreed and Hakim (P) appealed.

ISSUE: Are the costs of remedial efforts to prevent further contamination of property excluded from coverage by the owned property clause if there was contamination of adjacent property?

HOLDING AND DECISION: (Marshall, J.) No. The costs of remedial efforts to prevent further contamination of property are not excluded from coverage by the owned property clause if there was contamination of adjacent property. In cases where environmental contaminants migrate from an insured's property to adjacent property, the courts have generally agreed that the exclusion does relieve the insurer of all liability. The cleanup is invariably designed to remediate, prevent or abate further migration. This court will follow this majority rule. However, in this case, the insurer argues that the cleanup of the Hakim (P) property itself is not covered, regardless of the reason for the cleanup. Hakim (P) insists that all costs because of contamination of adjacent property, is covered. It doesn't

appear that the policy language unequivocally supports either view. Thus, it is appropriate to consider the reasonable expectations of the insured. In the present case, Hakim (P) could expect that the costs incurred in preventing continuing contamination of the waterways and adjacent property would be covered. But costs incurred for the sole purpose of remediating the Hakim (P) property could not be expected to be covered given the exclusion. The available record does not provide enough information to make this determination here. Thus, the case is remanded for further proceedings and summary judgment vacated.

▶ ANALYSIS

Although this decision seems to suggest that the insurer (D) might not be responsible for the soil remediation, it is highly unlikely in practice. Contaminants in soil generally will migrate, even if very slowly. Thus, the insured will always argue that if not remedied the adjacent property or groundwater will eventually be contaminated.

Argue it's already in soil and will eventually contaminate others

■=■

Quicknotes

SUMMARY JUDGMENT Judgment rendered by a court in response to a motion made by one of the parties, claiming that the lack of a question of material fact in respect to an issue warrants disposition of the issue without consideration by the jury.

■=■

Weedo v. Stone-E-Brick, Inc.

Homeowner (P) v. Contractor (D)

N.J. Sup. Ct., 405 A.2d 788 (1979).

NATURE OF CASE: Appeal from reversal of summary judgment for defendant in action to determine insurance coverage liability.

FACT SUMMARY: Pennsylvania National Mutual Insurance Company (D) refused coverage of Stone-E-Brick, Inc.'s (D) liability to a homeowner for faulty workmanship.

> **RULE OF LAW**
> The insured products, work performed and business risk exclusions are valid to exclude coverage for the insured's faulty work that does not cause other property damage.

FACTS: The Weedos (P) contracted with Stone-E-Brick, Inc. (D) to pour a concrete floor and to apply stucco masonry to the exterior of their home. Stone-E-Brick (D) had a comprehensive general liability (CGL) policy with Pennsylvania National Mutual Insurance Company (Pennsylvania National) (D) that included exclusion clauses for insured products and work performed. After the Weedos (P) sued Stone-E-Brick (D) for faulty workmanship that required that the work be redone, Stone-E-Brick (D) sought defense and indemnification from Pennsylvania National (D) through a third-party complaint. Pennsylvania National (D) was granted dismissal through summary judgment, but the state's intermediate appellate court reversed. The state's highest court granted review. Pennsylvania National (D) appealed.

ISSUE: Are the insured products, work performed and business risk exclusions valid to exclude coverage for the insured's faulty work that does not cause other property damage?

HOLDING AND DECISION: (Clifford, J.) The insured products, work performed and business risk exclusions are valid to exclude coverage for the insured's faulty work that does not cause other property damage. A comprehensive general liability (CGL) policy generally provides coverage for property damage of the type that is provided for in the policy. It is helpful to look at the nature of the construction business to determine the extent of coverage. Stone-E-Brick (D) work for homeowner carries with it an implied warranty of merchantability that arises through operation of law. Repair or replacement costs are generally the measure of damages for a breach of this warranty. The insured-contractor can control this risk through the quality of goods and services that are provided. However, the insured-contractor has much less control over a related risk. If faulty work causes an accidental injury to property or persons, almost limitless liability is possible. This type of injury and resulting damages are what the CGL policy means to cover. The insured products and work performed exclusions directly address this concept. In the present case, the only damages sought against Stone-E-Brick (D) by Weedo (P) are for repair and replacement. Thus, it is clear that either exclusion applies. The business risk exclusion operates the same way. While some claim that it is ambiguous when read in conjunction with the insuring clause, this exclusion operates to exclude coverage for faulty workmanship alone. Reversed and remanded.

ANALYSIS

This decision is in accord with the majority view. However, the decision is not that clear in providing the exact reason for exclusion. It seems to be both that the exclusions are plain and unambiguous and that it generally doesn't make sense to provide coverage in cases such as this.

Quicknotes

BREACH OF WARRANTY The breach of a promise made by one party to a contract on which the other party may rely, relieving that party from the obligation of determining whether the fact is true and indemnifying the other party from liability if that fact is shown to be false.

SUMMARY JUDGMENT Judgment rendered by a court in response to a motion made by one of the parties, claiming that the lack of a question of material fact in respect to an issue warrants disposition of the issue without consideration by the jury.

American States Insurance Co. v. Koloms

Insurer (P) v. Insured (D)

Ill. Sup. Ct., 687 N.E.2d 72 (1997).

NATURE OF CASE: Appeal from affirmance of judgment for defendant insured in action to determine insurance coverage liability.

FACT SUMMARY: American States Insurance Co. (P) claimed that the absolute pollution exclusion applied when a faulty furnace in Koloms's (D) building leaked carbon monoxide.

🏛 RULE OF LAW
The absolute pollution exclusion applies only to those injuries and damages caused by traditional environmental pollution.

FACTS: Koloms (D) owned a commercial building. A furnace in the building began to emit carbon monoxide that caused employees working in the building to become ill. These people filed suit against Koloms (D) for negligently maintaining the furnace. Koloms (D) tendered the defense of the claims to American States Insurance Co. (ASI) (P), its insurer, who agreed to defend subject to a reservation of rights. ASI (P) reserved the right to contest coverage on the basis of the absolute pollution exclusion in the policy. This clause provides that "bodily injury arising out of actual discharge, dispersal, release or escape of pollutants at premises you own" is excluded from coverage. ASI (P) then instituted an action seeking a declaration that it had no duty to defend or indemnify Koloms (D). In response, Koloms (D) maintained that the policy exclusion was ambiguous and was not meant to apply to injuries caused by a leaking furnace. The trial court granted judgment for Koloms (D), and the state's intermediate appellate court affirmed. The state's highest court granted review.

ISSUE: Does the absolute pollution exclusion apply only to those injuries and damages caused by traditional environmental pollution?

HOLDING AND DECISION: (McMorrow, J.) Yes. The absolute pollution exclusion applies only to those injuries and damages caused by traditional environmental pollution. The plain language of the absolute pollution exclusion clearly includes a release of carbon monoxide. Some courts have applied the exclusion as broadly as it is written. However, others have found that exclusion was never intended to apply to routine commercial hazards such as the one in the present case. There has been no clear consensus with regard to this exclusion. The source of the disagreement is that the language of the clause is specific on its face, yet results in an extremely broad application. This breadth raises an issue as to whether it is so general as to be meaningless. The drafting history of the exclusion guides our decision. It is obvious from this history that the exclusion was adopted in 1985 so that insurers could avoid the enormous expense and exposure resulting from the explosion of environmental litigation. The exclusion employs environmental contamination terms of art such as "discharge" and "dispersal." Accordingly, the exclusion should not be used to disclaim defense and indemnity of claims that have nothing to do with traditional environmental pollution. The leaking furnace in Koloms's (D) building is not this type of pollution. Affirmed.

▶ ANALYSIS

The courts are all over the map on the scope and application of the absolute pollution exclusion. Some have found that it cannot be applied as it is written because the exception would swallow up the main risk that the insurance was meant to cover. The absolute pollution exclusion came about after the sudden and accidental exclusion failed to protect the insurers as they intended.

Quicknotes

DECLARATORY JUDGMENT A judgment of the court establishing the rights of the parties.

RESERVATION OF RIGHTS A clause in a deed or other instrument reserving particular rights to the grantor of the property.

Mighty Midgets, Inc. v. Centennial Insurance Company

Insured (P) v. Insurer (D)

N.Y. Ct. App., 389 N.E.2d 1080 (1979).

NATURE OF CASE: Appeal from affirmance of order in action for determination of insurance coverage.

FACT SUMMARY: Mighty Midgets, Inc. (P) did not provide official written notice of a claim to Centennial Insurance Company (D) until seven and a half months after the incident.

🏛 RULE OF LAW
The timeliness of notice of a claim to the insurer depends on the facts and circumstances of the particular case.

FACTS: Mighty Midgets, Inc. (P) is a nonprofit group that supports boys' football teams. Mighty Midgets (P) obtained a liability policy from Centennial Insurance Company (Centennial) (D) and an accident and health policy from Hartford through Dunn & Fowler (Dunn). Dunn collected the premiums, issued the policy and was designated as agent or broker. Nine-year-old Glenn De Temple suffered a serious injury after a football game in October 1970. Halle, the president of Mighty Midgets (P), called Dunn, informed them about the incident and asked about the procedure for presenting a claim. Dunn instructed Halle that the claim should be made to Hartford and provided a Hartford form. In April 1971, Hartford notified Mighty Midgets (P) that its policy did not cover the incident because it occurred after the game. This led to De Temple's lawyer sending a letter in May to Mighty Midgets (P) that a liability lawsuit was imminent. Mighty Midgets (P) immediately forwarded the letter to Centennial (D) and Dunn. Centennial (D) denied coverage on the basis that notice was not "as soon as practicable" as required in the policy. In a subsequent lawsuit, the trial court ruled that Mighty Midgets (P) had acted reasonably in light of the circumstances, including Dunn's negligent handling of the original oral notice. The state's intermediate appellate court affirmed, and the state's highest court granted review.

ISSUE: Does the timeliness of notice of a claim to the insurer depend on the facts and circumstances of the particular case?

HOLDING AND DECISION: (Fuchsberg, J.) Yes. The timeliness of notice of a claim to the insurer depends on the facts and circumstances of the particular case. The requirement that notice be "as soon as practicable" does not mandate immediate or prompt notice. Compliance is not to be measured simply by measuring the time. The requirement acknowledges that the reasonableness of the notice timing must be judged in light of the facts and circumstances. The conduct and representations of the insurer and its agents may be considered in this determination. The experience and expertise of the insured is also a factor. In the present case, there was a seven and a half month period between the accident and written notice. But the trial judge found that the reason was the Mighty Midgets (P) genuine, if misguided, belief that it had already provided notice by calling Dunn. Although this call did not provide the required notice, it was relevant in that it affected the time it took before written notice was given. There is no evidence that Mighty Midgets (P) had any motive for not complying or was not ready to provide any information that was required. It seems entirely reasonable that Halle of Mighty Midgets (P) would rely on Dunn's advice. This advice and subsequent silence lulled Mighty Midgets (P) into believing that notice had been given. Given all these factors, the trial court certainly had enough evidence to find that the Mighty Midgets (P) failure to provide notice before it did was not unreasonable. Affirmed.

▶ ANALYSIS

Some courts have considered situations like this to involve waiver of the notice requirement. The problem with this view is that policies often provide that agents can't waive notice provisions. Most courts also have ruled that even a requirement of immediate notice is actually tempered by a reasonableness standard.

Quicknotes

NOTICE Communication of information to a person by one authorized or by an otherwise proper source.

West Bay Exploration v. AIG Specialty Agencies

Commercial insured (P) v. Insurance company (D)

915 F.2d 1030 (6th Cir. 1990).

NATURE OF CASE: Appeal from summary judgment for defendant insurers in insurance coverage action.

FACT SUMMARY: Several insurers (D) that had issued commercial general liability insurance policies to West Bay Exploration Company (West Bay) (P) contended that West Bay's (P) untimely notice of claims materially prejudiced them and, therefore, relieved them of any liability under the policies.

> ## 🏛 RULE OF LAW
> An insured's untimely notice under a commercial general liability insurance policy that materially prejudices an insurer relieves the insurer of any liability under the policy.

FACTS: West Bay Exploration Company (West Bay) (P) operated gas and oil wells. Several insurers (D) each issued commercial general liability insurance policies to West Bay (P). The state, through its department of natural resources, notified West Bay (P) that there were various toxins, known as BTEX, in unacceptable levels in seven of its wells. The department issued West Bay (P) a Letter of Noncompliance on October 31, 1985, stating that the department had reason to believe that West Bay (P) had improperly disposed of toxins and thereby unlawfully "committed waste in the development of oil," in violation of state law. The department ordered West Bay (P) to either replace a leaking drip barrel or shut down the wells, and to take samples of the groundwater beneath the unsound barrel. It also indicated that at least one of West Bay's (P) drip barrels had been intentionally perforated so as to allow collected water to seep into the ground. The department ordered cleanup and remediation. West Bay (P) did not notify the insurers (D) of its claims for the cleanup costs until two and three years after incurring them, when it commenced a declaratory judgment action against the insurers (D) in federal district court. The insurers (D) moved for summary judgment on the grounds that West Bay (P) had failed to satisfy a condition precedent to their duty under the insurance contracts by not notifying them of the facts underlying the claim "as soon as practicable." Finding that West Bay's (P) delay had materially prejudiced the insurers (D), the district court granted the summary judgment motions. The court of appeals granted review.

ISSUE: Does an insured's untimely notice under a commercial general liability insurance policy that materially prejudices an insurer relieve the insurer of any liability under the policy?

HOLDING AND DECISION: (Guy, Jr., J.) Yes. An insured's untimely notice under a commercial general liability insurance policy that materially prejudices an insurer relieves the insurer of any liability under the policy. The terms of the policies require that notice be provided to an "authorized agent[]" of the insurers (D), and that the notice be provided "as soon as practicable." A review of the record shows that West Bay (P) satisfied neither of these requirements as they are construed under state law. Under state law, late notice to an insurance company will not eliminate an insurer's obligations under a policy unless the insurer can demonstrate that it has been prejudiced by the delay; the insurer carries the burden on this issue. Prejudice will be found where the delay "materially" impairs an insurer's ability to contest its liability to an insured or the liability of the insured to a third party. Here, the facts are so clear that the insurers (D) have been prejudiced, that the question is one as a matter of law. The insurers' (D) policies contained a "pollution exclusion" which excluded from coverage pollution, unless it occurred suddenly or accidentally. Here, West Bay's (P) failure to notify the insurers (D) before disposing of the drip barrels from which the BTEX escaped, obviously prejudiced the insurers (D). If this action proceeded to trial, the insurers (D) could escape liability under this provision only by showing that the discharge of BTEX occurred either gradually or intentionally. Both showings could best be made by presenting evidence of the condition of the discharge barrels at the time the discharge was discovered. If the state was correct that at least one of the barrels was perforated, the insurers (D) would make out a powerful case that the discharge was both intentional and gradual. By destroying the drip barrels in its clean-up effort, West Bay (P) materially compromised the insurers' (D) ability to present their most powerful defense to liability under the policy. In addition, through its lengthy delay, West Bay (P) left the insurers without the option of suggesting, or even mandating, the use of less costly, more efficient procedures in responding to the state's request for cleanup. Affirmed.

▶ ANALYSIS

Some courts have found not only that the insured is under an obligation to give prompt notice, but that the insurer also has a corresponding duty to notify the insured within a reasonable time that it is denying coverage. For example, in New York, a court ruled that a 48-day delay by the insurer in providing notice of denial of coverage was unreasonable as a matter of law under the circumstances.

■═■

Continued on next page.

Quicknotes

DECLARATORY JUDGMENT A judgment of the court establishing the rights of the parties.

MATERIALITY Importance; the degree of relevance or necessity to the particular matter.

PREJUDICE A preference of the court towards one party prior to litigation.

SUMMARY JUDGMENT Judgment rendered by a court in response to a motion made by one of the parties, claiming that the lack of a question of material fact in respect to an issue warrants disposition of the issue without consideration by the jury.

■━━■

Alstrin v. St. Paul Mercury Insurance Company

Corporate director/officer (P) v. Insurance companies (D)

179 F. Supp. 2d 376 (D. Del. 2002).

NATURE OF CASE: Motion for summary judgment on claims for directors and officers (D & O) liability insurance coverage.

FACT SUMMARY: Former directors and officers (P) of Cole Taylor Financial Group, Inc., who were defendants in a securities class action and related bankruptcy adversary proceedings, contended that certain exclusions in a directors and officers liability insurance policy issued by National Union Fire Insurance Company of Pittsburgh, PA (D) did not apply to their claims as a matter of law.

🏛 **RULE OF LAW**

(1) As a matter of law, an exclusion in a directors and officers insurance liability policy that purports to exclude coverage for claims "arising out of, based upon or attributable to the committing in fact of any criminal or deliberate fraud" does not exclude coverage for securities fraud claims where the policy purports to cover "Securities Claims" brought under the federal securities acts of 1933 and 1934.

(2) As a matter of law, an exclusion in a directors and officers insurance liability policy that purports to exclude coverage for claims "arising out of, based upon or attributable to the gaining in fact of any profit or advantage to which an insured was not legally entitled" does not exclude coverage for securities and breach of fiduciary duties claims where the policy purports to cover "Securities Claims" brought under the federal securities acts of 1933 and 1934.

(3) As a matter of law, an exclusion in a directors and officers insurance liability policy that purports to exclude coverage for claims made against an insured by "any Insured or by the Company" does not exclude coverage for claims brought by a bankruptcy estate representative against the former directors and officers of a debtor company where the debtor company is the insured entity.

FACTS: Former directors and officers (the D & O plaintiffs) (P) of Cole Taylor Financial Group, Inc., who were defendants in a securities class action and related bankruptcy adversary proceedings (brought by the bankruptcy estate representative) involving claims of fraudulent conveyance and breach of fiduciary duties, asserted claims under a directors and officers (D & O) liability insurance policy issued by National Union Fire Insurance Company of Pittsburgh, PA (National Union) (D). National Union

(D) denied the claims, arguing that exclusions in section 4 of the policy—4(a), (c), and (i)—excluded coverage. The officers and directors (P) contended that the exclusions did not apply to their claims as a matter of law, and moved for summary judgment on this issue. They also contended that National Union (D) attempted to interpret its exclusions so as to swallow up the very coverage the policy purported to offer. The federal district court reviewed each of the four exclusions.

ISSUE:

(1) As a matter of law, does an exclusion in a directors and officers insurance liability policy that purports to exclude coverage for claims "arising out of, based upon or attributable to the committing in fact of any criminal or deliberate fraud" exclude coverage for securities fraud claims where the policy purports to cover "Securities Claims" brought under the federal securities acts of 1933 and 1934?

(2) As a matter of law, does an exclusion in a directors and officers insurance liability policy that purports to exclude coverage for claims "arising out of, based upon or attributable to the gaining in fact of any profit or advantage to which an insured was not legally entitled" exclude coverage for securities and breach of fiduciary duties claims where the policy purports to cover "Securities Claims" brought under the federal securities acts of 1933 and 1934?

(3) As a matter of law, does an exclusion in a directors and officers insurance liability policy that purports to exclude coverage for claims made against an insured by "any Insured or by the Company" exclude coverage for claims brought by a bankruptcy estate representative against the former directors and officers of a debtor company where the debtor company is the insured entity?

HOLDING AND DECISION: (McKelvie, J.)

(1) No. As a matter of law, an exclusion in a directors and officers insurance liability policy that purports to exclude coverage for claims "arising out of, based upon or attributable to the committing in fact of any criminal or deliberate fraud" does not exclude coverage for securities fraud claims where the policy purports to cover "Securities Claims" brought under the federal securities acts of 1933 and 1934. According to the definitions set forth in the policy, the National Union (D) policy provides an explicit and broad grant of coverage for securities fraud claims. With respect to individual officers and directors, the securities fraud coverage includes even criminal proceedings commenced by indictment.

Continued on next page.

Given that the National Union (D) policy explicitly covers securities fraud claims, the issue before the court is whether exclusion 4(c), which excludes claims "arising out of, based upon or attributable to the committing in fact of any criminal or deliberate fraud," can be properly construed to exclude coverage for securities fraud claims. The D&O plaintiffs (P) argue that it cannot and submit that if exclusion 4(c) is so interpreted it will directly conflict with the coverage grant of the policy. The D&O plaintiffs (P) reason that when one provision of an insurance policy appears to cancel coverage provided for in another provision, this creates an ambiguity that must be construed in favor of the insured. National Union (D) argues that securities fraud coverage would not be eliminated by the deliberate fraud exclusion because certain securities fraud claims can be sustained based on recklessness or negligence, and exclusion 4(c) only applies to "deliberate fraud." However, given that the policy purports to provide broad coverage for securities claims brought under the Securities Act of 1933 or the Securities Exchange Act of 1934, National Union's (D) argument is unconvincing. The fact that some limited amount of coverage might survive the intentional act exclusion is not sufficient grounds to apply an exclusion that is irreconcilable with the coverage grant itself, because no one purchasing a policy that provides coverage for securities claims under the '33 and '34 Acts would intend to purchase such restricted coverage, especially given that securities fraud claims are among the most common claims filed against officers and directors. Summary judgment is granted to the D & O plaintiffs (P) on this issue.

(2) No. As a matter of law, an exclusion in a directors and officers insurance liability policy that purports to exclude coverage for claims "arising out of, based upon or attributable to the gaining in fact of any profit or advantage to which an insured was not legally entitled" does not exclude coverage for securities and breach of fiduciary duties claims where the policy purports to cover "Securities Claims" brought under the federal securities acts of 1933 and 1934. Exclusion 4(a) excludes claims "arising out of, based upon or attributable to the gaining in fact of any profit or advantage to which an insured was not legally entitled." The successful invocation of this exclusion requires National Union (D) to identify allegations in the complaints that allege that the D&O plaintiffs (P) gained "any profit or advantage to which [they] were not entitled." Almost all securities fraud complaints will allege that the defendants did what they did in order to benefit themselves in some way. If such an allegation were sufficient to invoke the protections of 4(a), the broad coverage for "Securities Claims" provided by the National Union (D) policy would be rendered valueless by this exclusion. The proper inquiry, therefore, must focus not only on the factual allegations, but on the elements of the causes of action that are alleged. If an element of the

cause of action that must be proved requires that the insured gained a profit or advantage to which he was not legally entitled, then, if proved, this exclusion would be applicable. That is not the case here. Exclusion 4(a), by its terms, requires a profit or gain that is illegal; not an illegal act that produces a profit or gain to the insured as a by-product. This exclusion, therefore, would be applicable in cases of theft, such as insider trading, but is inapplicable to illegalities such as securities misrepresentation to which a private gain might be incidental. While the securities complaint arguably alleges that financial benefit to some of the D & O plaintiffs (P) was a reason for their conduct, the only illegalities alleged are false and misleading disclosures in violation of the federal securities law. The "illegal" conduct is the alleged dissemination of false information. Similarly, the breach of fiduciary duty claim alleges that some of the D & O plaintiffs (P) breached their duty of loyalty to the company in the manner in which they ran the company and in various actions concerning a split-off transaction. The alleged "illegal" conduct is the breach of this duty; not the incidental gains therefrom. Summary judgment is granted to the D & O plaintiffs (P) on this issue relating to securities and breach of fiduciary duty claims.

(3) No. As a matter of law, an exclusion in a directors and officers insurance liability policy that purports to exclude coverage for claims made against an insured by "any Insured or by the Company" does not exclude coverage for claims brought by a bankruptcy estate representative against the former directors and officers of a debtor company where the debtor company is the insured entity. Exclusion 4(i), the insured v. insured exclusion, excludes from coverage any claim made against an Insured "which is brought by any Insured or by the Company . . . ." The intent behind the "insured v. insured" exclusion in a D & O policy is to protect the insurance companies against collusive suits between the insured corporation and its insured officers and directors. When the plaintiff is not the corporation but a bankruptcy trustee acting as a genuinely adverse party to the defendant officers and directors, there is no threat of collusion. Here, there is no collusion between the estate representative and the D & O plaintiffs (P). While it is true that the company itself could have brought such claims against its directors and officers, the estate's claims are asserted on behalf of the debtor company's creditors and not on behalf of the debtor company itself. Thus, the estate representative is acting as a genuinely adverse party to the debtor's former directors and officers. In determining that the estate is not the debtor, the court resolves the insured v. insured dispute by determining that due to the status of the debtor estate, the adversary proceeding claims do not fall within the plain language of the exclusion.

Continued on next page.

Accordingly, the court finds that exclusion 4(i) may not be relied upon by National Union (D) to defeat coverage for the claims asserted by the D & O plaintiffs (P). Summary judgment is granted to the D & O plaintiffs (P) on this issue.

▌ *ANALYSIS*

With regard to the fraudulent transfer claims brought against the D & O plaintiffs (P) by the bankruptcy estate representative, the D & O plaintiffs (P) conceded that these claims fell within the scope of the illegal profit or gain exclusion (section 4(a)). However, they contended that National Union (D) had to prove these claims on the merits. The court found that the D & O plaintiffs (P) failed to meet their burden on summary judgment, saying that should National Union (D) be able to use facts developed during discovery to prove that the allegations of fraudulent transfer were true, National Union (D) could rely on exclusion 4(a) to deny coverage. Accordingly, the court denied the D & O plaintiffs' motion for partial summary judgment on this portion of National Union's (D) defense.

■▬■

Quicknotes

BREACH OF FIDUCIARY DUTY The failure of a fiduciary to observe the standard of care exercised by professionals of similar education and experience.

CLASS ACTION A suit commenced by a representative on behalf of an ascertainable group that is too large to appear in court, who shares a commonality of interests and who will benefit from a successful result.

DUTY OF LOYALTY A director's duty to refrain from self-dealing or to take a position that is adverse to the corporation's best interests.

SECURITIES EXCHANGE ACT OF 1934 Federal statute regulating stock exchanges and trading and requiring the disclosure of certain information in relation to securities traded.

SUMMARY JUDGMENT Judgment rendered by a court in response to a motion made by one of the parties, claiming that the lack of a question of material fact in respect to an issue warrants disposition of the issue without consideration by the jury.

■▬■

Owens Corning v. National Union Fire Insurance Company of Pittsburgh, Pennsylvania

Corporate insured (P) v. Insurance company (D)

257 F.3d 484 (6th Cir. 2001).

NATURE OF CASE: Appeal from summary judgment for plaintiff in declaratory judgment action for insurance coverage of indemnification.

FACT SUMMARY: Owens Corning (P) contended that under its directors and officers insurance policy with National Union Insurance (D) it was not required to allocate settlement and defense costs between covered directors and the corporation itself, which was not covered.

RULE OF LAW
Where a directors and officers (D & O) insurance policy does not specify a method of allocating settlement and defense costs between an insured director or officer and the uninsured corporation, the corporation does not have to allocate costs to itself where uninsured claims have not increased the insurer's liability.

FACTS: Owens Corning (P), a corporation, had a directors and officers (D & O) insurance policy with National Union Insurance (National Union) (D), which insured Owens Corning (P) for expenses incurred when Owens Corning (P) indemnified its directors and officers against certain liabilities incurred in their capacities as directors and officers, and which was subject to a $2.5 million deductible. Owens Corning (P) and six of its directors were named as defendants in a class action lawsuit (the *Lavalle* suit), *Gaetana Lavalle v. Owens Corning Fiberglass Corp.*, Case No. 3:91 CV 7640 (N.D. Ohio 1991). National Union (D) was apprised of the litigation, but did not participate in the defense or eventual settlement of the action. It was not required to allocate settlement and defense costs between covered directors and the corporation itself, which was not covered. After indemnifying its directors and officers for their defense and settlement costs, Owens Corning (P) requested reimbursement from National Union (D), which denied coverage. One issue was whether Owens Corning (P) was obliged to have allocated some portion of the settlement of $9.975 million to itself (a non-covered entity under the insurance contract), since National Union provided insurance against liabilities of the directors, rather than against those of the company generally. The district court granted summary judgment to Owens Corning (P) on this issue, and the court of appeals granted review.

ISSUE: Where a directors and officers (D & O) insurance policy does not specify a method of allocating

settlement and defense costs between an insured director or officer and the uninsured corporation, does the corporation have to allocate costs to itself where uninsured claims have not increased the insurer's liability?

HOLDING AND DECISION: (Boggs, J.) No. Where a directors and officers (D & O) insurance policy does not specify a method of allocating settlement and defense costs between an insured director or officer and the uninsured corporation, the corporation does not have to allocate costs to itself where uninsured claims have not increased the insurer's liability. National Union (D) argued that the costs of the *Lavalle* settlement should have been allocated among potentially liable parties. This would cause the exposure of the directors (and thus Owens Corning's (P) claim under the policy) to represent only a fraction of the total paid out. If the fraction of the $9.975 million allocated to the directors resulted in a figure below the $2.5 million deductible, National Union (D) could, hypothetically, avoid payment altogether. To determine whether allocation is warranted, one of two rules may be applied: the "larger settlement" rule or the "relative exposure rule." The larger settlement rule allows allocation of the costs of a settlement only where that settlement is larger because of the activities of uninsured persons who were sued or persons who were not sued but whose actions may have contributed to the suit. Hence, if an uninsured corporate defendant makes the settlement larger than it otherwise would have been with only the insured directors as defendants, allocation of the excess can be made and coverage partially denied. Alternatively, the relative exposure rule allocates a settlement based on comparing the potential exposure of the uninsured and insured defendants had the litigation proceeded. Because the relative exposure rule "envisions a somewhat elaborate inquiry into what happened in a settlement and who really paid for what relief[,]" National Union (D) endorses the rule in its effort to resist summary judgment. The state has not indicated whether it would favor one or the other of these rules. Nor does the policy state which method of allocation should be used. Instead it suggests that, post-settlement, the insurer and the policyholder will use their best efforts to determine a "fair and proper allocation of the amounts as between the Company and the Insureds," with this latter term referring to the directors and officers. The label "fair" does not uniquely designate one of a number of rival legal principles. Therefore, although settlement allocation between covered and uncovered claims is clearly contemplated by

Continued on next page.

the policy, where appropriate, the nature of the method of allocation is ambiguous. Therefore, the policy is to be strictly construed against the insurer. Because allocation is in effect a partial exclusion of the insurer's liability, under state law such exclusion must be clear and exact in order to be given effect. In the absence of clearer language in the policy, state law favors the larger settlement rule in this instance, and supports coverage of the settlement except to the extent that uninsured claims have actually increased National Union's (D) liability. If the uninsured claims would not impose a marginal cost on National Union (D), their presence in the settled suit should not operate to exclude Owens Corning (P) from coverage for the insured claims. Here, Owens Corning (P) carried its burden by showing that insured defendant directors were sued on all claims; there were no separate claims attributable solely to other corporate employees or to the corporation. If there were any general corporate motives driving the settlement, these were not distinct from the directors' motives. Affirmed.

▶ ANALYSIS

There is some economic rationale behind the larger settlement rule, related to the likely intent of an entity purchasing insurance. The type of corporate liability involved is premised on indirect responsibility for the risky acts of directors, and the combined effect (and reasonable intent) of an indemnification provision and a D & O policy is to shift the risk of directorial acts first to the corporation, but then on to the insurer. However, the Private Securities Litigation Reform Act of 1995 (PSLRA) sharply limited joint and several liability in shareholder actions, possibly altering the rationale behind the rule in the post-PSLRA environment. The case here occurred under the old pre-PSLRA regime.

■══■

Quicknotes

AMBIGUITY Language that is capable of being understood to have more than one interpretation.

DECLARATORY JUDGMENT A judgment of the court establishing the rights of the parties.

SUMMARY JUDGMENT Judgment rendered by a court in response to a motion made by one of the parties, claiming that the lack of a question of material fact in respect to an issue warrants disposition of the issue without consideration by the jury.

■══■

Thoracic Cardiovascular Associates, Ltd. v. St. Paul Fire and Marine Insurance Company

Insured (P) v. Insurer (D)

Ariz. Ct. App., 891 P.2d 916 (1994).

NATURE OF CASE: Appeal from summary judgment for plaintiff in declaratory judgment action for insurance coverage.

FACT SUMMARY: Thoracic Cardiovascular Associates, Ltd. (P), insured by a claims-made professional liability policy, was sued during the policy period but not served with the summons until after expiration of the policy.

🏛 RULE OF LAW
The notice period for a claims-made policy will not be extended because the claim was not discovered during the policy period.

FACTS: St. Paul Fire and Marine Insurance Company (St. Paul) (D) issued a professional liability policy to Thoracic Cardiovascular Associates, Ltd. (Thoracic) (P) for the period between November 1, 1987 and May 1, 1988. The policy covered claims that were made during the policy period and the date of the claim was considered to be the date that Thoracic (P) reported an incident or injury to St. Paul (D). Before the end of the policy term, Thoracic (P) canceled the policy. St. Paul (D) wrote Thoracic (P) twice, explaining that if an optional reporting endorsement was not purchased there would be no coverage for claims arising out of acts performed prior to termination, but reported after. Thoracic (P) declined to buy this extension and the policy expired. Subsequently, Grimaldi served a summons and complaint for medical malpractice against Thoracic (P). The suit had been filed almost a year earlier but the summons wasn't served and Thoracic (P) had no notice of the claim until after the St. Paul (D) policy was terminated. Thoracic (P) notified St. Paul (D) of the claim and requested defense and indemnity. St. Paul (D) declined but a trial court ruled for Thoracic (P).

ISSUE: Will the notice period for a claims-made policy be extended because the claim was not discovered during the policy period?

HOLDING AND DECISION: (Toci, J.) No. The notice period for a claims-made policy will not be extended because the claim was not discovered during the policy period. An occurrence policy covers an act or omission that occurs within the policy period, regardless of the date of discovery or the date the claim is made. These policies create a "tail," or time lapse between the date of alleged negligence and the claim. In order to better compute accurate premiums, insurers mostly shifted to claims made policies for professional liability. Transmittal of the notice of the claim to the insurer is the most important aspect of these policies because it triggers coverage. The essence is notice to the insurer within the policy period. Such language was plain and unambiguous in the St. Paul (D) policy at issue here. The reporting requirement was a condition precedent to coverage. There is no exception for a delay in notice for a reasonable excuse. Such an exception would convert the claims made policy into an occurrence policy. In the present case, it is undisputed that Thoracic (P) provided notice of the Grimaldi claim months after the St. Paul (D) policy was terminated. Thus, there is no coverage owed for the claim. Reversed.

▶ ANALYSIS

The court suggested that Thoracic (P) could have protected itself in a different manner. Had Thoracic (P) reported the Grimaldi incident to St. Paul even before the suit was filed, this would have been timely and sufficient notice. It would follow then that insureds who want to be particularly careful in these situations could report any potential claim, even where a later claim is highly unlikely.

Quicknotes

NOTICE Communication of information to a person by one authorized or by an otherwise proper source.

Liability Insurance Defense and Settlement

Quick Reference Rules of Law

Beckwith Machinery Company v. Travelers Indemnity Company

Insured (P) v. Insurer (D)

638 F. Supp. 1179 (W.D. Pa. 1986).

NATURE OF CASE: Motions for summary judgment in breach of insurance contract action.

FACT SUMMARY: Travelers Indemnity Company (D) withdrew its defense of Beckwith Machinery Company (P) in the middle of the underlying litigation.

🏛 RULE OF LAW
If an insurer assumes the insured's defense without reserving its right to deny coverage, it is precluded from later denying coverage.

FACTS: Travelers Indemnity Company (Travelers) (D) provided Beckwith Machinery Company (Beckwith) (P), a seller of equipment, with comprehensive general liability coverage. The policy provided that Travelers (D) would defend any suit brought against Beckwith (P), even if any of the allegations were groundless, as the suit alleged covered damage. Beckwith (P) sold tractor scrapers to Trumbull, which apparently broke down. Trumbull sued Beckwith (P) for selling defective equipment and Beckwith (P) tendered the claim to Travelers (D). The Trumbull suit alleged various breach of warranties and Travelers (D) assumed the defense, although it notified Beckwith (P) it wouldn't provide coverage for the claimed punitive damages. As the case proceeded, Travelers (D) was unsure whether to continue the defense and then suddenly withdrew its defense. Beckwith (P) obtained new representation and the Trumbull case was eventually settled for $100,000 from Beckwith (P). Beckwith (P) then filed suit against Travelers (D) to recover this amount and the entire costs of the defense. Each party moved for summary judgment.

ISSUE: If an insurer assumes the insured's defense without reserving its right to deny coverage, is it precluded from later denying coverage?

HOLDING AND DECISION: (Cohill, C.J.) Yes. If an insurer assumes the insured's defense without reserving its right to deny coverage, it is precluded from later denying coverage. The duty to defend arises whenever allegations against the insured state a claim that is potentially within the scope of coverage. This duty is separate from the indemnification duty and is broader. This defense obligation continues until the insurer can confine the possibility of recovery to claims outside the policy coverage terms. Thus, an insurer can assume the defense at the outset while reserving its right to later terminate the defense if the facts and allegations show that there is no potential for coverage. If there is reservation of rights, the insurer is estopped from later claiming that the loss was not covered, even if the defense is valid. This reservation of

rights is necessary so that the insured can protect its own rights by obtaining separate counsel. In the present case, Travelers (D) assumed the defense of the Trumbull suit without reserving its rights as to the indemnification of compensatory damages. The abrupt denial of coverage and defense after Beckwith (P) had relied on it means that Travelers (D) is estopped from raising any valid coverage defenses. The appropriate measure of damages for this breach of the duty to defend is the entire defense costs expended and the entire loss in the underlying litigation. Thus, Travelers (D) is liable for the $100,000 settlement amount in addition to the defense costs paid by Beckwith (P) after Travelers (D) left the defense. Summary judgment for Beckwith (P).

▶ ANALYSIS

The court also ruled in any case that the allegations of the Trumbull suit were potentially covered and Travelers (D) should have continued its defense, reservation of rights or not. The court noted that insurers stand in a fiduciary relationship with the insured and have a duty of good faith in representing the insured's interest. In the instant case, the court was clear in holding that Travelers (D) showed a greater concern for its own interests than for Beckwith (P).

⬛▬⬛

Quicknotes

COMPENSATORY DAMAGES Measure of damages necessary to compensate victim for actual injuries suffered.

DUTY OF GOOD FAITH AND FAIR DEALINGS An implied duty in a contract that the parties will deal honestly in the satisfaction of their obligations and without intent to defraud.

ESTOPPEL An equitable doctrine precluding a party from asserting a right to the detriment of another who justifiably relied on the conduct.

INDEMNIFICATION Reimbursement for losses sustained or security against anticipated loss or damages.

RESERVATION OF RIGHTS A clause in a deed or other instrument reserving particular rights to the grantor of the property.

⬛▬⬛

Gray v. Zurich Insurance Company

Insured victim of assault (P) v. Insurance company (D)

Cal. Sup. Ct., 419 P.2d 168 (1966).

NATURE OF CASE: Appeal from dismissal of an action for breach of an insurance contract.

FACT SUMMARY: Gray (P) asserted that Zurich Insurance Company (D), his insurer, was obligated to defend an assault claim against him even though intentional acts were excluded from coverage.

🏛 RULE OF LAW
Insurers have a duty to defend a suit which potentially seeks damages within the coverage of the policy.

FACTS: Zurich Insurance Company (Zurich) (D) issued a comprehensive personal liability policy to Gray (P). An exclusion clause provided that coverage was not extended to damages caused intentionally by the insured. Gray (P) had an altercation with Jones, who filed a complaint alleging that Gray (P) had willfully and intentionally assaulted him. Gray (P) requested that Zurich (D) defend the suit, stating that he had acted in self-defense. Zurich (D) refused on the ground that the complaint alleged an intentional tort, which was not covered by Gray's (P) policy. Jones obtained a judgment against Gray (P) for $6,000, and Gray (P) filed suit against Zurich (D) for breach of its duty to defend. The trial court ruled for Zurich (D), and Gray (P) appealed.

ISSUE: Do insurers have a duty to defend a suit which potentially seeks damages within the coverage of the policy?

HOLDING AND DECISION: (Tobriner, J.) Yes. Insurers have a duty to defend a suit which potentially seeks damages within the coverage of the policy. In adhesion contracts where one party has a significantly better bargaining position, the reasonable expectations of the weaker party should control interpretation. Since insurance policies are contracts of adhesion, the expectations of the insured should determine the extent of coverage. In a comprehensive personal liability policy, the language of the duty-to-defend provision states that the insurer will defend even groundless allegations. This would lead an insured to reasonably expect that the insurer would defend any suit for bodily injury. Any exclusion of this broad duty must be conspicuous, plain, and clear. The word "intentional" does not have a plain meaning to an insured because it might suggest a planned action beyond the notion of intentional torts. Therefore, an insurer has a duty to defend which may be broader than the indemnification obligation. Furthermore, pleadings are amendable and may not be the sole basis for determining the defense duty. Therefore, an insurer bears a duty to defend its insured whenever it ascertains facts that give rise to the potential of liability under the policy. Jones' complaint against Gray (P) clearly presented the possibility that he might obtain damages that were covered within the provisions of Zurich's (D) policy since Gray (P) might have been able to demonstrate that the injury was caused by negligence or exceeding the bounds of self-defense. This obligation to defend does not violate any public policy because only the indemnification of intentional torts is prohibited. Furthermore, there is no conflict of interest in the defense because the question of intentional conduct is not an issue that would be resolved in an action for assault, outside the punitive damages question. Accordingly, Zurich (D) breached its duty to defend the action against Gray (P) because the action was potentially a claim which was covered by the comprehensive policy. Reversed.

▶ ANALYSIS

The court also rejected Zurich's (D) argument that it should only be responsible for the defense costs and not the payment of the judgment since it was outside the policy coverage. The court noted that it would be impossible for the insured to prove the extent of the loss caused by the breach. It proceeded to apply the general rule that an insurer who breaches the duty to defend is responsible for the ensuing judgment.

■=■

Quicknotes

DUTY TO DEFEND An insurer's obligation to provide an insured with a legal defense against a liability claim arising within the terms of an insurance policy.

■=■

Shoshone First Bank v. Pacific Employers Insurance Company

Insured corporation (D) v. Insurance company (P)

Wyo. Sup. Ct., 2 P.3d 510 (2000).

NATURE OF CASE: Question certified to state's highest court from federal district court regarding allocation of costs in an insurance action.

FACT SUMMARY: Shoshone First Bank (Shoshone) (D) contended that allocation and recovery of litigation costs by Pacific Employers Insurance Company (Pacific) (P) was not permitted under the commercial general liability insurance issued to Shoshone (D) by Pacific (P) for non-covered claims and counterclaims.

RULE OF LAW
(1) The allocation and recovery by an insurer of the costs attributable to the defense of claims that are not covered by the insurer's policy is not permitted so long as one or more of the claims alleged is covered by the insurance policy.
(2) The allocation and recovery by an insurer of the costs attributable to the prosecution of a counterclaim belonging to an insured is permitted, regardless of any tactical or strategic justification for asserting the counterclaim.

FACTS: Pacific Employers Insurance Company (Pacific) (P) issued a commercial general liability insurance policy to Shoshone First Bank (Shoshone) (D). The policy covered claims brought against Shoshone (D) for invasion of privacy. A disgruntled former Shoshone (D) director brought suit against Shoshone (D) for breach of contract, breach of the covenant of good faith and fair dealing, invasion of privacy, infliction of severe emotional distress, and abuse of process. Shoshone (D) filed a counterclaim for indemnity and breach of duty of loyalty against the director. Pacific (P) agreed to defend Shoshone (D) under a reservation of rights. The suit was settled for a fraction of the defense costs and fees. Pacific (P) sued Shoshone (D) seeking recovery of the portion of the defense costs paid to defend the uncovered claims and to assert the counterclaim. Whether allocation of the costs was permissible was certified as a question to the state's highest court by the federal district court.

ISSUE:
(1) Is the allocation and recovery by an insurer of the costs attributable to the defense of claims that are not covered by the insurer's policy permitted so long as one or more of the claims alleged is covered by the insurance policy?
(2) Is the allocation and recovery by an insurer of the costs attributable to the prosecution of a counterclaim belonging to an insured permitted, regardless of any tactical or strategic justification for asserting the counterclaim?

HOLDING AND DECISION: (Thomas, J.)
(1) No. The allocation and recovery by an insurer of the costs attributable to the defense of claims that are not covered by the insurer's policy is not permitted so long as one or more of the claims alleged is covered by the insurance policy. Here, the policy extended to the claim for invasion of privacy. Pacific (P) contends that it is responsible for those defense costs attributable to the claim for invasion of privacy only. It contends that it is entitled to allocate the defense costs between the claim for invasion of privacy and all the other claims involved and seek compensation from Shoshone (D) for the costs of defending the other claims. The duty to defend extends to the entire suit brought against the insured. Thus, unless an agreement to the contrary is found in the policy, the insurer is liable for all of the costs of defending the action. Here, there was no definition of the "duty to defend" or of "claims." An ambiguity arises, therefore, and must be construed against Pacific (P). To hold otherwise would give rise to problems involving an insured's predicament of having to obtain separate counsel to defend non-covered claims and potential disagreements between members of the defense team. Such a public policy necessarily would lead to inefficiency and perhaps inconsistency in the resolution of disputes. Moreover, it is obvious that no right of allocation should exist if the costs incurred for the defense of a non-covered claim were necessarily incurred or would have had to be incurred because of the defense of a covered claim. Because an allocation is not permitted to unilaterally modify and change policy coverage, Pacific's (P) reservation of rights letter does not relieve Pacific (P) of its duty to defend or of the costs associated with a defense undertaken pursuant to that duty. If an insurance carrier believes that no coverage exists, then it should deny the insured a defense at the beginning instead of defending and later attempting to recoup from its insured the costs of defending the underlying action. Where the insurance carrier is uncertain over insurance coverage for the underlying claim, the proper course is for the insurance carrier to tender a defense and seek a declaratory judgment as to coverage under the policy.
(2) Yes. The allocation and recovery by an insurer of the costs attributable to the prosecution of a counterclaim belonging to an insured is permitted, regardless of any tactical or strategic justification for asserting the counterclaim. If an insurance policy fails to specify coverage for prosecuting counterclaims, the policy language will not be "tortured"

Continued on next page.

to create an ambiguity. The policy issued to Shoshone (D) by Pacific (P) did not obligate Pacific (P) to prosecute any claims. For that reason, we will not require Pacific (P) to assume any of the costs incurred with respect to Shoshone's (D) counterclaims for indemnity and breach of duty of loyalty against the director.

▶ ANALYSIS

The court in this case joined the minority of jurisdictions in rejecting the allocation of defense costs. The majority position permits allocation of litigation expenses when the action against the insured involves both covered and uncovered claims. However even those courts that do permit allocation, do so only under particular circumstances, as where there was never any duty to defend the non-covered portion of a suit to begin with.

■■■

Quicknotes

BREACH OF CONTRACT   Unlawful failure by a party to perform its obligations pursuant to contract.

COUNTERCLAIM   An independent cause of action brought by a defendant to a lawsuit in order to oppose or deduct from the plaintiff's claim.

DUTY OF LOYALTY   A director's duty to refrain from self-dealing or to take a position that is adverse to the corporation's best interests.

INDEMNITY   The duty of a party to compensate another for damages sustained.

INVASION OF PRIVACY   The violation of an individual's right to be protected against unwarranted interference in his personal affairs, falling into one of four categories: (1) appropriating the individual's likeness or name for commercial benefit; (2) intrusion into the individual's seclusion; (3) public disclosure of private facts regarding the individual; and (4) disclosure of facts placing the individual in a false light.

RESERVATION OF RIGHTS   A clause in a deed or other instrument reserving particular rights to the grantor of the property.

■■■

Parsons v. Continental National American Group

Injured (P) v. Insurance company (D)

Ariz. Sup. Ct., 113 Ariz. 223 (1976).

NATURE OF CASE: Appeal from judgment for garnishee in a garnishment proceeding.

FACT SUMMARY: The Parsons (P) appealed from a judgment in favor of Continental National American Group (CNA) (D) in a garnishment proceeding, contending that CNA (D) was estopped from asserting the intentional act exclusion because CNA's (D) attorney obtained confidential information as a result of his representation of the insured, Smithey (D), in a prior proceeding.

RULE OF LAW
When an attorney who is the agent of an insurance company uses the confidential attorney client relationship to obtain information so as to deny the insured coverage under the policy in a garnishment proceeding, such conduct constitutes a waiver of any defense and the insurance company is estopped from disclaiming liability under an exclusionary clause in the liability policy.

FACTS: Smithey (D) brutally assaulted his neighbors, Ruth, Dawn and Gail Parsons (P). Candelaria, Continental National American Group's (CNA) (D) claims representative, told Smithey's (D) attorney to contact the Parsons' (P) attorney to see what type of settlement they would accept. Candelaria tried to settle with the Parsons (P) and failed to reach an agreement. The Parsons (P) then filed a complaint against Smithey (D), claiming he assaulted the Parsons (P) and that his parents were negligent in not obtaining the necessary treatment for their son. They tendered a demand settlement offer of $22,500, which CNA (D) rejected. CNA (D) retained counsel to defend Smithey (D). The trial court entered a directed verdict for Smithey's (D) parents, finding they were not negligent. This court affirmed. The trial court also entered a directed verdict for the Parsons (P) as to Smithey's (D) liability and judgment was entered against him for $50,000. The Parsons (P) garnished CNA (D). CNA (D) successfully defended against the garnishment action by claiming the intentional act exclusion defense. The same law firm and attorney that defended Smithey (D) also represented CNA (D). The Parsons (P) contend that CNA (D) should be estopped from denying coverage and waived the intentional act exclusion since it took advantage of the fiduciary relationship between its attorney and Smithey (D).

ISSUE: When an attorney who is the agent of an insurance company uses the confidential attorney client relationship to obtain information so as to deny the insured coverage under the policy in a garnishment proceeding, does such conduct constitute a waiver of any defense and is the

insurance company estopped from disclaiming liability under an exclusionary clause in the liability policy?

HOLDING AND DECISION: (Gordon, J.) Yes. When an attorney who is the agent of an insurance company uses the confidential attorney client relationship to obtain information so as to deny the insured coverage under the policy in a garnishment proceeding, such conduct constitutes a waiver of any defense and the insurance company is estopped from disclaiming liability under an exclusionary clause in the liability policy. Here the attorneys retained by CNA (D) represented Smithey (D) at the personal liability trial and obtained confidential information regarding Smithey (D) in the course of that representation. The ABA Committee on Ethics and Professional Responsibility and the Arizona State Bar Committee on Professional Responsibility have both held that an attorney who has represented the insured at the request of the insurer owed undivided loyalty to the insured and may not reveal any information or conclusions derived from that representation to the insurer that may be detrimental to the insured in a later action. Both Committees have also issued opinions stating that in garnishment proceedings, the attorney who represented the insured should not be expected to provide information learned in the previous representation for the benefit of the garnishee insurance company. Where the attorney represents both the insured and the insurer, the highest duty of loyalty is to the insured and the attorney cannot be used by the insurance company to obtain information received in confidence that is detrimental to the insured. This duty is owed regardless of who compensates the attorney. Here the attorney should have notified CNA (D) that he could not represent them when he obtained information from Smithey (D) detrimental to Smithey's (D) interests under the liability policy. Reversed.

ANALYSIS

CNA (D) also argued that the reservation of rights agreement under which the personal liability matter was defended permitted CNA (D) to investigate the claim without waiving any defenses. The court stated that the agreement was ineffective here since the same attorney represented both the insured and the insurer, whose interests were in conflict. Such a potential conflict allows the insured to estop the insurer from hiring the same attorney due to the risk of undue prejudice.

■=■

Continued on next page.

Quicknotes

ATTORNEY-CLIENT RELATIONSHIP The confidential relationship established when a lawyer enters into employment with a client.

DIRECTED VERDICT A verdict ordered by the court in a jury trial.

ESTOPPEL An equitable doctrine precluding a party from asserting a right to the detriment of another who justifiably relied on the conduct.

GARNISHEE A party against whom a garnishment has been ordered; party holding the property of a judgment creditor who is directed to hold the property until a court determination of the proper disposition thereof.

GARNISHMENT Satisfaction of a debt by deducting payments directly from the debtor's wages before the wages are paid to him by his employer; due process requires that the debtor be first given notice and an opportunity to be heard.

WAIVER The intentional or voluntary forfeiture of a recognized right.

Crisci v. Security Insurance Company of New Haven, Connecticut

Insured apartment building owner (P) v. Insurance company (D)

Cal. Sup. Ct., 66 Cal.2d 425, 426 P.2d 173 (1967).

NATURE OF CASE: Appeal from affirmance of damages awarded for breach of contract and personal injury.

FACT SUMMARY: Crisci (P), having suffered personal liability resulting from a judgment, sought to recover from her insurance company for its earlier failure to settle within policy limits.

🏛 RULE OF LAW
An insurer who fails to settle within policy limits will be liable to the insured for any judgment in excess of policy limits.

FACTS: After DiMare, a tenant in a building owned by Crisci (P), fell through the building's staircase, she brought suit against Crisci (P). DiMare's attorney demanded $10,000, the limits of Crisci's (P) liability policy with Security Insurance Company of New Haven, Connecticut (Security) (D). Security (D) offered only $3,000, and the case went to trial. DiMare received a judgment of $101,000. Security (D) paid $10,000, and DiMare executed the remainder of her judgment against Crisci's (P) personal assets, leaving her indigent. Crisci (P) later brought an action against Security (D). A jury awarded $91,000 for breach of contract and $25,000 for mental distress. The court of appeals affirmed, and the California Supreme Court granted review.

ISSUE: Will an insurer who fails to settle within policy limits be liable to the insured for any judgment in excess of policy limits?

HOLDING AND DECISION: (Peters, J.) Yes. An insurer who fails to settle within policy limits will be liable to the insured for any judgment in excess of policy limits. Every contract carries with it an implied covenant of good faith and fair dealing. In the context of liability insurance, this means that an insurer will defend an insured and, if possible, settle within the policy limits. An insurance carrier may not gamble with its insured's financial well-being by electing to "roll the dice" in hopes of a verdict of less than the policy limits. If an insurer decides to gamble in this fashion, it must be responsible for any negative consequences. Here, Security (D) had the opportunity to settle for the policy limits. It did not do so, believing it could do better at trial. Its judgment was wrong, and it, not Crisci (P), should bear the consequences of its misjudgment. Affirmed.

▶ ANALYSIS

Although the terminology was not in use at the time, this case is an excellent example of the concept of first-party bad faith. Essentially, first-party bad faith occurs when an insurer abuses its policyholder in some manner. The cause of action arises in some states from statute, in other states, such as California, here, from the implied covenant of good faith and fair dealing.

Quicknotes

BREACH OF CONTRACT Unlawful failure by a party to perform its obligations pursuant to contract.

IMPLIED COVENANT OF GOOD FAITH AND FAIR DEALING An implied warranty that the parties will deal honestly in the satisfaction of their obligations and without an intent to defraud.

Commercial Union Assurance Companies v. Safeway Stores, Inc.

Excess insurer (P) v. Insured (D)

Cal. Sup. Ct., 610 P.2d 1038 (1980).

NATURE OF CASE: Appeal from affirmance of dismissal of action to recover insurance payments.

FACT SUMMARY: Commercial Union Assurance Companies (P), an excess insurer, claimed that Safeway Stores, Inc. (D) had a duty to settle the case within the policy limits of the underlying policies.

RULE OF LAW
The insured has no implied duty to accept a settlement offer which would avoid exposing the excess insurer to liability.

FACTS: Safeway Stores, Inc. (Safeway) (D) had primary liability coverage from Travelers up to $50,000. Safeway (D) insured itself for losses between $50,000 and $100,000 and the top layer of excess coverage was provided by Commercial Union Assurance Companies (Commercial Union) (P). Callies brought an action against Safeway. Commercial Union (P) alleged that Safeway (D) and Travelers had an opportunity to settle the case for $60,000 but refused. Later, Callies obtained a judgment for $125,000. Thus, Commercial Union (P) was required to pay $25,000. Commercial Union (P) filed suit against Safeway (D) claiming that it owed a duty to accept a reasonable settlement offer so as to avoid exposing the excess liability coverage owned by Commercial Union (P). The trial court dismissed the action.

ISSUE: Does the insured have an implied duty to accept a settlement offer which would avoid exposing the excess insurer to liability?

HOLDING AND DECISION: (Per curiam) No. The insured has no implied duty to accept a settlement offer which would avoid exposing the excess insurer to liability. It is well established that an insurer may be held liable for a judgment against the insured in excess of its policy limits where it has breached its implied covenant of good faith and fair dealing by unreasonably refusing to accept a settlement offer within the policy limits. The insurer must settle within the limits if there is a substantial likelihood or recovery in excess of those limits. This duty does not come from the policy itself, but from an implied covenant. Thus, the insurer must take into account the interest of the insured in deciding whether a claim should be compromised. Similarly, an excess insurer can maintain an action against the primary insurer for the wrongful refusal to settle within the latter's policy limits. However, this is based on equitable subrogation, where the excess insurer steps into the shoes of the insured. There is no reason to hold that the implied covenant is reciprocal. The essence of the covenant is that neither party will do anything to prevent the other from receiving the benefits of the agreement. The excess insurer can have no such expectation that its insured will give as much consideration to the insurer's interest as its own. In the present case, Safeway (D) made no such implied promise when it purchased the excess liability coverage. Affirmed.

ANALYSIS

The court noted that a contrary conclusion was reached in another case and overruled that case. Equitable subrogation obviously didn't work in this case because Commercial Union (D) was faced with a self-insured. It also doesn't work in situations in which the insured and the primary insurer jointly agree on a settlement.

Quicknotes

EQUITABLE SUBROGATION Doctrine that holds that one who assumes and pays a debt for another assumes the same position as the holder of the previous encumbrance and is subrogated to all the holder's rights and remedies.

IMPLIED COVENANT OF GOOD FAITH AND FAIR DEALING An implied warranty that the parties will deal honestly in the satisfaction of their obligations and without an intent to defraud.

SELF-INSURANCE The practice of setting aside funds to cover losses instead of purchasing insurance against such losses.

Mission National Insurance Company v. Duke Transportation Company

Excess insurer (D) v. Insured (P)

792 F.2d 550 (5th Cir. 1986).

NATURE OF CASE: Appeal from summary judgment for defendant in declaratory judgment action for insurance coverage.

FACT SUMMARY: Duke Transportation Company (P) claimed that Mission National Insurance Company (D), an excess insurer, had to take over the primary coverage when the primary carrier went bankrupt.

🏛 RULE OF LAW
An excess insurer does not agree to drop down and assume primary coverage obligations when the primary insurer is insolvent unless the policy expressly assumes the responsibility for losses that are "uncollectible" or "unrecoverable."

FACTS: Duke Transportation Company (Duke) (P) purchased primary insurance coverage from Northwest Insurance Company (Northwest). The policy provided for general liability coverage up to a maximum of $300,000. Duke (P) also purchased excess coverage from Mission National Insurance Company (Mission) (D) for up to $5 million. The excess policy provided that it would cover losses above $300,000 or for losses that were "not covered" by the primary insurance. Subsequently, Northwest was insolvent and Duke (P) requested that Mission (D) provide primary coverage and defense. Mission (D) refused the request and Duke (P) filed suit. The trial court granted summary judgment for Mission (D) and Duke (P) appealed.

ISSUE: Does an excess insurer agree to drop down and assume primary coverage obligations when the primary insurer is insolvent?

HOLDING AND DECISION: (Hill, J.) No. An excess insurer does not agree to drop down and assume primary coverage obligations when the primary insurer is insolvent unless the policy expressly assumes the responsibility for losses that are "uncollectible" or "unrecoverable." When an excess policy provides that it will cover losses that are "not covered" by an underlying policy, this refers to losses that fit within the primary coverage terms. An "uncovered" loss is not one that is covered but uncollectible. The responsibility of an excess insurer to drop down and assume primary coverage obligations depends on this language in the policy. In the present case, the Mission (D) policy provided that it would cover losses that were "not covered" by the primary insurance. Thus, it agreed to take over the defense and indemnity of claims not within the primary coverage. In this situation, Northwest was insolvent and could not cover or defend Duke's (P) claims.

However, its primary policy still provided the terms for when Mission (D) was obligated to drop down and assume defense and coverage. Mission (D) had no responsibility to drop down unless a claim was outside the primary coverage terms. Affirmed.

▶ ANALYSIS

The court also rejected Duke's (P) contention that Mission (D) was obligated because the primary coverage was "exhausted." The court found the exhaustion had to be from losses paid under the policy. This decision is in accord with other courts addressing this issue. Obviously, the result is determined by the exact language used in the policy.

■━■

Quicknotes

DECLARATORY JUDGMENT A judgment of the court establishing the rights of the parties.

■━■

Automobile Insurance

Quick Reference Rules of Law

St. Paul Fire & Marine Insurance Company v. Smith

Insurance company (P) v. Drivers' estates (D)

Ill. Ct. App., 337 Ill. App. 3d 1054, 272 Ill. Dec. 666, 787 N.E.2d 852 (2003).

NATURE OF CASE: Appeal from summary judgment for defendant insureds in wrongful death action.

FACT SUMMARY: St. Paul Fire & Marine Insurance Company (P) argued that a named driver exclusion in its automobile liability insurance policy did not violate public policy or the state's mandatory insurance statute.

🏛 RULE OF LAW
Named driver exclusion in an automobile liability insurance policy does not violate public policy.

FACTS: While driving his father's car, William Smith collided with another vehicle carrying two individuals; all three died. At the time of the accident, William had an automobile liability insurance policy issued by Valor Insurance Company (Valor). The car was insured by St. Paul Fire & Marine Insurance Company (St. Paul) (P), under a personal insurance package policy including homeowners and automobile liability insurance procured by William's parents, Allen (D) and June Smith. The St. Paul (P) policy initially listed Allen (D) and June as insureds and drivers covered under the policy. William was added as a covered driver to Allen (D) and June's policy. However, when St. Paul (P) learned that William's license had previously been suspended and revoked because he had been convicted of driving under the influence of alcohol twice and driving with a revoked license, St. Paul (P) removed William as a covered driver from Allen (D) and June's policy and required Allen (D) and June to sign a named driver exclusion, which excluded liability for any accidents or losses incurred while the car was driven by William. Valor paid its policy limits in actions brought against William for wrongful death and Allen (D) for negligent entrustment. A verdict of $5 million was returned against Allen (D) and William's estate (D). St. Paul (P) then filed a complaint for declaratory judgment, seeking a declaration that it did not owe a duty to defend and/or indemnify Allen (D) or William's estate (D) in the underlying suit because the named driver exclusion in Allen's (D) insurance policy barred coverage for any accident involving a vehicle driven by William. The trial court, finding that the named driver exclusion violated public policy, granted summary judgment to the defendants. The appellate court granted review.

ISSUE: Does named driver exclusion in an automobile liability insurance policy violate public policy?

HOLDING AND DECISION: (Theis, J.) No. Named driver exclusion in an automobile liability insurance

policy does not violate public policy. Courts apply terms in an insurance policy as written unless those terms contravene public policy. Statutes are an expression of public policy. Accordingly, insurance policy provisions that conflict with a statute are void. The state's mandatory insurance provision requires that all vehicles be insured through a liability insurance policy. Case law has interpreted state statutory law to require a liability insurance policy issued to the owner of a vehicle to cover the named insured and "any other person" using the vehicle with the named insured's permission. The defendants (D) in this case contend that the definition of the term "any other person" necessarily includes the driver who was purportedly excluded from coverage by the named driver exclusion, assuming he had the insured's permission to operate the vehicle. Thus, defendants (D) argue, the exclusion conflicts with the statute and is void. St. Paul (P) retorts that there is a limited exception for named driver exclusions in the mandatory insurance laws. St. Paul (P) is correct. The section of the state's laws pertaining to insurance cards (which immediately precedes the mandatory insurance provision) appears to recognize that insurance policies may exclude named drivers from coverage, and, therefore, conflicts with the mandatory insurance provision. When there is an alleged conflict between two statutes, a court interprets those statutes to avoid inconsistency and give effect to both statutes where such an interpretation is reasonably possible. Because these two statutory provisions were enacted together and are next to each other, it seems that the legislature's intent was to create a limited exception for named driver exclusions to the mandatory insurance laws. This is supported by administrative regulations that provide that insurance cards specify excluded drivers, as well as public policy reasons, such as keeping unfit drivers off the road. Therefore, St. Paul's (P) insurance policy is valid and does not violate public policy. Reversed and remanded.

> *[handwritten margin note: vehicle, not person]*

▌ *ANALYSIS*

States upholding the validity of named driver exclusions have delineated several public policy reasons supporting the exclusions. A Texas appeals court found that named driver exclusions furthered Texas's public policy of protecting all potential claimants from damages resulting from automobile accidents by enabling drivers with family members having poor driving records to procure affordable insurance, rather than obtaining coverage from an assigned risk pool at a greater cost or not securing insurance at all. Further, these exclusions deterred insured drivers from entrusting their vehicles to unsafe excluded

Continued on next page.

drivers, which kept those unfit drivers off the road. Utah has found that named driver exclusions ensure continued coverage of an automobile where the driving record of a household member warrants non-issuance or cancellation.

■══■

Quicknotes

PUBLIC POLICY Policy administered by the state with respect to the health, safety and morals of its people in accordance with common notions of fairness and decency.

■══■

Curtis v. State Farm Mutual Automobile Insurance Company

Injured auto passenger (P) v. Insurer (D)

591 F.2d 572 (10th Cir. 1979).

NATURE OF CASE: Appeal from declaratory judgment for plaintiff in action for insurance coverage.

FACT SUMMARY: A friend of a 14-year-old who had taken the family car got into an accident. State Farm Mutual Automobile Insurance Company (D) denied coverage.

RULE OF LAW
The implied permission to use an insured vehicle is dependent on the relationship of the parties and their course of conduct.

FACTS: The Ahrens family had a VW auto insured by State Farm Mutual Automobile Insurance Company (State Farm) (D), with the parents as the named insureds. This car was mainly used by the two daughters Beth and Shawnna, particularly because their mother was unable to drive for medical reasons. Another daughter, Deborah, was 14 years old and not licensed to drive. She took the VW with a friend, Curtis (P), to meet some friends, including Wallace. Beth may have known that Deborah was taking the car, but it was not discussed and she didn't know that Deborah was taking it to meet friends. Later that evening, Wallace asked Deborah if he could drive and immediately got into an accident that injured Curtis (P). State Farm (D) denied coverage of the subsequent claim, maintaining that Wallace was not a permitted and insured user of the car under the policy. The trial jury ruled against State Farm (D).

ISSUE: Is the implied permission to use an insured vehicle dependent on the relationship of the parties and their course of conduct?

HOLDING AND DECISION: (Holloway, J.) Yes. The implied permission to use an insured vehicle is dependent on the relationship of the parties and their course of conduct. Permission to use an auto for purposes of insurance coverage can be either actual or implied. In the present case, it is unquestioned that Wallace did not have the actual permission of a named insured. Thus, Wallace was only a permitted user through implied permission. The only plausible theory for finding this permission is that the Ahrens parents gave Beth and Shawnna permission, that Beth gave Deborah permission and that Deborah gave Wallace permission. Thus, Wallace would be a third level permittee. Additionally, the parents did not expect that Deborah would be driving the car, nor did Beth expect that Wallace would be driving. Given all of these facts, the implied permission cannot be stretched so far to as to include Wallace. Therefore, State Farm (D) did not have to assume coverage for Curtis's (P) injuries. Reversed.

ANALYSIS

The court also rejected the argument that the two older daughters should be considered named insureds. The court was not inclined to rewrite the express terms of the policy even if the family circumstances were relevant. A public policy argument also failed, with Curtis (P) asserting that the public has contrary expectations in cases such as this one.

Quicknotes

PUBLIC POLICY Policy administered by the state with respect to the health, safety and morals of its people in accordance with common notions of fairness and decency.

First look for actual then permissive

Farm Bureau Mutual Insurance Company v. Evans

Insurance company (D) v. Injured person (P)

Kan. Ct. App., 7 Kan. App. 2d 60, 637 P.2d 491 (1981).

NATURE OF CASE: Appeal from summary judgment for plaintiff in insurance coverage dispute.

FACT SUMMARY: Farm Bureau Mutual Insurance Company, Inc. and Farmers Insurance Company, Inc. (collectively "insurers") (D) argued that their automobile insurance policies did not cover bodily injuries sustained from the throwing of a lighted M-80 firecracker from the rear of a parked station wagon because the injuries did not arise "out of the use of an automobile."

> ### RULE OF LAW
> Bodily injuries caused by the throwing of a lighted firecracker from the rear of a parked automobile do not arise "out of the use of an automobile."

FACTS: On a cold and rainy day, during a going-away party for Evans (P), Ehinger, Rose and Ireland sought shelter in the back of Rose's parked station wagon, the back of which was open. From the rear of the station wagon, Ehinger, with the help of Rose and Ireland, threw an explosive device known as an M-80, which landed in Evans's (P) glass of beer. When it exploded, Evans (P) received extensive damage to her hand and wounds to her body. Evans (P) brought a personal injury action against Ehinger, Rose and Ireland. Farm Bureau Mutual Insurance Company, Inc. (D) insured the Rose automobile and Farmers Insurance Company, Inc. (D) insured an automobile owned by Ehinger. The policies of both insurers (D) provided coverage for bodily injury "arising out of the ownership, maintenance or use" of the insured vehicle. The issue before the trial court was whether the two policies provided coverage for Ehinger, Ireland and Rose, or any of them, with regard to Evans's (P) claims. The trial court determined that there was coverage because the automobile was being used as shelter, a reasonable incident of its use and one reasonably contemplated by the parties to the insurance contract. Accordingly, it granted summary judgment for Evans (P). The appellate court granted review.

ISSUE: Do bodily injuries caused by the throwing of a lighted firecracker from the rear of a parked automobile arise "out of the use of an automobile"?

HOLDING AND DECISION: (Abbott, J.) No. Bodily injuries caused by the throwing of a lighted firecracker from the rear of a parked automobile do not arise "out of the use of an automobile." The policy provision in question is mandated by the legislature, and as an automobile liability coverage clause, it is to be interpreted broadly to afford the greatest possible protection to the insured. However, mere use of a vehicle, standing alone, is not sufficient to trigger coverage. Thus, even though the vehicle was being used within the meaning of the automobile liability policies, the question remains whether that use is so remote from the negligent act that it can be said there was no causal relationship between the use of the car and the injuries sustained. In other words, an injury does not arise out of the "use" of a vehicle within the meaning of the coverage clause of an automobile liability policy if it is caused by some intervening cause not identifiable with normal ownership, maintenance and use of the insured vehicle and the injury complained of. The throwing of an explosive device from a car, however, has generally been held to be so remotely connected with the use of the vehicle that it is not causally related to the injury. The fact that the M-80 was lit inside the vehicle and the defendants might have had difficulty lighting it if no shelter had been available is so remote that it does not furnish the necessary causal relationship between the use of the car and Evans's (P) injuries. There is no more difference in the use of the vehicle here under the facts present than if the owner of the vehicle had been outside the car and in order to avoid the rain had held the device under the car or stood on the "leeward" side of it to light the device. Reversed. Judgment entered for the insurance carriers on their motions for summary judgment.

ANALYSIS

The court in this case followed the majority rule that there must be some causal connection between the use of the insured vehicle and the injury. The court must consider whether the injury sustained was a natural and reasonable incident or consequence of the use of the vehicle involved for the purposes shown by the declarations of the policy though not foreseen or expected. This notion, however, imparts a more liberal concept of causation than "proximate cause" in its traditional, legal sense. See, e.g., 12 *Couch on Insurance*, 2d, § 45:56, p. 147.

■=■

Quicknotes

CAUSATION The aggregate effect of preceding events that bring about a tortious result; the causal connection between the actions of a tortfeasor and the injury that follows.

PROXIMATE CAUSE The natural sequence of events without which an injury would not have been sustained.

■=■

State Farm Mutual Automobile Insurance Company v. Davies

Insurer (D) v. Injured motorist (P)

Va. Sup. Ct., 310 S.E.2d 167 (1983).

NATURE OF CASE: Appeal from judgment against defendant insurer in declaratory judgment action for insurance coverage.

FACT SUMMARY: Turner, State Farm Mutual Automobile Insurance Company's (D) insured, failed to show up at the trial arising out of an accident she was in.

🏛 **RULE OF LAW**
An insurer is not liable where the insured's willful failure to cooperate deprives the insurer with evidence that would have made a jury issue of the insured's liability.

FACTS: Turner, insured by State Farm Mutual Automobile Insurance Company (State Farm) (D), got into an auto accident with Davies (P). Turner reported the accident to State Farm (D) and told a claims representative that the accident wasn't her fault. Smith, a passenger in the car, corroborated her account. Davies (P) filed suit for personal injury and State Farm (D) took over the defense of Turner. As trial approached, both Turner and Smith became unavailable and neither appeared at the trial. Davies (P) testified that Turner was at fault and three police officers heard Turner admit fault. The trial jury gave a verdict to Davies (P). After State Farm (D) disclaimed liability because Turner's failure to appear constituted a material breach of the cooperation clause, the trial court ruled that State Farm (D) had not been prejudiced and entered judgment against them.

ISSUE: Is an insurer liable where the insured's willful failure to cooperate deprives the insurer with evidence that would have made a jury issue of the insured's liability?

HOLDING AND DECISION: (Carrico, C.J.) An insurer is not liable where the insured's willful failure to cooperate deprives the insurer with evidence that would have made a jury issue of the insured's liability. A showing of prejudice is the dispositive factor in a failure to cooperate situation. There is no *per se* rule that an insured's failure to appear at trial is prejudice. Conversely, the insurer is not required to demonstrate that had its insured appeared, the result would have been different. The insurer must only establish a reasonable likelihood that the result would have been favorable. In the instant case, Turner's failure to appear meant that State Farm (D) had no opportunity to present any evidence with regard to her account of the accident. Given that the eyewitness testimony here depends on a jury determination of credibility, Turner's testimony would have at least raised a jury issue. Deprived of this evidence, State Farm (D) was prejudiced by the breach of cooperation clause. Accordingly, State Farm (D) is not liable for the judgment. Reversed.

▌ *ANALYSIS*

The court ordered that the judgment be paid by GEICO, Turner's insurer who provided uninsured motorist coverage. The problem with this decision is that it doesn't really encourage an insurer to locate an insured for testimony where the case seems to suggest that liability will be proven. Thus, some courts favor insurers who have made strong efforts to assist or assure cooperation.

■══■

Quicknotes

MATERIAL BREACH Breach of a contract's terms by one party that is so substantial as to relieve the other party from its obligations pursuant thereto.

PER SE By itself; not requiring additional evidence for proof.

PREJUDICE A preference of the court towards one party prior to litigation.

■══■

Miller v. Shugart

Injured automobile passenger (P) v. Driver (D)

Minn. Sup. Ct., 316 N.W.2d 729 (1982).

NATURE OF CASE: Appeal from summary judgment for plaintiff in garnishment action.

FACT SUMMARY: Milbank Mutual Insurance Company (Milbank) (D) contended that Miller (P), who had been injured in a car driven by Shugart and owned by Locoshonas (Milbank's (D) insured), could not collect from Milbank (D) in a garnishment proceeding on Shugart and Locoshonas's settlement judgment with Miller (P); that the judgment stipulated to was not covered by Milbank's (D) policy; and that Milbank (D) did not have to pay interest on any amount over its policy limit.

🏛 RULE OF LAW

(1) Garnishment lies against an automobile insurer on a judgment stipulated by its insured and a plaintiff that provides that it can only be collected from insurance proceeds, with no personal liability to the insured.

(2) An insured does not breach the duty to cooperate with the insurer by not waiting to settle a suit until after the issue of policy coverage has been decided in a declaratory action.

(3) A stipulated judgment that is entered into by an insured without the insurer's participation and over the insurer's objections, because the insurer is litigating its coverage liability, and that is for an amount greater than the insurance policy limits, is not *per se* collusive and fraudulent.

(4) A stipulated judgment is reasonable and prudent as a matter of law where the effect of the settlement is to substitute the claimant in an action for an insured in a claim against an insurer, and where the amount of the settlement, up to the limits of the insured's policy, is most likely less than the amount of potential damages.

(5) Where an insurance policy provides that the insurer will pay interest on an entered judgment that does not exceed the limit of the insurer's liability, an insurer does not have to pay interest on an entire settlement judgment that exceeds the insurer's liability limits.

FACTS: Miller (P) was a passenger in a car driven by Shugart and owned by Locoshonas. Shugart accidentally drove the car into a tree, and Miller (P) sustained injuries. Milbank Mutual Insurance Company (Milbank) (D) had provided auto insurance to Locoshonas. While Milbank (D) was litigating whether it had to provide coverage for both Locoshonas and Shugart in a pending declaratory action,

Shugart and Locoshonas entered into a settlement stipulation in favor of Miller (P) in the amount of $ 100,000, upon the condition that the judgment was satisfied from Milbank's (D) liability insurance only. However, before entering into the settlement, they advised Milbank (D) of what they were doing, and waited to settle until after the district court had found coverage to exist (but not before an appeal was taken). The policy limit was $50,000. Milbank (P) brought a garnishment action against Milbank (D) to collect on the stipulated judgment, and Milbank (D) contended that garnishment proceeding against it for the confessed judgment was improper. The trial court granted summary judgment for Miller (P), and ruled that Milbank (D) was liable for the $50,000 policy limits, and interest on the entire $100,000. The state's highest court granted review.

ISSUE:

(1) Does garnishment lie against an automobile insurer on a judgment stipulated by its insured and a plaintiff that provides that it can only be collected from insurance proceeds, with no personal liability to the insured?

(2) Does an insured breach the duty to cooperate with the insurer by not waiting to settle a suit until after the issue of policy coverage has been decided in a declaratory action?

(3) Is a stipulated judgment that is entered into by an insured without the insurer's participation and over the insurer's objections, because the insurer is litigating its coverage liability, and that is for an amount greater than the insurance policy limits, *per se* collusive and fraudulent?

(4) Is a stipulated judgment reasonable and prudent as a matter of law where the effect of the settlement is to substitute the claimant in an action for an insured in a claim against an insurer, and where the amount of the settlement, up to the limits of the insured's policy, is most likely less than the amount of potential damages?

(5) Where an insurance policy provides that the insurer will pay interest on an entered judgment that does not exceed the limit of the insurer's liability, does an insurer have to pay interest on an entire settlement judgment that exceeds the insurer's liability limits?

HOLDING AND DECISION: (Simonett, J.)

(1) Yes. Garnishment lies against an automobile insurer on a judgment stipulated by its insured and a plaintiff that provides that it can only be collected from insurance proceeds, with no personal liability to the insured. Milbank (D) argues that because there has never been a trial on the merits, the purported judgment is an unliquidated tort claim and the sum due Miller (P) is not due absolutely, so garnishment cannot lie. However, as

Continued on next page.

between Miller (P) and Shugart and Locoshonas, the claim has been liquidated and reduced to a judgment. Therefore, there is a basis for garnishment. In other words, the judgment effectively liquidates the personal liability of Shugart and Locoshonas, so that Miller (P) may seek to collect on that judgment. Affirmed on this issue.

(2) No. An insured does not breach the duty to cooperate with the insurer by not waiting to settle a suit until after the issue of policy coverage has been decided in a declaratory action. Here, the insurer had a right to determine if its policy afforded coverage for the accident claim. Thus, while it did not abandon its insureds, neither did it accept responsibility for the insured's liability exposure. While the defendant insureds have a duty to cooperate with the insurer, they also have a right to protect themselves against plaintiff's claim. If, as here, the insureds are offered a settlement that effectively relieves them of any personal liability, at a time when their insurance coverage is in doubt, surely it cannot be said that it is not in their best interest to accept the offer. Nor, can the insurer who is disputing coverage compel the insureds to forego a settlement which is in their best interests. Affirmed on this issue.

(3) No. A stipulated judgment that is entered into by an insured without the insurer's participation and over the insurer's objections, because the insurer is litigating its coverage liability, and that is for an amount greater than the insurance policy limits, is not *per se* collusive and fraudulent. A money judgment confessed to by an insured is not binding on the insurer if obtained through fraud or collusion. Here, however, Milbank (D) makes a showing of neither collusion nor fraud. Milbank's (D) argument is that the fraud and collusion consist of the defendant insureds settling the claims over Milbank's objections and contrary to the insurer's best interests, and in confessing judgment for a sum twice the amount of the policy limits. This conduct, however, need be neither fraudulent nor collusive, given that the insureds had a right to make a settlement relieving them of liability. They also advised Milbank (D) of what they were doing, and waited to settle until after the district court had found coverage to exist. There is, therefore, nothing improper in the insureds' conduct. Affirmed on this issue.

(4) Yes. A stipulated judgment is reasonable and prudent as a matter of law where the effect of the settlement is to substitute the claimant in an action for an insured in a claim against an insurer, and where the amount of the settlement, up to the limits of the insured's policy, is most likely less than the amount of potential damages. Here, although the judgment is binding and valid as between the stipulating parties, it is not conclusive on Milbank (D). The burden of proof is on Miller (P) to show that the settlement is reasonable and prudent. The test as to whether the settlement is reasonable and prudent is, what a reasonably prudent person in the position

of the insured would have settled for on the merits of Miller's (P) claim. This involves a consideration of the facts bearing on the liability and damage aspects of her claim, as well as the risks of going to trial. The record reveals that "there was a substantial likelihood that ultimately judgment would be entered against [the insureds] . . . for more than any possible insurance coverage." On this undisputed showing, the settlement was reasonable and prudent, and the trial court did not err in granting summary judgment to Miller (P) to the extent of $50,000 (the policy limit). Affirmed on this issue.

(5) No. Where an insurance policy provides that the insurer will pay interest on an entered judgment that does not exceed the limit of the insurer's liability, an insurer does not have to pay interest on an entire settlement judgment that exceeds the insurer's liability limits. Milbank's (D) policy provides "the company will pay . . . all interest on the entire amount of any judgment therein which accrues after the entry of judgment and before the company has paid or tendered or deposited in court that part of the judgment which does not exceed the limit of the company's liability thereon." The stipulated judgment was not conclusive as to Milbank (D) until it had a chance to litigate that issue in the garnishment action, when it was determined that Milbank (D) was liable for $50,000. Therefore, Milbank (D) is liable for interest only on interest accruing on $50,000 from the time judgment was entered in the garnishment proceeding. It is not liable for any interest on the remaining $50,000 of the stipulated judgment. Reversed on this issue.

▶ ANALYSIS

The facts of this case present a "no-win" situation for the insurer. If the insurer ignores the "invitation" to participate in the settlement negotiations, it may run the risk of being required to pay, even within its policy limits, an inflated judgment. On the other hand, if the insurer decides to participate in the settlement discussions, ordinarily it can hardly do so meaningfully without abandoning its policy defense. In this case, the court acknowledged the insurer's predicament, but concluded that if a risk is to be borne, it is better to have the insurer who makes the decision to contest coverage bear the risk. Of course, the insurer escapes the risk if it should be successful on the coverage issue, and, in that event, it is the claimant who loses.

■■■

Quicknotes

COLLUSION An agreement between two or more parties to engage in unlawful conduct or in other activities with an unlawful goal, typically involving fraud.

GARNISHMENT Satisfaction of a debt by deducting payments directly from the debtor's wages before the wages

Continued on next page.

are paid to him by his employer; due process requires that the debtor be first given notice and an opportunity to be heard.

PER SE By itself; not requiring additional evidence for proof.

STIPULATION An agreement by the parties regarding an issue before the court so as to avoid unnecessary expense and delay.

SUMMARY JUDGMENT Judgment rendered by a court in response to a motion made by one of the parties, claiming that the lack of a question of material fact in respect to an issue warrants disposition of the issue without consideration by the jury.

Carriers Insurance Company v. American Policyholders' Insurance Company

Insurer (P) v. Insurer (D)

Me. Sup. Jud. Ct., 404 A.2d 216 (1979).

NATURE OF CASE: Appeal from judgment in contribution action.

FACT SUMMARY: Carriers Insurance Company (P) and American Policyholders' Insurance Company (D) each had other insurance clauses in their policies and disputed which one was applicable.

🏛 RULE OF LAW
Where two policies covering a risk have other insurance clauses, both insurers must share the loss by prorating the loss up to the limits of the lower policy.

FACTS: Cummings leased vehicles from Merrill. Pursuant to the lease, Merrill provided insurance coverage through Carriers Insurance Company (Carriers) (P) for its vehicles while they were operated by Cummings' employees. The policy had liability coverage for personal injury up to $3 million. Cummings independently procured $250,000 of liability coverage through American Policyholders' Insurance Company (American) (D). Both policies contained nearly identical other insurance clauses, providing that if there was other insurance against an occurrence then the policy would be considered excess. Subsequently, a Cummings employee driving a vehicle leased by Merrill negligently caused an accident and killed the other driver. Carriers (P) settled the wrongful death claim for $200,000 and property damage claim for $8,000. Carriers (P) sought contribution from American (D) which was denied. After filing suit, Carriers (P) won a judgment of $104,000 from American (D).

ISSUE: Where two policies covering a risk have other insurance clauses, must both insurers share the loss by prorating the loss up to the limits of the lower policy?

HOLDING AND DECISION: (Delahanty, J.) Yes. Where two policies covering a risk have other insurance clauses, both insurers must share the loss by prorating the loss up to the limits of the lower policy. Other insurance clauses were designed to prevent fraudulent claims induced by overinsuring and violate no public policy. There are three basic types of other insurance clauses: (1) a pro-rata clause limits the liability of an insurer to the proportion of the total loss; (2) an escape clause seeks to avoid all liability; and (3) an excess clause provides that the insurance will only be excess. The latter type is at issue here. There is no problem when only one policy on a risk contains another insurance clause since it can be given effect as written. However, where the clauses conflict,

there is no logical way to reconcile the two provisions. Courts have adopted numerous manners of resolving the conflict. However, here where the clauses are virtually identical, any methodology would be arbitrary. Thus, the best resolution is to hold that the insurers share the loss. This method is best for advancing certainty and uniformity into the industry and enabling underwriters to more accurately predict losses. There are three basic methods of proration when the insurers share a loss. The majority prorates liability according to the limits of the policies. A seldom followed method prorates on premiums paid. A growing minority prorates the loss equally up to the limits of the lower policy. This latter method does not unfairly discriminate against larger policy limits in the face of a policy that agreed to cover the loss. Therefore, it is the best method and should be used as did the trial court. Affirmed.

▶ ANALYSIS

The court noted that the majority rule on proration does not encourage an insurer to increase coverage where it is aware of a lesser policy. The court left open the possibility that the particular language of a clause should be interpreted in order to find any consistency. Some favor a *per se* rule that the clauses always conflict.

Quicknotes

PRO RATA In proportion.

Roth v. Amica Mutual Insurance Company

Insured car owner (P) v. Insurance company (D)

Mass. Sup. Jud. Ct., 440 Mass. 1013, 796 N.E.2d 1281 (2003).

NATURE OF CASE: Appeal from partial summary judgment for defendant insurer and from denial of class certification in insurance coverage action.

FACT SUMMARY: Roth (P) contended that only original equipment manufacturer (OEM) parts could satisfy Amica Mutual Insurance Company's (D) obligation under its policy to repair her damaged car, and that because non-OEM parts were used she suffered "inherent diminished value," and she sought class certification for like-situated insureds.

🏛 RULE OF LAW
An insurer's specification of non-original equipment manufacturer (non-OEM) parts to repair a damaged automobile does not constitute an automatic violation of its obligations under a standard automobile insurance policy's collision provisions to repair the automobile.

FACTS: Amica Mutual Insurance Company (Amica) (D) issued to Roth (P) a standard automobile policy with optional collision coverage to insure her car. Her car suffered damage, including damage to the front fender. When the vehicle was repaired, pursuant to an appraisal by Amica (D), the damaged fender was replaced with a fender that had been manufactured by someone other than the original equipment manufacturer (OEM). Roth (P) protested that only a fender from the OEM would satisfy Amica's (D) obligation to repair the vehicle under the language of the standard policy and the applicable regulations. She also contended that, notwithstanding the repair of her vehicle, she had sustained damage in the form of "inherent diminished value," and demanded compensation for that damage. She filed suit, individually and as a representative of all persons similarly situated. The trial court ruled that Roth (P) was not entitled to collect inherent diminished value from Amica (D) under the policy, and that the use of non-OEM parts on her car (driven over 15,000 miles at the time of the accident) was not a regulatory violation. It also ruled, however, that a genuine issue of material fact existed as to the quality of the particular non-OEM fender placed on Roth's (P) car. Roth's (P) motion for class certification was denied, as she was unable to bring forward any other similarly situated persons. The state's highest court granted direct appellate review.

ISSUE: Does an insurer's specification of non-original equipment manufacturer (non-OEM) parts to repair a damaged automobile constitute an automatic violation of its obligations under a standard automobile insurance policy's collision provisions to repair the automobile?

HOLDING AND DECISION: [Judge not stated in casebook excerpt.] No. An insurer's specification of non-original equipment manufacturer (non-OEM) parts to repair a damaged automobile does not constitute an automatic violation of its obligations under a standard automobile insurance policy's collision provisions to repair the automobile. Roth's (P) assertion that all non-OEM parts are inherently inferior to OEM parts in every circumstance flies in the face of common sense, common experience, and contrary conclusions reached by the legislature and regulatory bodies. The regulatory scheme unambiguously allows for use of non-OEM parts. In an appropriate case, a plaintiff may successfully claim damages based on an insurer's specification of a substandard non-OEM part, or successfully demonstrate that the insurer's duty under the policy to repair or replace can only be satisfied by the designation of a particular OEM part to repair the specific damage to that automobile—there are certainly some parts of some vehicles where unique dimensions or specifications of the part are such that only a replacement part from the original manufacturer will suffice to restore the vehicle to its proper functioning condition. That, however, is not the case presented, here. Affirmed.

▶ ANALYSIS

In this case, the court almost summarily disposed of the issue of inherent diminished value (the diminished value of the vehicle that results from the mere fact that it has been in an accident, even when fully repaired), stating merely that the state does not permit insureds to recover for alleged inherent diminished value under the standard automobile insurance policy. While most courts have rendered similar opinions on this issue, some courts have found in favor of coverage. Usually, the difference in outcome hinges on differences in policy language.

■══■

Quicknotes

CLASS CERTIFICATION Certification by a court's granting of a motion to allow individual litigants to join as one plaintiff in a class action against the defendant.

MATERIAL FACT A fact without the existence of which a contract would not have been entered.

PARTIAL SUMMARY JUDGMENT Judgment rendered by a court in response to a motion by one of the parties, claiming that the lack of a question of material fact in respect to one of the issues warrants disposition of that issue without going to the jury.

■══■

Allison v. Iowa Mutual Insurance Company

Insured (P) v. Insurer (D)

N.C. Ct. App., 258 S.E.2d 489 (1979).

NATURE OF CASE: Appeal from judgment in action for property damage coverage.

FACT SUMMARY: Allison's (P) car was damaged when the bridge it was on collapsed. Allison's (P) insurer, Iowa Mutual Insurance Company (D) denied coverage on the grounds that the accident did not constitute a collision.

> ## 🏛 RULE OF LAW
> Contact with the road itself does not constitute a collision within the meaning of the term used in a collision insurance policy.

FACTS: Allison (P) had automobile insurance through Iowa Mutual Insurance Company (Iowa Mutual) (D). The policy provided coverage for damage to the vehicle from any cause except collisions. Subsequently, Allison (P) was driving across a bridge when it collapsed and the truck slid into the river causing damages of $8,500. Iowa Mutual (D) denied coverage, claiming the incident was a collision and not covered. At the trial, the trial judge ruled that the bridge collapse did not constitute a collision and ruled for Allison (P). Iowa Mutual (D) appealed.

ISSUE: Does contact with road itself constitute a collision within the meaning of the term used in a collision insurance policy?

HOLDING AND DECISION: (Hedrick, J.) No. Contact with road itself does not constitute a collision within the meaning of the term used in a collision insurance policy. Collision is typically defined as the collision of the covered vehicle with another object or upset of the vehicle. Thus, it implies an impact or sudden contact of two bodies, both in motion or one stationary. Other courts interpreting this term and provision have found that a giving way of the roadbed over which the insured car is traveling is not a collision within the popular and usual meaning of the term. In the present case, there was plainly no driver control with respect to the collapse of the bridge. Allison (P) did nothing to set in force the succeeding events. The collapse of the bridge alone was the occurrence and cause of the damage. Thus, it was not a collision within the meaning of the coverage exclusion. Affirmed.

▌ ANALYSIS

The court distinguished a case in which the insured car was being used to launch a boat and ended up rolling into the water. The court found that this situation was different because the driver was responsible for leaving the car in a situation in which it could roll. This decision is in accord with section 65 of *American Jurisprudence* 2d, "Automobile Insurance."

■■■

Rodemich v. State Farm Mutual Automobile Insurance Company

Insured (P) v. Insurer (D)

Ariz. Ct. App., 637 P.2d 748 (1981).

NATURE OF CASE: Appeal from directed verdict for plaintiff in action for recovery of property damage.

FACT SUMMARY: Rodemich's (P) motor home was damaged when he swerved to avoid an animal in the roadway.

🏛 RULE OF LAW
The term "colliding with animals" in a policy should be read as to require the actual striking of the vehicle and the animal.

FACTS: Rodemich (P) owned a motor home that was insured by State Farm Mutual Automobile Insurance Company (State Farm) (D). The policy had only comprehensive coverage and did not insure for loss by collision except if the loss was caused by colliding with birds or other animals. Rodemich (P) was driving through a state park when he claimed that a gray four-legged animal appeared in the roadway. Rodemich (P) swerved to avoid the collision and ended up severely damaging the motor home. Neither the animal, nor any hair or blood was found on the vehicle, but Rodemich (P) did claim he heard a thump. State Farm (D) denied coverage based on the collision exclusion. However, the trial court directed a verdict to Rodemich (P) on the coverage issue in a subsequent lawsuit on the basis that swerving to miss the animal was covered. The jury found that there was an animal that caused the accident. State Farm (D) appealed.

ISSUE: Should the term "colliding with animals" in a policy be read as to require the actual striking of the vehicle and the animal?

HOLDING AND DECISION: (Eubank, J.) Yes. The term "colliding with animals" in a policy should be read as to require the actual striking of the vehicle and the animal. Here, the State Farm (D) policy excluded coverage for collisions, including the upset of the vehicle. This is what appears to have happened to the Rodemich (P) motor home. Thus, the loss would not be covered except if there was an exception. The clause expressly provides that if the vehicle collides with an animal, then there is coverage under the policy despite the collision exclusion. Rodemich (P) argued that where a risk insured against operates to subject the insured property to a risk not insured against, the loss is covered. However, the language of the policy does not support this interpretation. The plain meaning requires an actual striking of the animal. Therefore, the trial court did not present the proper fact question to the jury. Since reasonable minds could differ as to whether Rodemich (P) actually struck the animal with the motor

home, the judgment must be reversed and remanded for a new trial.

▶ ANALYSIS

The result of the policy language and its strict interpretation here results in a very odd result—colliding with an animal results in coverage under the policy that excludes coverage for a collision and a loss caused by not colliding with an animal is not covered because it is considered an excluded collision.

▪▬▪

Quicknotes

DIRECTED VERDICT A verdict ordered by the court in a jury trial.

PLAIN LANGUAGE RULE Rule that the meaning of a document should be construed in accordance with the ordinary meaning of the language used.

▪▬▪

Allstate Insurance v. Boynton

Insurer (D) v. Insured (P)

Fla. Sup. Ct., 486 So. 2d 552 (1986).

NATURE OF CASE: Appeal from reversal of summary judgment for defendant insurer in action to recover under uninsured motorist coverage.

FACT SUMMARY: Boynton (P), a mechanic, was struck by a car that was being worked on by a co-employee.

RULE OF LAW
(1) A vehicle may be considered an "uninsured motor vehicle" where it is covered by a liability insurance policy but that policy does not provide coverage for a particular occurrence that causes damages.
(2) An insured is not "legally entitled to recover" from the operator of an insured motor vehicle when there is a statutory bar to an action against the operator, but for which bar, recovery would lie.

FACTS: Boynton (P) worked as a mechanic at Sears. He was injured when struck by a car that co-worker, Luke, was working on. The car was leased to Xerox and left at Sears for repairs. Boynton (P) filed suit against Xerox and Sears. However, Sears was immune from suit under the provisions of the workers compensation laws. Xerox was dismissed on the basis that the owner is not liable for the negligent operation of a vehicle left at a repair shop. Boynton (P) then sought recovery from Luke's insurer, but coverage was precluded by a clause that excluded injuries occurring during the pursuit of a business. Boynton (P) then sued Allstate Insurance (Allstate) (D), his own insurer, for recovery under the uninsured motorist provisions. The trial court ruled for Allstate (D) and Boynton (P) appealed and the appellate court reversed.

ISSUE:
(1) May a vehicle may be considered an "uninsured motor vehicle" where it is covered by a liability insurance policy but that policy does not provide coverage for a particular occurrence that causes damages?
(2) Is an insured "legally entitled to recover" from the operator of an insured motor vehicle when there is a statutory bar to an action against the operator, but for which bar, recovery would lie?

HOLDING AND DECISION: (Ehrlich, J.)
(1) Yes. A vehicle may be considered an "uninsured motor vehicle" where it is covered by a liability insurance policy but that policy does not provide coverage for a particular occurrence that causes damages. The fact that an owner of vehicle has a liability policy does not always mean that the vehicle is insured for purposes of uninsured motorist coverage. In this context, a vehicle is only insured when the insurance in question is available to the injured plaintiff. In the present case, it is clear that the Xerox policy was not available to Boynton (P) and could not be held responsible for Luke's negligence. Since Luke's own policy also excluded coverage for the occurrence, it also was unavailable. Therefore, the vehicle that injured Boynton (P) was technically uninsured.
(2) No. An insured is not "legally entitled to recover" from the operator of an insured motor vehicle when there is a statutory bar to an action against the operator, but for which bar, recovery would lie. To recover, Boynton still had to be legally entitled to recover from the owner or operator of the vehicle. Thus, the insured must have a claim against a tortfeasor that could be reduced to judgment. In this context, the insurer has available all substantive defenses the tortfeasor could have raised. Such a holding supports the basic reasoning behind uninsured motorist coverage. It is not first party coverage, even though the insured pays the premiums. Fault is not an issue in first party coverage. In uninsured motorist coverage, the insurer steps into the shoes of the tortfeasor. This subrogation right would be frustrated if the insurer was forced to pay claims when it would be barred by a substantive defense from winning a judgment against the tortfeasor. In the present case, Boynton's (P) lawsuits were barred by the provisions of the state workers compensation laws. Thus, Allstate (D) had this defense available to the action to collect on the uninsured motorist coverage. Accordingly, the appellate court's decision is quashed and remanded.

ANALYSIS

The court went on to note that since Boynton (P) was taken care of by workers compensation, this case showed that public policy supported the decision. In some states, uninsured motorist coverage is mandatory. Others require that insurers at least offer it to their insureds.

Quicknotes

TORTFEASOR Party that commits a tort or wrongful act.

UNINSURED MOTORIST COVERAGE Protection afforded against bodily injury inflicted by an uninsured motorist; coverage intended to close the gaps inherent in motor vehicle financial responsibility and compulsory insurance legislation.

Simpson v. Farmers Insurance Company, Inc.

Insured (P) v. Insurer (D)

Kan. Sup. Ct., 592 P.2d 445 (1979).

NATURE OF CASE: Appeal from summary judgment for defendant insurer in action for uninsured motorist coverage.

FACT SUMMARY: Simpson (P) was injured when she was forced to swerve to avoid a collision with a hit-and-run driver. Her insurer, Farmers Insurance Company, Inc. (D), denied coverage because there had been no physical contact with the other car.

RULE OF LAW
A hit-and-run provision of uninsured motorist coverage that requires actual physical contact is void and unenforceable.

FACTS: Simpson (P) was forced to drive her car into a ditch to avoid a collision with another vehicle. Simpson (P) suffered personal injuries and the other vehicle fled the scene before it could be identified. Simpson (P) sought to recover damages for her injuries under the uninsured motorist (UM) coverage of her Farmers Insurance Company, Inc. (Farmers) (D) policy. The policy provided that uninsured vehicle included hit-and-run cars that caused injury arising out of physical contact. Farmers (D) denied coverage based on this provision and the fact that the hit and run car never struck Simpson's (P) auto. The trial court granted summary judgment to Farmers (D) and Simpson (P) appealed, asserting that public policy made the provision void and unenforceable.

ISSUE: Is a hit-and-run provision of uninsured motorist coverage that requires actual physical contact void and unenforceable?

HOLDING AND DECISION: (Prager, J.) Yes. A hit-and-run provision of uninsured motorist coverage that requires actual physical contact is void and unenforceable. Kansas adopted a law that required insurers to provide UM coverage to their insureds. The purpose of the legislation was to provide financial recompense to innocent persons who are damaged by the acts of those that cannot respond in damages. This court has already determined that as remedial legislation, it should be liberally construed to provide the intended protection. Since adoption of the law, insurers have made various attempts to dilute the broad coverage contemplated by the statute. This court has held all these clauses to be void. The hit-and-run provision at issue here is another clause that seeks to dilute this broad coverage. Other jurisdictions have split on whether physical contact can be required between the hit-and-run vehicle and insured auto. Those who have allowed the clause have done so on the basis that it will prevent fraud. However, the prevention of fraud is an unreasonable basis for applying the provision. Other standards are far better suited to preventing fraud and don't cause unrecoverable losses to innocent victims. Therefore, the Farmers (D) hit-and-run provision requiring physical contact is void and unenforceable. Summary judgment is reversed.

▶ ANALYSIS

While most states require UM coverage, not all mandate coverage for hit-and-run situations. However, virtually all jurisdictions have found that a hit-and-run vehicle is an uninsured vehicle for purposes of coverage. The court correctly noted that the physical contact requirement was not very well suited for fraud prevention. An insured could still point to any mark on the car to demonstrate contact, without having any witnesses.

◼▬◼

Quicknotes

PUBLIC POLICY Policy administered by the state with respect to the health, safety and morals of its people in accordance with common notions of fairness and decency.

UNINSURED MOTORIST COVERAGE Protection afforded against bodily injury inflicted by an uninsured motorist; coverage intended to close the gaps inherent in motor vehicle financial responsibility and compulsory insurance legislation.

◼▬◼

Taft v. Cerwonka

Decedent's father (P) v. Motorist (D)

R.I. Sup. Ct., 433 A.2d 215 (1981).

NATURE OF CASE: Appeal from judgment for plaintiff insured in wrongful death action.

FACT SUMMARY: Taft (P) sought to stack their uninsured motorist coverage when his daughter died in an accident with an uninsured motorist.

> ## 🏛 RULE OF LAW
> An insured who has paid separate premiums providing two vehicles with uninsured motorist coverage is entitled to stack the coverage and recover up to the aggregate sum of the two vehicles' coverages.

FACTS: Beverly Taft died in an auto accident with Cerwonka (D), an uninsured motorist driving an uninsured vehicle. Earl Taft (P), Beverly's father, filed suit for wrongful death due to negligent operation of a motor vehicle. Taft (P) also filed suit against Allstate Insurance Company (Allstate) (D), the insurer of Taft's two vehicles, pursuant to the uninsured motorist provisions of the policy. Taft (P) asserted at trial that the Allstate (D) coverage could be stacked so that the uninsured coverage limits for each vehicle, $10,000, could be combined. The trial court ultimately agreed and entered judgment against Allstate (D) for $20,000. Allstate (D) appealed.

ISSUE: Is an insured who has paid separate premiums providing two vehicles with uninsured motorist coverage entitled to stack the coverage and recover up to the aggregate sum of the two vehicles' coverages?

HOLDING AND DECISION: (Murray, J.) Yes. An insured who has paid separate premiums providing two vehicles with uninsured motorist coverage is entitled to stack the coverage and recover up to the aggregate sum of the two vehicles' coverages. When the stacking is the aggregation of limits for coverage of each car covered in one policy it is deemed intra-policy stacking. Other jurisdictions have allowed intra-policy stacking for three general reasons. One theory is that the policy provisions are ambiguous with respect to stacking and the ambiguity should be resolved in favor of the insured. Another theory is that the state's uninsured motorist statute requires stacking. The other theory is that the payment of separate premiums for the coverage on each vehicle entitles the insured to stack. Some jurisdictions have disallowed stacking, finding that multiple vehicles involve greater risk that justify the additional premiums. This court holds that to not allow stacking would defeat the reasonable expectations of the insured. When two premiums are paid to insure two cars under a single policy, the insured expects that the combination coverage will allow for the stacking of limits.

Therefore, Taft (P) was entitled to stack the coverage limits for the uninsured motorist coverage of Allstate (D). The judgment is affirmed.

▶ ANALYSIS

The court went on to suggest that it probably wouldn't allow the stacking of multiple coverages where an entire fleet of cars was insured under a policy. Apparently, such stacking would not be within the reasonable expectations of the insured. One key factor in this decision is that inter-policy stacking, combining coverage limits from policies issued by two different insurers, would have been allowed for Taft (P) in this case. Thus, it would hardly have been fair to disallow the intra-policy stacking.

■══■

Quicknotes

AMBIGUITY Language that is capable of being understood to have more than one interpretation.

UNINSURED MOTORIST COVERAGE Protection afforded against bodily injury inflicted by an uninsured motorist; coverage intended to close the gaps inherent in motor vehicle financial responsibility and compulsory insurance legislation.

WRONGFUL DEATH An action brought by the beneficiaries of a deceased person, claiming that the deceased's death was the result of wrongful conduct by the defendant.

■══■

The Secondary Market

Quick Reference Rules of Law

Allendale Mutual Insurance Company v. Excess Insurance Co. Limited

Insurer (P) v. Reinsurer (D)

992 F. Supp. 278 (S.D.N.Y. 1998).

NATURE OF CASE: Action for recovery of reinsurance proceeds.

FACT SUMMARY: Factory Mutual International (P), obtained reinsurance coverage from Excess Insurance Co. Ltd. (D) of a warehouse, but did not disclose fire safety problems.

🏛 RULE OF LAW
A reinsured owes to its reinsurer a duty to disclose all material facts regarding the original risk of loss so that failure to do so renders the agreement voidable.

FACTS: Factory Mutual International (FMI) (P), a subsidiary of Allendale Mutual Insurance Company (Allendale) (P), issued an insurance policy to Zenith Data Systems France and Zenith Data System Europe (Zenith) covering a warehouse in Seclin, France for up to $48 million. The policy was reinsured by Allendale (P) who, in turn, reinsured most of the risk itself. A $7 million layer of reinsurance coverage was offered to Excess Insurance Co. Ltd. (Excess) (D). Excess (D) was advised that the warehouse was "non sprinklered." Before accepting, Excess added a note that its acceptance was subject to compliance with recommendations in a survey of the warehouse. This initial reinsurance policy covered January 1 to June 1, 1991. In late January, the Seclin warehouse was surveyed and a report included a recommendation section that included several entries for ways to reduce the fire risk. Neither Zenith nor Allendale (P) took any action with regard to the recommendations, nor did Allendale (P) provide Excess (D) with a copy. When the first policy period ended June 1, it was extended for another year. This time there was no clause about it being subject to compliance with the recommendations and Excess (D) still had no knowledge of the survey results. Two weeks later, the Seclin warehouse was completely destroyed by fire. Excess (D) sought to rescind the reinsurance policy due to Allendale's (P) failure to disclose the survey recommendations. Allendale (P) filed suit.

ISSUE: Does a reinsured owe to its reinsurer a duty to disclose all material facts regarding the original risk of loss so that failure to do so renders the agreement voidable?

HOLDING AND DECISION: (Scheindlin, J.) Yes. A reinsured owes to its reinsurer a duty to disclose all material facts regarding the original risk of loss so that failure to do so renders the agreement voidable. This doctrine imposes no duty of inquiry upon the reinsurer. The burden is on the reassured to volunteer all material facts since the reinsured is in the best position to know the

relevant circumstances. A reinsured need not possess a specific intent to conceal information to make the reinsurance policy voidable. An innocent failure to disclose material information is sufficient. A fact is material if it would have prevented the reinsurer from issuing the policy or prompted it to charge a higher premium. In the present case, it seems clear that the survey recommendations were material facts that should have been disclosed to Excess (D) by Allendale (P). Excess (D) even specifically included a provision with regard to the recommendations in the first policy. It does not matter that the second policy was issued without mention of the recommendations because the reinsurer has no positive duty to inquire. It cannot be said here that the information had become stale because Excess (D) hadn't shown any interest in such facts for many years. There is no doubt that Excess (D) would have found the recommendations to be material in deciding whether to reinsure. Accordingly, Allendale's (P) failure to disclose constituted a violation of its duty of utmost good faith and Excess (D) was entitled to rescind coverage.

▶ ANALYSIS

The court rejected Allendale's (P) various arguments that the recommendations were not material. Allendale (P) argued that an Excess (D) executive testified that he didn't know what he would have done if given the information. The court correctly held that this was hardly an admission of immateriality.

Quicknotes

DUTY OF GOOD FAITH OF FAIR DEALINGS An implied duty in a contract that the parties will deal honestly in the satisfaction of their obligations and without intent to defraud.

DUTY TO DISCLOSE The duty owed by a fiduciary to reveal those facts that have a material effect on the interests of the party that must be informed.

MATERIAL FACT A fact without the existence of which a contract would not have been entered.

REINSURANCE A contract between an insurer and a third party to insure the insurer against potential loss or liability resulting from a previous insurance contract.

SPECIFIC INTENT The intent to commit a specific unlawful act that is a required element for criminal liability for certain crimes.

Travelers Casualty and Surety Company v. Certain Underwriters at Lloyd's of London

Reinsured (P) v. Reinsurer (D)

N.Y. Ct. App., 96 N.Y.2d 583, 734 N.Y.S.2d 531, 760 N.E.2d 319 (2001).

NATURE OF CASE: Appeals in two actions from affirmance of summary judgment for defendant reinsurers in reinsurance action.

FACT SUMMARY: Travelers Casualty and Surety Company (P), a reinsured insurance company, contended that it properly aggregated losses from environmental injury claims involving decades of commercial activities at numerous industrial and waste disposal sites as a single "disaster and/or casualty" under certain reinsurance treaties.

🏛 **RULE OF LAW**
(1) A reinsurance treaty that defines the term "disaster and/or casualty" as including "all loss resulting from a series of accidents, occurrences and/or causative incidents having a common origin and/or being traceable to the same act, omission, error and/or mistake" does not encompass a reinsured's single allocation of its losses arising out of multiple occurrences that are not linked spatially or temporally.
(2) A "follow the fortunes" clause in a reinsurance policy does not override the policy's other limitations.

FACTS: Travelers Casualty and Surety Company (Travelers) (P), an insurance company, provided primary, excess, and umbrella general liability insurance policies to Koppers Company (Koppers), a chemical manufacturer, and to E.I. DuPont de Nemours & Company (DuPont), the largest chemical company in the world. Travelers (P) purchased various types of reinsurance in connection with its policies issued to Koppers and DuPont. In particular, Travelers (P) purchased facultative reinsurance for 50 percent of the limits of its excess liability policies issued to Koppers. In addition, it secured catastrophic excess of loss reinsurance from a number of foreign reinsurance companies (reinsurers) (D). These reinsurance treaties obligated the reinsurers (D) to pay Travelers (P) for "each and every loss" incurred by Travelers (P) that exceeded the retentions established under the treaties. With regard to its DuPont insurance, Travelers (P) secured three catastrophic excess of loss treaties from the reinsurers (D) to cover a "disaster and/or casualty" in excess of a $10 million retention. The relevant provisions in those treaties—including the definitions of "each and every loss," "disaster and/or casualty" and a "follow the fortunes" clause—were identical. The treaties defined "each and every loss" as "all loss arising

out of any one disaster and/or casualty under coverage of any or all insureds of the Companies. . . ." They defined "disaster and/or casualty" as "each and every accident, occurrence and/or causative incident, it being further understood that all loss resulting from a series of accidents, occurrences and/or causative incidents having a common origin and/or being traceable to the same act, omission, error and/or mistake shall be considered as having resulted from a single accident, occurrence and/or causative incident." Finally, all the treaties contained a so-called "follow the fortunes" clause that provided that "Any and all payments made by [Travelers] in settlement of loss or losses under [its] policies, whether in satisfaction of a judgment in any Court against the Insured or [Travelers] or made voluntarily by [Travelers] before judgment, in full settlement or as a compromise, shall be unconditionally binding upon the [Reinsurers] and amounts falling to the share of the [Reinsurers] shall be immediately payable to [Travelers] by [the Reinsurers] upon reasonable evidence of the amount paid by [Travelers] being presented. . . ." Both Kopper and DuPont sought, and received, insurance coverage from Travelers (P) for pollution-related claims arising from multiple hazardous waste sites that involved decades of commercial activities. Travelers (P) paid Koppers about $140 million, which Travelers (P) apportioned among its underlying direct insurance policies, treating each of the over 160 Koppers sites as a separate occurrence. Travelers ceded approximately $61.5 million of this settlement to its facultative reinsurance policies. In determining how much of the settlement to allocate to the reinsurers (D) under the applicable reinsurance treaties, Travelers (P) treated the entire settlement as a single "disaster and/or casualty" and appropriated the settlement monies correspondingly among the implicated treaties. Travelers' (P) rationale was that the Koppers loss resulted from a "common origin" and/or was "traceable to the same act, omission, error and/or mistake," namely, "Koppers' companywide waste-disposal practice." Based on this approach, the total amount Travelers (P) ceded to the reinsurers (D) was approximately $13 million of Koppers' claims, or about 9 percent of the total settlement. Travelers (P) paid $72.5 million, and it attributed $69 million to an umbrella policy, with 25 different sites identified as separate occurrences for allocation purposes. Travelers (P) ceded over $34 million of the settlement to certain facultative reinsurance policies. After deducting this amount and its retention under the excess of loss reinsurance treaties, Travelers (P)

Continued on next page.

billed the reinsurers (D) approximately $7.4 million, or about 9 percent of the total settlement. As it did with the Koppers' allocation, Travelers (P) calculated this amount by treating the environmental contamination at the DuPont sites as a single loss with a common origin, namely, a managerial failure by DuPont in the implementation and enforcement of its companywide environmental policy. Travelers (P) then sued the reinsurers (D) seeking monetary damages and declaratory relief. The reinsurers (D) answered and asserted a counterclaim for declaratory relief. The reinsurers (D) moved for summary judgment dismissing the complaint and for a declaration that they had no further obligation to Travelers (P) with respect to the settlement of insurance claims. The trial court ruled for the reinsurers (D), the intermediate appellate court affirmed, and the state's highest court granted review.

ISSUE:

(1) Does a reinsurance treaty that defines the term "disaster and/or casualty" as including "all loss resulting from a series of accidents, occurrences and/or causative incidents having a common origin and/or being traceable to the same act, omission, error and/or mistake" encompass a reinsured's single allocation of its losses arising out of multiple occurrences that are not linked spatially or temporally?

(2) Does a "follow the fortunes" clause in a reinsurance policy override the policy's other limitations?

HOLDING AND DECISION: (Graffeo, J.)

(1) No. A reinsurance treaty that defines the term "disaster and/or casualty" as including "all loss resulting from a series of accidents, occurrences and/or causative incidents having a common origin and/or being traceable to the same act, omission, error and/or mistake" does not encompass a reinsured's single allocation of its losses arising out of multiple occurrences that are not linked spatially or temporally. In defining "origin" Travelers (P) contends that the plain language of the treaties requires the "widest possible search for a unifying factor among the underlying claims." However, in the treaties, the terms "common origin" and "traceable to" are modified by the phrase "series of" in the definition of "disaster and/or casualty." Using Travelers' (P) definition would operate to excise the words "series of" from the language of the treaties in derogation of a basic principle of contract interpretation. This result should be avoided by incorporating the inherent spatial or temporal boundaries of the phrase "series of" in interpreting the treaties. Moreover, this construction permits a reinsured to properly aggregate claims if the underlying occurrences have a spatial or temporal relationship to one another and a "common origin." Where such a relationship is lacking, however, a reinsured cannot simply ignore the words "series of" and point to any event however remote in place or time, which could possibly be considered of "common

origin." This construction also comports with the broad definition of "each and every loss," which sets forth the overall parameters of the reinsurer's (D) liability, i.e., that loss is limited to "any one disaster and/or casualty." This interpretation demonstrates that the parties did not intend for the reinsured to simply group together all other losses as a single "disaster and/or casualty," but sought to allow aggregation only where the losses are linked spatially or temporally and share a "common origin." Here, the record clearly establishes that none of the contaminated sites bore a spatial or temporal relationship to each other, so that aggregating them was not proper. Because the treatment of each site as a separate "disaster and/or casualty" fails to pierce any of the retention levels of the reinsurance treaties, summary judgment was properly granted in favor of the reinsurers (D) in both actions.

(2) No. A "follow the fortunes" clause in a reinsurance policy does not override the policy's other limitations. Travelers (P) argues, that the "follow the fortunes" clauses in the treaties mandate that the reinsurers (D) reimburse it for losses it allocates to them reasonably and in good faith. The "follow the fortunes" doctrine provides that "a reinsurer is required to indemnify for payments reasonably within the terms of the original policy, even if technically not covered by it." Although a "follow the fortunes" clause in most reinsurance agreements leaves reinsurers little room to dispute the reinsured's conduct of the case, such a clause does not alter the terms or override the language of reinsurance policies. To hold that the "follow the fortunes" clauses supplant the definition of "disaster and/or casualty" in the reinsurance treaties and allow Travelers (P) to recover under its single allocation theory would effectively negate the phrase. The practical result of such an application would be that a reinsurance contract that contains a "follow the fortunes" clause would bind a reinsurer to indemnify a reinsured whenever it paid a claim, regardless of the contractual language defining loss. This clearly would be contrary to the parties' express agreement and to the settled law of contract interpretation. Affirmed.

▶ ANALYSIS

This case illustrates the inherent tension between "follow the fortunes" clauses and limitations on the liability of reinsurers. Commentators concur that a "follow the fortunes" clause does not supersede specific language in a reinsurance contract. Under this view, the reinsurer follows the insurer's fortunes under the latter's insurance policies, subject to the stated exclusions and limitations in the reinsurance agreement. In other words, according to these commentators, "following the fortunes" means that, so long as the reinsured acts in good faith, its losses from

Continued on next page.

underwriting that looks improvident in retrospect or was simply unlucky will be indemnified within the terms of the reinsurance contract. Increasingly, courts are viewing "follow the fortunes" as existing only if provided for in the insurance contract, and find no "follow the fortunes" duty in the absence of such a provision. Nonetheless, some courts still hold that such a duty exists even absent an express obligation to "follow the fortunes."

■≡■

Quicknotes

REINSURANCE A contract between an insurer and a third party to insure the insurer against potential loss or liability resulting from a previous insurance contract.

■≡■

Travelers Casualty & Surety Company v. Gerling Global Reinsurance Corporation of America

Insurer (P) v. Excess reinsurer (D)

419 F.3d 181 (2d Cir. 2005).

NATURE OF CASE: Appeal from grant of summary judgment to defendant reinsurer, and request for summary judgment for plaintiff insurer, in action for reinsurance coverage.

FACT SUMMARY: Travelers Casualty & Surety Company (Travelers) (P) contended that its reinsurer on excess policies issued to Owens-Corning Fiberglas Corporation (OCF), Gerling Global Reinsurance Corporation (D), was required to follow the fortunes of Traveler's (P) allocation of its good faith settlement with OCF regardless of whether the allocation, based on a single-occurrence position, was inconsistent with the multiple-occurrence position Travelers (P) adopted in reaching settlement with OCF.

🏛 RULE OF LAW

(1) A reinsurer is required to follow the fortunes of a cedent's post-settlement allocation regardless of whether the allocation reflects a position initially taken by the cedent as to a particular coverage issue, provided the allocation is reasonable and made in good faith.

(2) A reinsurer will be required, as a matter of law, to follow the fortunes of a cedent's post-settlement allocation where the reinsurer cannot show that the allocation was made in bad faith or was unreasonable.

FACTS: Travelers Casualty & Surety Company (Travelers) (P) issued annual primary policies to Owens-Corning Fiberglas Corporation (OCF), one of the world's largest manufacturers of asbestos-containing products. These policies distinguished between "products" and "non-products" claims. Each primary policy had a $1 million "per occurrence" limit of liability, regardless of whether the claims arising from that occurrence fell within the products or non-products category, and each policy also had a $1 million aggregate limit of liability for products coverage, but not for non-products coverage, thus exposing Travelers (P) to unlimited liability for claims arising from multiple occurrences triggering non-products coverage. Travelers (P) also issued to OCF a number of excess policies, and obtained reinsurance on those excess policies from several reinsurers, including Gerling Global Reinsurance Corporation (Gerling) (D). The combined "per occurrence" limit of all of the OCF-Travelers' policies—both primary and excess—was $ 273.5 million. Gerling (D) agreed to be bound by any loss settlements entered into between Travelers (P) and OCF, provided the

settlements comported with the terms of the original policies and Gerling's (D) reinsurance certificates. After Travelers (P) had paid OCF over $400 million on products coverage, which was then exhausted, OCF began to submit its asbestos claims as non-products claims, which Travelers (P) disputed. OCF contended its non-products claims were separate, multiple occurrences, rather than single occurrences. The dispute went to arbitration, but Travelers (P) and OCF settled before a final arbitral determination. Travelers (P) agreed to pay around $273.5 million, which was approximately one additional occurrence limit. OCF and Travelers (P) "explicitly disclaimed any particular theory of coverage," and they never reached agreement as to whether the claims arose from a single occurrence or multiple occurrences. Although the settlement did not resolve the occurrence issue, Travelers (P) had to choose an occurrence position to allocate the settlement between its primary and excess policies. In doing so, it allocated most of the settlement amount as a single occurrence using a "rising bathtub" methodology whereby the settlement amount was allocated evenly among policy years. However, because each year's primary policy had a $1 million per occurrence limit, the primary policies were quickly depleted, and the remaining amounts were spread among the excess policies, including Gerling's (D). Gerling (D) refused to pay the amount allocated to it, contending that Travelers (P) should have made the allocation on a multiple-occurrence basis, in accord with Travelers' (P) implicit settlement position. Because there was no aggregate limit on liability for non-products coverage, allocation on a multiple-occurrence basis would necessarily assign a larger portion of the settlement amount to the primary policies, and a much smaller portion to the excess policies that Gerling (D) had reinsured. Travelers (P) brought a breach of contract action against Gerling (D). The district court granted summary judgment to Gerling (D), finding that the follow-the-fortunes doctrine was inapplicable. Travelers (P) appealed, seeking not only to reverse summary judgment for Gerling (D), but also requesting summary judgment in its favor. The court of appeals granted review.

ISSUE:

(1) Is a reinsurer required to follow the fortunes of a cedent's post-settlement allocation regardless of whether the allocation reflects a position initially taken by the cedent as to a particular coverage issue, provided the allocation is reasonable and made in good faith?

(2) Will a reinsurer be required, as a matter of law, to follow the fortunes of a cedent's post-settlement allocation

Continued on next page.

where the reinsurer cannot show that the allocation was made in bad faith or was unreasonable?

HOLDING AND DECISION: (Walker, C.J.)

(1) Yes. A reinsurer is required to follow the fortunes of a cedent's post-settlement allocation regardless of whether the allocation reflects a position initially taken by the cedent as to a particular coverage issue, provided the allocation is reasonable and made in good faith. The argument that there has to be mutuality of interest between the cedent and the insurer has been rejected, since the main rationale for the follow-the-fortunes doctrine is to foster the goals of maximum coverage and settlement and to prevent courts from undermining the cedent-reinsurer relationship through *de novo* review of the cedent's decision-making process. Prior case law has held that the cedent's pre-settlement risk analysis may differ from its post-settlement allocation position for the doctrine to be applicable. Here, the only factual difference is that Travelers (P) implicitly took a position on occurrences in settlement that it then abandoned in its allocation determination. If anything, this difference weakens Gerling's (D) position since here it is not at all clear that Travelers (P) ever accepted, as a legal matter, OCF's multiple-occurrence stance, whereas a cedent that has conducted a risk analysis has considered an alternative allocation posture. Thus, in a case such as the one at bar, where the cedent's earlier position is not clear as to a coverage issue, it is even less appropriate for the reinsurer to claim an inconsistency between that earlier position and the cedent's subsequent allocation. Also, as here, where a number of occurrence positions were on the settlement negotiation table, the purpose of the follow-the-fortunes doctrine is served by preventing judicial inquiry into the propriety of the cedent's allocation method if the settlement and allocation were themselves made in good faith, were reasonable, and were within the terms of the policies. Reversed and remanded as to this issue.

(2) Yes. A reinsurer will be required, as a matter of law, to follow the fortunes of a cedent's post-settlement allocation where the reinsurer cannot show that the allocation was made in bad faith or was unreasonable. First, follow-the-fortunes applies only to good-faith claims. However, to demonstrate bad faith, the reinsurer must make an "extraordinary" showing of a disingenuous or dishonest failure. Gerling (D) has failed to make such a showing. Gerling's (D) argument that the allocation of all non-products claims to a single occurrence was inconsistent with the definition of "occurrence" in the underlying policies and rested on a construction of that term that was so legally baseless that it had never been adopted by any court in any jurisdiction fails to demonstrate bad faith, since allocation on a legally novel theory does not itself constitute dishonesty or disingenuousness. Moreover, Gerling (D) cannot substantiate its claim that had a multiple-occurrence

allocation method been used, it would have faced "virtually no exposure" because only the primary policies would have been implicated. Second, follow-the-fortunes requires that a settlement be reasonable. Here, Travelers' (P) settlement was reasonable, given that it was reasonable for it to take a single-occurrence position when disputing OCF's non-product claims. Traveler's (P) allocation method was also reasonable in light of then-prevailing case law, which predominantly treated asbestos-related claims as arising from single occurrences. Thus, there was a reasonable basis for Travelers' (P) claims here, and it is entitled to summary judgment.

ANALYSIS

As a practical matter, this decision will have minimal impact on disputes between insurers and reinsurers, the vast majority of which are arbitrated and not bound by case law precedent. Nevertheless, some commentators have criticized the court for crafting an opinion that seems to ignore that a reinsurer would not ordinarily give an insurer broad discretion in determining its allocation, which would create a conflict of interest between the ceding insurer, which is seeking to maximize its recovery, and the reinsurer. By contrast, if an allocation were based on the insurer's settlement position, there would arguably be no conflict of interest. Additionally, there is developing case law that holds that the reinsurer must follow-the-fortunes only if it expressly agreed to do so, and that absent a contractual agreement, the duty does not exist.

Quicknotes

ARBITRATION AGREEMENT A mutual understanding entered into by parties wishing to submit to the decision-making authority of a neutral third party, selected by the parties and charged with rendering a decision.

BAD FAITH Conduct that is intentionally misleading or deceptive.

DE NOVO The review of a lower court decision by an appellate court, which is hearing the case as if it had not been previously heard and as if no judgment had been rendered.

GOOD FAITH An honest intention to abstain from taking advantage of another.

Ainsworth v. General Reinsurance Corporation

Receiver of insolvent insurer (P) v. Reinsurer (D)

751 F.2d 962 (8th Cir. 1985).

NATURE OF CASE: Appeal from judgment in action on reinsurance contract.

FACT SUMMARY: General Reinsurance Corporation (D) settled directly with the insured when the insurer was insolvent.

RULE OF LAW
Reinsurers may not discharge their liability to the insurer by settling directly with the insured, regardless of whether the insurer is insolvent.

FACTS: Medallion, an insurer, obtained reinsurance from General Reinsurance Corporation (General Reinsurance) (D). Medallion was declared insolvent and a receiver was appointed. In the meantime, Pittsburgh and New England Trucking Company (P&NE), an insured of Medallion, lost a judgment of $485,000 for injuries arising out of an accident. P&NE sought payment from Medallion's receiver and General Reinsurance (D). Initially, General Reinsurance (D) maintained that the reinsurance assets belonged to the receiver and that it could not legally make any payments. However, later it negotiated a settlement, without involving the receiver, of $25,000 for a release discharging Medallion and the receiver. The receiver then filed suit to recover the full amount of the reinsurance proceeds from the P&NE liability. The district court awarded judgment to the receiver and General Reinsurance (D) appealed.

ISSUE: May reinsurers discharge their liability to the insurer by settling directly with the insured, regardless of whether the insurer is insolvent?

HOLDING AND DECISION: (Fairchild, J.) No. Reinsurers may not discharge their liability to the insurer by settling directly with the insured, regardless of whether the insurer is insolvent. When an insurer becomes insolvent, the reinsurer's obligation with respect to outstanding liability becomes an asset of the insolvency estate. The obligation is not to be diminished because of the insolvency. While the reinsurer has a right to defend against a claim on it merits, it does not have the right to reduce its obligation by taking advantage of the insured's obligee to take less because of the insolvency. Generally, the beneficiary of reinsurance is the insurer and not the insured. Liability runs solely to the reinsured, except where the reinsurance contract expressly provides for liability directly to the original insured. Where the insurer becomes insolvent, the reinsurance assets go directly to the receiver to be distributed generally among the creditors. Otherwise, reinsurers could deny general creditors their interest in reinsurance proceeds while also making cheap settlements with insureds facing the prospect of not receiving the full amount of their claims from the insolvent insurer. Accordingly, General Reinsurance (D) had no right to settle directly with Medallion's insured and their obligee. The judgment is affirmed.

ANALYSIS

This decision shows that there is no privity between an insured and the reinsurer. Many states require the inclusion of an insolvency clause in reinsurance contracts. A few jurisdictions allow the reinsurer to be obligated directly to the insured.

Quicknotes

INSOLVENT One's liabilities exceed one's assets; inability to pay one's debts.

LIABILITY Any obligation or responsibility.

PRIVITY Commonality of rights or interests between parties.

RECEIVER An individual who is appointed by the court to maintain the holdings of a corporation, individual or other entity involved in a legal proceeding.

O'Connor v. Insurance Company of North America

Liquidator (P) v. Reinsurer (D)

622 F. Supp. 611 (N.D. Ill. 1985).

NATURE OF CASE: Cross-motions for partial summary judgment in action to recover reinsurance proceeds.

FACT SUMMARY: O'Connor (P), Reserve Insurance Company's liquidator, sought to recover reinsurance proceeds without any set-off claims.

🏛 RULE OF LAW
Set-off may be asserted in bankruptcy proceedings by reinsurers for debts owed them by an insolvent insurer even though at the time of filing a debt is owing but not presently due, or where a definite liability has accrued but is as yet unliquidated.

FACTS: Reserve Insurance Company (Reserve) wrote many petroleum and petrochemical insurance policies. A portion of the risks was reinsured with various reinsurers (D). Reserve also acted as reinsurer on policies written by other insurance companies as part of a pooling agreement. When Reserve began to suffer losses, the pool manager at the time, American Reserve Insurance Brokers International, Inc. (ARIB), canceled the Reserve policies and issued new policies in the name of one of the other ceding companies. Reserve became insolvent, and a liquidator, O'Connor (P) was appointed. O'Connor (P) later filed suit to collect reinsurance proceeds for losses incurred by Reserve's insureds and other monies that the reinsurers (D) and pool manager owed to Reserve, claiming, inter alia, that ARIB's cancellation and rewriting of policies prior to Reserve's insolvency was unlawful. The reinsurers (D) maintained that they were entitled to reduce any amounts they might be found to owe by the amount of debts that Reserve owed to them under the reinsurance contracts, and the reinsurers (D) moved for partial summary judgment on this set-off issue. O'Connor (P) cross-moved for partial summary judgment on this issue.

ISSUE: May set-off be asserted in bankruptcy proceedings by reinsurers for debts owed them by an insolvent insurer even though at the time of filing a debt is owing but not presently due, or where a definite liability has accrued but is as yet unliquidated?

HOLDING AND DECISION: (Plunkett, J.) Yes. Set-off may be asserted in bankruptcy proceedings by reinsurers for debts owed them by an insolvent insurer even though at the time of filing a debt is owing but not presently due, or where a definite liability has accrued but is as yet unliquidated. O'Connor (P) argues that as a jurisdictional matter, the Insurance Code provides an exclusive procedure for the determination of claims against an insolvent insurer,

including set-off rights, and that the injunctions in the liquidation order present a bar to the reinsurers' (D) set-off claims in an insolvency proceeding. However, when the language of the statutes is examined, it seems that set-off rights are not included with the general bar against "claims" against an insolvent insurer. The only exception to this right is that the reinsurers (D) would have to file affirmative counterclaims with the liquidation court if the set-off amounts exceed the claims of O'Connor (P). Here, however, the reinsurers (D) seek only to show that O'Connor (P) has no claim or a lesser claim against them than he asserts. Accordingly, the reinsurers (D) may seek set-off in this forum. In order for a set-off to be valid it must be for a mutual debt. Thus, pre-liquidation debts owed by Reserve can only set off pre-liquidation debts owed to Reserve. Here, any liability that the reinsurers (D) may incur to pay reinsurance proceeds or return unearned premiums arises as a result of provisions in the previously executed reinsurance agreements. Thus, although the claims giving rise to liability were not paid prior to the insolvency, they were susceptible of liquidation. Accordingly, the reinsurers' (D) debts are pre-liquidation debts, mutuality of obligation exists, and set-off is permitted. The reinsurers' (D) motion for partial summary judgment is granted, and O'Connor's motion for partial summary judgment is denied.

▶ ANALYSIS

The right to set-off is important because it can have a large impact on creditors. It does make it much easier to handle the multiple debts and credits reinsurers and insurers have between them. Still, set-off of this type is not allowed in every jurisdiction.

Quicknotes

LIQUIDATION The reduction to cash of all assets for distribution to creditors.

SET-OFF A claim made pursuant to a counter-claim, arising from a cause of action unrelated to the underlying suit, in which the defendant seeks to have the plaintiff's claim of damages reduced.

Glossary

Common Latin Words and Phrases Encountered in the Law

A FORTIORI: Because one fact exists or has been proven, therefore a second fact that is related to the first fact must also exist.

A PRIORI: From the cause to the effect. A term of logic used to denote that when one generally accepted truth is shown to be a cause, another particular effect must necessarily follow.

AB INITIO: From the beginning; a condition which has existed throughout, as in a marriage which was void ab initio.

ACTUS REUS: The wrongful act; in criminal law, such action sufficient to trigger criminal liability.

AD VALOREM: According to value; an ad valorem tax is imposed upon an item located within the taxing jurisdiction calculated by the value of such item.

AMICUS CURIAE: Friend of the court. Its most common usage takes the form of an amicus curiae brief, filed by a person who is not a party to an action but is nonetheless allowed to offer an argument supporting his legal interests.

ARGUENDO: In arguing. A statement, possibly hypothetical, made for the purpose of argument, is one made arguendo.

BILL QUIA TIMET: A bill to quiet title (establish ownership) to real property.

BONA FIDE: True, honest, or genuine. May refer to a person's legal position based on good faith or lacking notice of fraud (such as a bona fide purchaser for value) or to the authenticity of a particular document (such as a bona fide last will and testament).

CAUSA MORTIS: With approaching death in mind. A gift causa mortis is a gift given by a party who feels certain that death is imminent.

CAVEAT EMPTOR: Let the buyer beware. This maxim is reflected in the rule of law that a buyer purchases at his own risk because it is his responsibility to examine, judge, test, and otherwise inspect what he is buying.

CERTIORARI: A writ of review. Petitions for review of a case by the United States Supreme Court are most often done by means of a writ of certiorari.

CONTRA: On the other hand. Opposite. Contrary to.

CORAM NOBIS: Before us; writs of error directed to the court that originally rendered the judgment.

CORAM VOBIS: Before you; writs of error directed by an appellate court to a lower court to correct a factual error.

CORPUS DELICTI: The body of the crime; the requisite elements of a crime amounting to objective proof that a crime has been committed.

CUM TESTAMENTO ANNEXO, ADMINISTRATOR (ADMINISTRATOR C.T.A.): With will annexed; an administrator c.t.a. settles an estate pursuant to a will in which he is not appointed.

DE BONIS NON, ADMINISTRATOR (ADMINISTRATOR D.B.N.): Of goods not administered; an administrator d.b.n. settles a partially settled estate.

DE FACTO: In fact; in reality; actually. Existing in fact but not officially approved or engendered.

DE JURE: By right; lawful. Describes a condition that is legitimate "as a matter of law," in contrast to the term "de facto," which connotes something existing in fact but not legally sanctioned or authorized. For example, de facto segregation refers to segregation brought about by housing patterns, etc., whereas de jure segregation refers to segregation created by law.

DE MINIMIS: Of minimal importance; insignificant; a trifle; not worth bothering about.

DE NOVO: Anew; a second time; afresh. A trial de novo is a new trial held at the appellate level as if the case originated there and the trial at a lower level had not taken place.

DICTA: Generally used as an abbreviated form of obiter dicta, a term describing those portions of a judicial opinion incidental or not necessary to resolution of the specific question before the court. Such nonessential statements and remarks are not considered to be binding precedent.

DUCES TECUM: Refers to a particular type of writ or subpoena requesting a party or organization to produce certain documents in their possession.

EN BANC: Full bench. Where a court sits with all justices present rather than the usual quorum.

EX PARTE: For one side or one party only. An ex parte proceeding is one undertaken for the benefit of only one party, without notice to, or an appearance by, an adverse party.

EX POST FACTO: After the fact. An ex post facto law is a law that retroactively changes the consequences of a prior act.

EX REL.: Abbreviated form of the term "ex relatione," meaning upon relation or information. When the state brings an action in which it has no interest against an individual at the instigation of one who has a private interest in the matter.

FORUM NON CONVENIENS: Inconvenient forum. Although a court may have jurisdiction over the case, the action should be tried in a more conveniently located court, one to which parties and witnesses may more easily travel, for example.

GUARDIAN AD LITEM: A guardian of an infant as to litigation, appointed to represent the infant and pursue his/her rights.

HABEAS CORPUS: You have the body. The modern writ of habeas corpus is a writ directing that a person (body) being detained (such as a prisoner) be brought before the court so that the legality of his detention can be judicially ascertained.

IN CAMERA: In private, in chambers. When a hearing is held before a judge in his chambers or when all spectators are excluded from the courtroom.

IN FORMA PAUPERIS: In the manner of a pauper. A party who proceeds in forma pauperis because of his poverty is one who is allowed to bring suit without liability for costs.

INFRA: Below, under. A word referring the reader to a later part of a book. (The opposite of supra.)

IN LOCO PARENTIS: In the place of a parent.

IN PARI DELICTO: Equally wrong; a court of equity will not grant requested relief to an applicant who is in pari delicto, or as much at fault in the transactions giving rise to the controversy as is the opponent of the applicant.

IN PARI MATERIA: On like subject matter or upon the same matter. Statutes relating to the same person or things are said to be in pari materia. It is a general rule of statutory construction that such statutes should be construed together, i.e., looked at as if they together constituted one law.

IN PERSONAM: Against the person. Jurisdiction over the person of an individual.

IN RE: In the matter of. Used to designate a proceeding involving an estate or other property.

IN REM: A term that signifies an action against the res, or thing. An action in rem is basically one that is taken directly against property, as distinguished from an action in personam, i.e., against the person.

INTER ALIA: Among other things. Used to show that the whole of a statement, pleading, list, statute, etc., has not been set forth in its entirety.

INTER PARTES: Between the parties. May refer to contracts, conveyances or other transactions having legal significance.

INTER VIVOS: Between the living. An inter vivos gift is a gift made by a living grantor, as distinguished from bequests contained in a will, which pass upon the death of the testator.

IPSO FACTO: By the mere fact itself.

JUS: Law or the entire body of law.

LEX LOCI: The law of the place; the notion that the rights of parties to a legal proceeding are governed by the law of the place where those rights arose.

MALUM IN SE: Evil or wrong in and of itself; inherently wrong. This term describes an act that is wrong by its very nature, as opposed to one which would not be wrong but for the fact that there is a specific legal prohibition against it (malum prohibitum).

MALUM PROHIBITUM: Wrong because prohibited, but not inherently evil. Used to describe something that is wrong because it is expressly forbidden by law but that is not in and of itself evil, e.g., speeding.

MANDAMUS: We command. A writ directing an official to take a certain action.

MENS REA: A guilty mind; a criminal intent. A term used to signify the mental state that accompanies a crime or other prohibited act. Some crimes require only a general mens rea (general intent to do the prohibited act), but others, like assault with intent to murder, require the existence of a specific mens rea.

MODUS OPERANDI: Method of operating; generally refers to the manner or style of a criminal in committing crimes, admissible in appropriate cases as evidence of the identity of a defendant.

NEXUS: A connection to.

NISI PRIUS: A court of first impression. A nisi prius court is one where issues of fact are tried before a judge or jury.

N.O.V. (NON OBSTANTE VEREDICTO): Notwithstanding the verdict. A judgment n.o.v. is a judgment given in favor of one party despite the fact that a verdict was returned in favor of the other party, the justification being that the verdict either had no reasonable support in fact or was contrary to law.

NUNC PRO TUNC: Now for then. This phrase refers to actions that may be taken and will then have full retroactive effect.

PENDENTE LITE: Pending the suit; pending litigation under way.

PER CAPITA: By head; beneficiaries of an estate, if they take in equal shares, take per capita.

PER CURIAM: By the court; signifies an opinion ostensibly written "by the whole court" and with no identified author.

PER SE: By itself, in itself; inherently.

PER STIRPES: By representation. Used primarily in the law of wills to describe the method of distribution where a person, generally because of death, is unable to take that which is left to him by the will of another, and therefore his heirs divide such property between them rather than take under the will individually.

PRIMA FACIE: On its face, at first sight. A prima facie case is one that is sufficient on its face, meaning that the evidence supporting it is adequate to establish the case until contradicted or overcome by other evidence.

PRO TANTO: For so much; as far as it goes. Often used in eminent domain cases when a property owner receives partial payment for his land without prejudice to his right to bring suit for the full amount he claims his land to be worth.

QUANTUM MERUIT: As much as he deserves. Refers to recovery based on the doctrine of unjust enrichment in those cases in which a party has rendered valuable services or furnished materials that were accepted and enjoyed by another under circumstances that would reasonably notify the recipient that the rendering party expected to be paid. In essence, the law implies a contract to pay the reasonable value of the services or materials furnished.

QUASI: Almost like; as if; nearly. This term is essentially used to signify that one subject or thing is almost analogous to another but that material differences between them do exist. For example, a quasi-criminal proceeding is one that is not strictly criminal but shares enough of the same characteristics to require some of the same safeguards (e.g., procedural due process must be followed in a parole hearing).

QUID PRO QUO: Something for something. In contract law, the consideration, something of value, passed between the parties to render the contract binding.

RES GESTAE: Things done; in evidence law, this principle justifies the admission of a statement that would otherwise be hearsay when it is made so closely to the event in question as to be said to be a part of it, or with such spontaneity as not to have the possibility of falsehood.

RES IPSA LOQUITUR: The thing speaks for itself. This doctrine gives rise to a rebuttable presumption of negligence when the instrumentality causing the injury was within the exclusive control of the defendant, and the injury was one that does not normally occur unless a person has been negligent.

RES JUDICATA: A matter adjudged. Doctrine which provides that once a court of competent jurisdiction has rendered a final judgment or decree on the merits, that judgment or decree is conclusive upon the parties to the case and prevents them from engaging in any other litigation on the points and issues determined therein.

RESPONDEAT SUPERIOR: Let the master reply. This doctrine holds the master liable for the wrongful acts of his servant (or the principal for his agent) in those cases in which the servant (or agent) was acting within the scope of his authority at the time of the injury.

STARE DECISIS: To stand by or adhere to that which has been decided. The common law doctrine of stare decisis attempts to give security and certainty to the law by following the policy that once a principle of law as applicable to a certain set of facts has been set forth in a decision, it forms a precedent which will subsequently be followed, even though a different decision might be made were it the first time the question had arisen. Of course, stare decisis is not an inviolable principle and is departed from in instances where there is good cause (e.g., considerations of public policy led the Supreme Court to disregard prior decisions sanctioning segregation).

SUPRA: Above. A word referring a reader to an earlier part of a book.

ULTRA VIRES: Beyond the power. This phrase is most commonly used to refer to actions taken by a corporation that are beyond the power or legal authority of the corporation.

Addendum of French Derivatives

IN PAIS: Not pursuant to legal proceedings.

CHATTEL: Tangible personal property.

CY PRES: Doctrine permitting courts to apply trust funds to purposes not expressed in the trust but necessary to carry out the settlor's intent.

PER AUTRE VIE: For another's life; during another's life. In property law, an estate may be granted that will terminate upon the death of someone other than the grantee.

PROFIT A PRENDRE: A license to remove minerals or other produce from land.

VOIR DIRE: Process of questioning jurors as to their predispositions about the case or parties to a proceeding in order to identify those jurors displaying bias or prejudice.

Casenote Legal Briefs